Demons at My Doorstep

Demons at My Doorstep

The search for my donor father...

As Told To Katherine Marsh

iUniverse, Inc.
New York Lincoln Shanghai

Demons at My Doorstep
The search for my donor father...

iUniverse, Inc.

For information address:
iUniverse, Inc.
2021 Pine Lake Road, Suite 100
Lincoln, NE 68512
www.iuniverse.com

ISBN: 0-595-32000-7

Printed in the United States of America

Contents

Introduction

✦

Donor Father, Donor Son: One Man's Quest to Find Identity

Imagine knowing that your life is out of control, you're a mess emotionally and psychologically and you're abusing yourself almost on a daily basis. But you don't know why; nor do you understand the reasons for the darkness behind the demons haunting you.

Then on your 28th birthday, your mother delivers the bomb; your father was sterile and you are donor offspring (children conceived through artificial insemination). What a wonderful birthday present! Suddenly you understand why your world is so amok. This explains your chaotic life.

However, that was just the beginning. A fellow donor offspring introduces you to the term of eugenics. More pieces of an ethereal puzzle. But what does it all mean? Now imagine you are the main character of this story, Scott, trying to make sense of it all.

Just coming to terms with the fact that he was a donor offspring would have been enough. But what was this eugenics and what did it have to do with him? He was not even remotely cognizant of the word, what it meant nor its relationship to his family. He hadn't even had time to decide if he really wanted to know. He knew only of his Father's trauma; that he'd been forcibly sterilized at the Beatrice State home in Nebraska in 1948 as a requisite to his release.

Learning the stealthy secret behind his true conception, he was considered a by-product of the trauma his father had experienced. Up to that point, he hadn't made any correlation to what his father had endured as being part of a mandate of eugenics. And why should he?

He viewed his Father's plight as most children would, a sterile man with a desperate plan, like many childless couples. How could he have known there existed a sinister darkness beyond that plan?

It would be years before Davis would learn exactly how much eugenics had been a part of his dad's world and subsequently, his own. What was meant by its benign definition: the movement devoted to improving the human species through the control of hereditary factors in mating.

At first glance, it seemed harmless, perhaps even a good ideal. Yet in his quest for knowledge, Davis uncovered some of societies´ best kept secrets that revealed a host of grisly undertakings endorsed by America's premiere citizens. He didn't want to believe it! It was too ugly to be true. And yet it was. In black, in white, in the scores of lives who were victims from it's ghastly tentacles. It was very real.

But before he could discover such irrefutable truths, Davis would have to learn to accept himself. Not an easy task for a man riddled with vices that ran the gamut from drug trafficking and abuse to sexual philandering to pornography and fleeting relationships.

In the process of finding himself, he would lose his father, two unborn children, several businesses, and himself.

In the midst of all the chaos, a voice inside would keep nagging him; a spiritual voice. But over and over again he denied it as he lied, cheated, and deceived those closest to him with broken promises and unraveled rehabilitative efforts. His life continued to spiral down a path of wayward living. Even going to jail didn't abate the inner turmoil.

His anger and indifference against his family and the world around him kept him bound in a revolving cycle of nightmarish living for almost twenty years.

He'd always known without truly knowing, that he was different from his father. He hadn't understood the glaring differences such as his light complexion in contrast to his Father's dark features. His innate intelligence and robust stature compared to his Father's small, slight build and methods of simple living. But in his heart he'd never dreamed or imagined the truth could be so repugnant. He had believed, or perhaps hoped, that the dark secret of his past meant he'd been adopted.

Instead, he would learn he was seed from a man who had no desire to meet him, know him or be a part of his life. Rejected again, but soothed with the knowledge of finally knowing his roots, it was a turning point. He might have been the son of a prominent professor, a man who looked like him, only older, but he wasn't his true father.

The rejection hurt, but not knowing his heritage had hurt worse. At least he knew his medical background, his ethnicity and an explanation for his high IQ. He'd never called his father stupid, but the inequities were so severe. Harry Davis, his father, had been an uneducated man. A product of his humble beginnings of poverty and deprivation.

With the truth of his biological father conquered Davis was strangely assuaged. He's lost more than his virtues along his journey of self revelation, but he had emerged a stronger man and better man.

The man he'd called his father was no longer there to guide him and love him, and yet Davis understood his dad better now. He didn't need his physical presence to feel him around. Now Scott understood what he was meant to do. Why his life had been spared through his many turbulent and perilous ventures.

He was to be a messenger, and his message would be the truth behind eugenics and the connections to sterilization, abortion, Nazi Germany and "Time Magazines Man Of The Year" in 1939, Adolf Hitler. The public needed to know what had happened to his father, to him, and to the many unsuspecting souls who were caught in that alternate microcosm simply by happenstance and the grip it has on today's society.

Things were happening that shouldn't be happening. Nightmares had been laid to rest, but he would excavate each grotesque skeleton. Bring to light the dark bones of past misdeeds. Davis knew he couldn't right the wrongs of the past, but perhaps he could be instrumental in preventing them from happening again.

Thus began Scott Davis's longest journey of forming liaisons with other donor offspring, public campaigns, raising a family, dealing with his Son's autism while doing research to uncover the murky truths. His story is a testament that the human spirit can triumph over evil if the sojourner has faith and truly believes. Scott Davis truly believes….

1

Sterilization

It was bitterly cold that morning in January. Snow pelted the dull brick building.

Angry bluish-black clouds seemed to hover over the home and dark shadows cast an eerie pall. Something was happening. The harsh glare of light escaped in slivers from the institution's windows. It was the only hint of life to the place.

But within the drab pea-green hallways, orderlies were busy keeping Beatrice's patients subdued. And in one room, Harry Davis lay on sterile white sheets, with restraints around his ankles and arms. A sheet was haphazardly placed over his naked body.

It was cold but he wasn't shaking from the temperature. He could feel his heartbeat as the blood coursed through his body. He looked at the clock on the wall. Two minutes to 10 AM. He was scheduled for his procedure at 10:30. Where was the doctor?

At 10:30 he would cease to be a man. The price for his "freedom."

The door opened and two nurses entered. One was blond, slender and carrying a tray of medical utensils. The other was shorter, dark-haired and held a blood pressure cuff. She curled it around Harry's arm and began pumping.

"How are you this morning, Harry?" she asked.

He looked at her, her brown eyes neutral. He wondered if she'd be as nonplussed if she was the one strapped down.

The door opened again and two orderlies entered with a doctor. He immediately recognized the doctor. His name was Malcom Hobbs. He'd seen him leaving this room many times. Now he knew what his visits meant.

"Good Morning, Harry. Are you comfortable? You will hardly feel a thing once I give you this shot. It'll all be over before you know it," he told him.

Harry looked at the hazel eyes behind the dark-rimmed glasses that matched his short auburn hair, cut close to his ears. Doctor Hobbs was a large man, nearly six feet and six inches. His expansive chest and square jaw gave him a military look. He wondered how many of these procedures he had done. Malcolm smiled down at him through yellowed teeth and took a deep breath.

"Rhonda, shall we?" he said turning his attention to the blond nurse. She handed him the syringe, averting her eyes. She did not want to see Harry, not now. It was enough that she had seen the blank muffled fear thick on his face when she'd entered the room. She felt sorry for him.

Harry watched the needle go in but he barely felt the prick against his skin over the whoosh of blood pounding in his ears. He knew then he was just another number on a long list of procedures that needed to be done. He closed his eyes turning his face as far away from them as possible. A tear escaped the corner of his left eye and rolled down his cheek. Within moments it was over.

2

Chance Encounter

It was hot for April, a sure sign that the summer of '49 would be warmer still with humid and miserable nights in Kansas. Sunshine blazed across the Kansas City streets. It was only nine o'clock in the morning, but already the heat waves were bouncing off the tired buildings of downtown Main Street.

Kansas City was in the middle of a dry spell, not unusual for the rural farmlands of the areas. The city held the heat like a frightened breath. Everywhere you looked, parched yellow and brown stubble replaced lawns, and the sickly-looking shrubs became the city's new decor.

Harry ran a handkerchief across his forehead as he stepped off the curb of Main Street. It felt strange to him to see the city again, to walk the streets he hadn't seen since he was a teenager. A sense of melancholy filled him as he crossed the street towards Frank's Place; a small, clay colored diner wedged between the two bigger, equally drab grey buildings of Owl's Drugs and Hanson's Lumber.

He drew a heavy breath as he carried the weight of his past like a duffel bag on his shoulders. He was an emancipated citizen, but he felt anything but free as the chains from years gone by bound him, holding him to his memories. He tried to convince himself that he was just as good as anyone except for his secret.

Barbara Moen was happy just to have a job working behind the counter of the local dinette. Jobs were hard to come by, and she knew she was lucky. She felt doubly lucky to be working in a place that boasted one of the few air conditioners in the city, a guarantee for good business, no matter what the quality of food.

Whenever the mercury climbed, folks would line up for an hour just to get a seat out of the heat and a plate full of Frank's infamous meat loaf special. That always made Barbara happy because among the customers would be the town's eligible bachelors, or so she hoped.

Barbara was just nineteen and fresh off a farm in Iowa. She had wholesome scrawled across her face. Kansas was her means to escape the cornfields and, hopefully, catch a man. But so far such a prize had eluded her.

At five feet and five inches, she was tall for a woman. Honey brown hair spilled over a pretty face. Being overweight and shy had hurt her chances for suitors. Compounding her plight, however, was a set of ill-fitting dentures in lieu of front teeth, courtesy of a freak childhood accident.

Like many newcomers, she'd fallen victim to the first kind face. It was her bad luck that he happened to be the son of her landlord. But interest had been fleeting, as quick as a butterfly lands, it soon departs. Not only were his interests clearly sordid but when he discovered she wouldn't give in to his wishes, he had quickly moved on.

It had left Barbara feeling lonely and homesick. Adjusting to the big city was proving to be quite the challenge. Almost every night she had cried herself to sleep while clutching a photograph of her parents.

She told herself she wasn't interested in just any man. She dreamed of a Prince Charming who would treat her like his princess, someone who would want to have babies, as desperately as she did, and plenty of them. After all, her family had been prolific, why not continue the tradition? Her fair prince didn't have to be movie star handsome or rich, just good-looking enough and nice. Then they'd simply settle down, buy a cute little house with a fenced yard for the children to play in, and live happily ever after. It wasn't a bad plan; all it lacked was the right man.

"Barbara, you ain't never satisfied," her father would scold whenever he'd catch her daydreaming. "And you never will be."

"I will, too," she had protested. "I don't need much."

But so far, except for the brief romance with the landlord's son that she preferred not to remember, she hadn't met anyone she even liked. Or they had no interest in a pudgy farm girl who hid her smile behind her hand.

"Looks like its going to rain," Frank said peering out the big storefront window. The sky had become a cluster of dark blue clouds. He glanced at Barbara behind the counter adjusting her hair net and white uniform as they prepared for the lunch rush.

"I hope so," Barbara replied, "it's so hot in my apartment, I can't sleep. And Susan and I are going to go dancing at the Star-lite Ballroom tonight."

"Barbara, you need to find you a man," he said looking at Barbara differently. He knew how it felt to be lonesome and single. He remembered his own days of searching.

"A pretty young girl like you should be married and home raising a family. You don't want to be a waitress all your life do you?"

"I ain't pretty," Barbara replied blushing but pleased by the compliment even if it came from old Frank. She pulled her purse from beneath the lunch counter and searched for her pack of cigarettes. A moment later, she was inhaling deeply. Slowly she blew the smoke out. Turning to lean against the counter, she looked at him. "Frank, you know I don't want to end up being a waitress forever. I want a big family, and a TV set in the living room, a swing on the front porch and a new Chevrolet in the driveway. But you tell me how I get those things?"

Frank grinned at her. Gray streaks shining through his thick black hair.
"You make sure you marry a rich one," he chuckled.

Barbara smiled, her hand unconsciously rising to her mouth.
"Oh come on, I can't even find a man who's broke, let alone one who's rich," she snickered.

Just then the bell above the door tinkled to announce the first lunch customer. Over the next two hours it tinkled almost nonstop. When alas it finally stopped, the meat loaf was gone and Barbara's white uniform was an unsightly mess of splattered sauce and other less identifiable stains.

The last couple hours of her shift seemed to pass like a tortoise crossing the highway. Finally, it was time. She hurried into the back room where Frank kept supplies and changed out of her soiled uniform into a dress. The dress was light blue with a simple cut, but flattering nonetheless.

She came out and sat at the counter doing her nails as she waited patiently for Susan to arrive. Suddenly the bell began to dance again. She turned in her seat to watch two young men entering. They settled in a corner booth. She could feel them giving her the eye, so she turned her back to them. She might be lonely, but she wasn't going to be ogled by a couple of strangers.

Susan arrived and took the seat next to Barbara. She noticed the strangers on her way in.

"Those two yokels in the booth are watching us," Susan said in a stage whisper.

"They good looking?" Barbara asked. She already thought the dark-haired one was cute, even though he didn't appear any taller than she was, a couple of inches over five foot, if that. But Susan was purportedly more worldly and wise in these sorts of things, so she deferred to her friend's opinion.

"Not bad," Susan said, turning boldly to appraise the young men. "But no money, honey." Turning back around, she added, "We'll do better at the Star-lite."

Barbara felt disappointment prick her. Susan was the one all the boys wanted to dance with at the Starlight; it held little for her, she considered herself lucky if she got asked more than once.

Perhaps taking Susan's stare as an invitation, the men sauntered to the counter. The taller, light-haired one pulled out cigarettes from a chest pocket and lit one for both himself and his friend, pretending to ignore the girls. He had small, nervous green eyes that flitted from Susan to Barbara and back.

Contrarily, his shorter companion, obviously the shyer of the two, hung back. Addressing Susan's back, he spoke.

"Say, what's a couple of swell-looking dames like you sitting alone for?"

Without turning, Susan shot back, "As you can see, we're not alone, so buzz off, Mac!"

As Susan spoke, Barbara glanced at the second man. He'd been smiling, but his smile quickly faded to hurt after Susan's remarks. Barbara wanted to tell him she didn't mean it but something stopped her.

"Hey, excuse me for liven'," the first man replied. "We were just going to offer to buy you a couple of Coca-Colas or somethin'."

"We don't need you to buy us anything," Susan snapped, this time turning to face him with a steely look.

"Take a hike, Mike."

"Okay, okay," the man said throwing up his hands in mock surrender. "The ice queen wins. Come on Harry, let's go find us a couple of girls who know how to have fun."

The first man pivoted angrily, and tugged on Harry's sleeve. He was still looking at Barbara with his soft brown, puppy-dog eyes. If she'd had the nerve, she would have said something but could only manage to give a half-smile as his friend pulled him away.

"You didn't have to be so mean," Barbara quipped to Susan after the men were gone.

"Take it from me, they were a pair of losers. Swell-looking dames. Ha! Who does he think he is, Bogart?" she scoffed.

Curls of blue smoke shot out of her nostrils. "Don't worry about it, Barbara-Boop. Let's wait a few minutes to make sure those jokers are gone; then we'll go dancing with some real men," she assured.

Barbara giggled behind her hand. She wanted to believe Susan was right. After all, Susan certainly had a lot more experience with men than Barbara did. Still, there was something sweet about that little fella with the warm puppy dog eyes and it nagged at her.

One last minute application of lipstick and the girls headed for the door. Susan stepped outside first, immediately a rush of heat swallowed her. Since the men were nowhere to be seen, they took it as a positive sign and walked to the corner bus stop.

Soon an old bus painted in ugly shades of green and gray coughed to the stop, quickly the girls got on. They found a seat near the front. Susan was still laughing about the bolder man's Hollywood shtick when the same two men suddenly climbed on just before the bus started to roll away.

"Goodness it's hot," Susan told Barbara fanning herself with a makeshift hand held fan that was nothing more than a ridged piece of paper. Barbara groaned uncomfortably.

"Frank said he heard it's supposed to rain, I pray he's right," she said shifting in her seat as if somehow that would make the heat more bearable. But the rickety city bus was unventilated. In fact, most of the windows would not open. It left the interior air stale and heavy. And on such sweltering days, it was nearly suffocating.

"Why, fancy meeting you two dames here," the light-haired stranger said grinning as they took a seat directly behind the women. Harry smiled shyly at Barbara as he slid into the seat.

"Ignore them," Susan instructed continuing to fan herself.

"Why, we were just going to go dancing," the man continued.

"Thought maybe you two dames would like to cut the rug a bit."

"I'd like to cut your tongue," Susan retorted, forgetting her own advice. The stranger gave her a disapproving look.

"I think we got us a coupla' cold ones here, Harry," he said, but then remained quiet for the rest of the ride to the dance hall. Barbara welcomed the silence; she didn't like Susan quarreling with him.

When they arrived, Susan hurriedly ushered Barbara off the bus without looking at their two erstwhile suitors. Barbara sighed inwardly. It was easy for Susan; she'd be dancing all night. It would have been nice to at least meet the dark-haired fella, maybe even dance, she thought. But their awkwardness bothered her, how would they ever connect? Did they even have a chance?

As expected, Susan was immediately off jitter-bugging. She wistfully watched her from across the modest dance floor littered with about a dozen couples. That left Barbara standing against a wall, along with a handful of other wall flowers, trying to look disinterested in dancing.

The Star-lite ballroom's name was far more glamorous than its interior. Two rows of chairs flanked each side of the dancing area. Close to the entrance, two long rectangular tables had been set up and were covered with plain white tablecloths. Each one held bowls of punch and home made confections for dessert along with rows of empty cups and saucers.

Barbara tapped her foot nervously. Several times, she had made eye contact with Harry but both quickly looked away, feeling embarrassed and gangly.

Finally, he stared at her as if something had been decided introspectively. He carefully sat down his cup of punch, straightened his oversized jacket and marched across the dance floor. Oh, God, he's coming over Barbara thought, unsure whether to look at him or look away.

"Would you like to d-d-dance," Harry stammered.

Barbara turned her head and got her first good look at him. He was short, but handsome with dark, wavy hair and sensitive brown eyes. His upper lip trembled as if he was afraid that she would turn him down. She nodded.

"Sure, that'd be nice," she said.

At first they danced as if they had four left feet. Harry stepped on Barbara's toes and Barbara dinged Harry's feet. Just as horrid, they seemed to swallow in unison. Loud swallows that belied innocence and nervousness. Harry feared his palms were sweating. While Barbara fought the urge to cover her mouth, fearing he'd notice her ill-fitting dentures. But then something magical happened. In spite of herself she was smiling and she wasn't hiding her face. Equally, Harry stopped stammering and sweating. Something intangible had been cemented between them.

After the first dance ended, he asked her again. And then again. For once Barbara understood what attracted Susan to the Starlight ballroom. She felt like the most beautiful and popular woman there, her heart all aglow from the new-found attention. She found herself wanting to know everything about this mysterious dark-haired stranger.

During a break, Barbara and Harry talked. Barbara was surprised to find herself babbling on like they were old friends. When alas Harry went to fetch her a cup of punch, she watched him with an appraising eye.

Harry was no rocket scientist, but he wasn't dumb either, she thought, just uneducated. Harry reminded her of uncle Syrus. A small, dark, quiet man with nice features who'd only completed the fifth grade. But it was his kindly soul that had won him everyone's admiration and strangely, inexplicably Barbara felt Harry was like him.

Barbara listened attentively as Harry told her that he had been raised in Kansas City. When she asked what he had been doing for a living, he hesitated a moment too long, then blurted he had been in the Navy over in the Pacific.

The way he said it and the look on his face, made her wonder if he was telling the truth. But then she heard her father's admonition hissing in her ears, she was never satisfied, always looking for something better than life was willing to give her. Something stirred in her soul. She liked this guy, Harry Davis.

They spent the entire evening together, dancing and talking. When the time came for them to leave, Harry politely asked if he could walk her to the bus. Barbara pretended to balk at the question. She didn't want to appear overanxious. After all, how much did she really know about this guy in the oversized jacket and dark-blue tweed pants? Memories of the landlord's sun flicked across her mind. Her eyes narrowed suspiciously. Trepidation was a snake slithering inside her. What should she do?

Susan was nowhere to be seen. She would have to make up her own mind. She hardly knew him, yet he seemed so honest and open, so genuinely interested in what she had to say, even with the topic of home and children. He couldn't be all bad if he liked children, she told herself.

"Sure," she said. "Why not?"

Harry's smile stretched across his face. It was like petting a puppy who has recently been in trouble. So quiet before, he suddenly couldn't stop talking. He was aghast with himself, but content too. He viewed the old diesel with different eyes as it came to a roaring halt. Everything in his life seemed better somehow. It baffled him.

Suddenly a loud clap of thunder roared across dark skies. Big, heavy drops began to trickle over them as they stood clumsily in front of the bus. Something made him offer Barbara his humble black umbrella. Perhaps it was the feelings she evoked, standing so close to her. He had never felt so elated. He had a feeling that things would be all right after all. He told himself he would get a job, win her heart and get married. Reluctantly she took the umbrella. Their eyes met. He watched her open it as if it were his promise ring. Yes, he thought, I will marry this woman, and my secret won't matter. Life was suddenly wonderful.

"Can I see you again?" he asked as the door swung open. She climbed onto the first step of the bus and paused.

The bus driver, an older man wearing a worn tan uniform with thick, dark glasses and gray puffs of hair escaping the edges of his cap stared at her, impatiently waiting for Barbara to board. Barbara looked down at Harry's hopeful face. How could she refuse? "Yes, Harry," she said. "I'd like that. Come see me at the drugstore, tomorrow if you can."

Not knowing what else to say, she turned and went to find a seat. Suddenly, another roll of thunder erupted as the cloudburst started. Looking out her window, she saw Harry standing there looking up, a smile still plastered on his face, completely undaunted by the rain drenching his simple jacket.

He anxiously waved, looking lost in the downpour as the bus pulled away from the curb. Barbara raised her hand and pressed her fingertips against the window. He was no Clark Gable, but then again, she was no Vivian Leigh.

Harry Davis. For a moment she tried the name out in her mind. Harry and Barbara Davis. Barbara Davis. Not bad, she thought, then laughed out loud. Mrs. Barbara Davis, just like the actress. Not bad at all.

3

White Lie

Harry stood in the rain on the street corner. Excitement danced along his skin. It was all he could do not to jump up and down flailing his arms. He wanted to tell the whole world how happy he was. But something kept him contained and proper as the bus pulled away. It was that same something that had ruled him at Beatrice that kept his excitement held to acceptable expression now. He knew about keeping up appearances.

Instinctively he ran for the next bus that would take him to his part of town, laughing and slapping his knees as he marveled over the night's events. Then he remembered, he didn't have enough money left for bus fare. He'd spent his paltry amount trying to impress Barbara. That meant walking. He began his trek, undaunted by the circumstance. He was too happy to care. He had a girl! A girl who genuinely seemed to like him for himself. It was a wonderful feeling that washed over him. Someone liked him. It could rain all week for all he cared. Life was good again.

It had been a very long time since he'd felt so jubilant. Even the rain and dusty old dirt roads made slick with the fresh rain smelled sweet. Slowly, with each step, he left the city behind. Storefront windows became glass shadows. Only the occasional car passing would throw some light his way. Crickets and croakers had begun their nightly song. Listening to their peaceful serenade while he walked towards the distant lights of houses was a comfort to him. Many times he'd walked home feeling lonesome or bored. But tonight his thoughts were centered around a certain chubby farm girl. He could still see her face and shy smile.

I should have kissed her, he thought suddenly in dismay. But just as quickly he brightened. There would be plenty of time for that. She said I could come see her at work, he reminded himself. Shame suddenly filled him; deceit was no way to start a relationship. He knew very little about the Navy. Why had he said that's what he'd been doing? Then again, that wasn't the lie he feared most.

Harry frowned. He wondered what she'd think if he'd told her everything about his past. Probably drop you on the spot, he scolded. After all, Barbara had raved about wanting babies. From there on, he would have to be especially careful about any references he made to his past.

It wasn't a pleasant tale. How do you delve into such sordid details with someone you've just met? Who would want to hear about an alcoholic and womanizing father you'd never known? It had established his life in and out of orphanages early on. It was also pretty apparent that his biological father knew very little about parenting. Eventually he abandoned the family altogether as he headed for Kansas City to continue his carousing ways.

It was not the sort of story one likes to share. He stopped for a moment to peer at the lonely moon partially hidden by clouds. It barely provided enough light to see vague shapes of the fence posts that skirted around much of the farmland along his path. Fortunately, he knew the way by heart.

The rain had subsided to just a drizzle but he was already soaked. Step after step, his shoes squeaked. He pulled the tuffs of his collar up around his ears. His thoughts shifted to his mother's life. Sade was a care-worn woman with a kind heart. In her day, she'd been considered quite a looker with striking features and long, auburn hair that fell in a feminine style across her shoulders.

She had done the best she could trying to raise nine kids with nothing. She was a frail woman with no real job skills. That fact, combined with having no relatives willing to help meant that they were always scraping to get by and often went hungry.

Harry, the youngest of the brood, had never had the privilege of new clothes or shoes. Without any positive male influence around and his mother constantly looking for work, Harry, a naturally rambunctious child with a talent for practical jokes, began a habit of getting into minor scrapes with the law.

Kansas social workers would occasionally look in on the family. They made note of the poverty and of Harry's waywardness, but did little to help. Instead, they warned his mother that they didn't approve of women raising children on their own. Abandoned and desperate to keep her family intact, she'd married Ed Foster. Ed was a one-time high school sweetheart who had let his amorous intentions be known shortly after her husband's departure.

Unfortunately, Ed Foster wasn't much of an improvement. He was only nice while sober and his propensity for bootleg whiskey guaranteed those times would be rare. The more he drank, the meaner he became. Harry was his favorite target. Ed never seemed to tire of pummeling on him to vent his frustrations. Regardless of how hard Ed worked during the day, every night he'd be at the same neighborhood pub drinking until he could hardly stand. When the money ran out, he'd stumble home.

Often foaming over with his own dissatisfactions, Harry knew a beating was looming. It was at such times that the boy tried to be invisible, keeping out of harms way.

From the start, Ed let Harry know that he wasn't wanted. The older siblings had scrambled to get away as soon as they were able, leaving Harry alone for Foster to exorcise his demons on. It didn't take long for Harry to recognize the signs; restlessness followed by spewing a host of slur's to the rage clearly visible in Ed's eyes.

It was during such times that his mother would feel so helpless to protect him. She was totally incapable of placating him. Then Ed's eyes would glaze over just before his hands would ball into a fist.

After a beating, Harry would steal away with his bruised body and bloody nose to wait for his mother to come home. He kept his suffering to himself, aware that his mother had heron abuse to contend with. From that moment on he promised himself that if he ever had kids, he'd never hit them or be so cruel as to tell them they weren't wanted. He'd be the perfect father, the kind that boys envied; playing ball, having long heart-to-heart talks with their sons and hugging them even when they squirmed to get away just to let them know they were loved. He would be all those things and more.

Barely more than a tadpole of ten Harry quit school to work at a local greenhouse for 10 cents an hour. The work was grueling for a youth, but Harry never complained. He irrigated, planted, separated, and hoed. Whatever was asked of him, he did. Anything to help his mother make ends meet. He told himself school was useless, he'd missed too many classes playing nurse for his and his mother's wounds. Academics had become a struggle. Scholastically his classmates were worlds ahead of him. Feeling resigned and figuring he'd never catch up, he'd just given up. But he never recovered from the embarrassment of not knowing how to read. It would be a blight on his future that would haunt him daily.

Finally, one evening after a particularly brutal beating that had left Harry a collection of bruises and scrapes, he ran away. With the wind at his back and the sun setting, he gathered a handful of clothes and the little bit of food he could find, stuffed them into a burlap sack and snuck out, leaving the little house with the tattered shutters and chipped green paint behind.

But each time he closed his eyes, the images of that night would return. The night had started like so many. Ed rummaging through the cupboards and icebox in search of food and blaming him and his mother for his demise. Of course there wasn't much food and what they had wasn't what he wanted. Ed was a big man with an equally big appetite. What he wanted was a hearty meal like a t-bone steak, potatoes and a salad.

His eyes shifted to Harry, who was sitting silently on the couch wearing a threadbare orange and brown stripped tee shirt. Harry was by the radio fiddling with a make shift sling shot. He was small for a boy and being so thin made him appear even smaller. Harry felt the weight of his stare but refused to look up. He didn't want to see Ed's disgust directed at him.

"If your mom didn't have so many damned kids…," Ed left the sentence dangling as he threw an empty milk carton against the window. That earned a peek. Harry could see anger like two fire dragons in Ed's eyes glaring at him. "I told her I didn't want any damned kids. Especially somebody else's brats!" he spat bitterly thumping the counter with one of his large hands. Hearing Ed slap the counter made Harry jump. He could feel terror growing; he knew the maelstrom coming.

"You!" Ed clutched Harry and slammed him against the wall, keeping him pinned.

"Leave me alone!" were the only words Harry managed to utter before he felt the first blow. It sent him flying. Harry landed haphazardly against the rocker sitting in front of the living room window. Although the rocker was old and rickety, it was still Sade's favorite piece of furniture. No sooner did Harry get to his feet when another blow sent him sailing against the archway that led into the small, cluttered dining room. Harry scrambled under the kitchen table.

"Think that's going to save you?" Ed mocked swiping at him. For a time Harry successfully dodged his lunges. But then lady luck turned on him as Ed's big hand curled around the boy's neck. Ed shook him like a loose sack of sawdust. Harry coughed and sputtered. The child's world began to spin, faster and faster while his feet dangled freely. Darkness flowed over him like a huge ink blot. The pain was gone and all the memories of his stepfather striking him gone too.

When Harry awoke, his eyes barely opened. It was then he knew he had to get out of there. If he didn't, Ed would surely kill him. Leaving was his only choice; so he'd left. Harry was determined to survive. Believing anything was better than the world he knew. But his new life proved to be quite the challenge for a crudely educated and unskilled youth. He tried to make do; working any kind of job he could find no matter how low the pay. There were times he wasn't sure if he was going to freeze, bake, or starve to death.

Stealing soon became a necessity of life. At least he wouldn't starve when he was stealing, and the practice became more common to Harry. It wasn't long before the police caught up with the wayward teen. In turn, they brought him before the Kansas juvenile authorities where he was deemed uncontrollable. His parents were notified of the hearing but no one came to speak up for him. It reinforced old fears, he was truly alone. No one cared. Not even his mother.

They provided him with two choices: Going home where there would inevitably be more beatings or being placed in the Kansas Institution for Feeble-minded Youth. It was an easy decision; he chose the institution; not realizing what that decision would mean. To a half-starved youth, three square meals a day and a roof over his head were quite enticing.

The institution had been opened by the Kansas state legislature in 1887 near the small farming community of Beatrice. Like so many institutions of the day, it began with high-minded aspirations. This one was designed to reclaim mentally retarded youths with the goal of making them "fit for use in society." Over the years, its mission changed to include the mentally ill and mentally "defective." That included boys like Harry Davis, who were not old enough or bad enough for prison but were still viewed outcasts. Reclamation was a standing joke because everyone knew that once you entered The Beatrice State Home, you never returned. It was a legal dumping ground for children whose parents either couldn't or wouldn't care for them.

Boys were trained in agriculture and girls in domestic work. The institution's farm, which included a large dairy, provided all of the necessary food for its residents while also producing a steady income for the home from surplus revenue. The grounds included forty acres of rolling farmland and trees. The entire estate was kept pristine at all times. Electricity for its 23 buildings was supplied by their own power plant, making Beatrice a very succinct unit.

In 1945 Harry became one more number among the more than 1,500 residents who already lived in the Beatrice State home. Except for semi-regular visits from his sister and Ed Harris, his brother-in-law, Harry had little contact with the outside world.

Once during a routine visit, Harris, an Army veteran who'd spent four years fighting the Nazis in Europe, didn't like what he saw at the institution. In fact, he found it appalling. Constant shrill wailing and screams echoed across the lawn escaping one of the nearby buildings. Heavy metal bars were anchored to the windows giving an eerie appearance. Here and there, small troops of mentally retarded residents shuffled along after their attendants, their faces dumb, their eyes blank. He cringed, it reminded him of his days in Germany and the concentration camps.

Ed looked back at Harry, lying on his back. He seemed preoccupied with watching the clouds in the sky. It was a beautiful fall day. Loose leaves that hadn't been raked into nice neat piles blew across the grounds in colors of burlaps browns, pear yellows and watermelon reds. Ed sat for awhile just studying his brother-in-law. He noticed how he recoiled at the sight of people in white uniforms and wondered what went on there when visiting hours were over.

Ed was puzzled. He knew Harry was no dummy and he sure didn't act crazy. In fact, as long as Ed had known him, Harry had always been a good-hearted kid, even if a bit wild in his younger days. And who could blame him for that, Ed thought, considering the two "fathers" he'd had in his life. Five years in the institution had mellowed him to where the sweet, childlike nature and his shy smile remained, but a lot of the spirit had been leached out of him.

The situation confused him. What was someone like Harry even doing in a place like Beatrice?

"So what in the hell are you doing here, Harry?" Ed asked. "You don't belong here. This place is for crazy people. Real crazy people."

Harry turned his head to look at his brother in law. For a long time he said nothing. Tears welled in his eyes and when he spoke his voice was barely above a whisper.

"I don't know, Ed. But if I'm here much longer, I'm afraid I'm gonna go crazy, too," Harry confessed.

"Then you've got to get out!" Ed insisted. He wondered why Harry was so resigned to getting his freedom, but then it occurred to him that perhaps if he'd been living there for long he might be just as broken. He knew he had to rescue him; somehow, some way.

As Harry watched Ed leaving, he could feel his mood plummeting. Before he realized it, he'd fallen into a deep depression. It was too much to hope for. He couldn't let himself believe he could get out. It was easier to endure the insanity than to get his hopes up and be disappointed yet again.

Ed kept his promise. In fact he was surprised to learn that Harry could leave the state home. After all he was nearly twenty-one and certainly no threat to society anymore. His days of petty thievery and mischief were long gone. There was only one catch, being a ward of the state, the state had the right to insist that Harry be sterilized before being released.

According to state officials, they didn't want to chance Harry's children showing proclivities for juvenile delinquency. Ed was shocked. Sterilized? How could they endorse such an outrageous requisite? Harris argued relentlessly with Beatrice on Harry's behalf, but in the end nothing changed. Those were the requirements. But not to worry, they assured Ed. It was a safe, simple procedure that wouldn't affect his sexual interests. He just wouldn't be able to father children.

Ed was horrified. He didn't know what he'd do if he was in the situation. Then again, it wasn't his decision to make. He told Harry. The younger man nodded his head solemnly. For years he had struggled to maintain his sanity by dreaming about the day he'd be free. Finally a light had opened in his world and Harry was going to be given his chance. He didn't want much from life, just a wife, children and a home to come back to every night.

He shuddered remembering the many nights he'd lay awake trying to shut out moans, screams and cries of his fellow inmates by trying to imagine what it would be like. His favorite dream had preserved him day after day; his vision of a loving wife kissing him each morning as he headed off for work. Then hugs from his children when he returned home to dinner on the table.

He had to make a choice. His freedom or his lineage. Children were a very important part of his dreams. But if he remained at the home, he'd have neither. He chose freedom. With it, there was hope; without it, there was none. Adoption, he thought. Yes, we could always adopt, he reassured himself.

Harry snapped out of the past and into the present as he rounded the final curve that took him to the driveway that led to the house where he had a room. The medium-size canary yellow house looked white by the pale moonlight. It was totally dark inside, meaning Mrs. Hansbury and Pete and Juliann Rose, the other two residents, were all asleep.

Carefully, he skipped up the porch steps trying not to disturb anyone inside. He fumbled for his key, but once inside, he crept down the hall to his room in perfect silence. His room was the last one on the right. He didn't even light the kerosene lamp. Instead he laid on his bed and began to softly hum Amazing Grace, his favorite song. Singing it or whistling it always made him feel better. He'd been through a lot. Only a year ago he'd gone under the knife now his potential wife was here. He thought about what the men in the white coats had done to him down there. Could she love a man who couldn't give her babies?

I can make her happy, he muttered to himself. I know I can. I've conquered the hardest, this is nothing. It's only a little white lie. She'll see, he thought. Then he closed his eyes letting the crickets and frogs lull him to sleep.

4

Preston's Truth

My father's world was a trek into hell. Learning what he'd endured just because he was born during a time of ignorance in this country, while equally ridiculous measures for dealing with societies' undesirables were applied, left me a very humble man. But I like to reflect back on his life. It helps me put things in perspective. Realizing what burdens he carried for the love of his family often made me feel petty when I complained about mine.

However, these were truths that would take me a long time to acknowledge and a longer time to learn. I'm still learning. But I'm getting ahead of myself. So let's begin where it begins with me and my family. My son Preston was born underneath the auspicious skies of Phoenix, Arizona on Ground Hog's day. His chestnut hair and cherubic-face belied his secret world. I guess you could say that he was a special child right from the start. On one hand he was a much-wanted kid but on the other hand he was unplanned, or what most people would say, unwanted.

The odds had been against him from his moment of conception, as most single and un-married young mothers in today's world are encouraged to abort rather than conceive. Whatever happened to adoption? It seemed it had become a dying art, littered by the corpses of millions of abandoned babies who longed to grow up but would never have the chance…Preston would be given that chance. He was lucky.

It was a brilliant Saturday morning. The smell of drying pine needles mixed with a crystalline frost permeated the air. I loaded up the car and carefully strapped my son Preston, wriggling all the while, into the car seat as we went for his 9:00 A.M. appointment.

"There is nothing wrong," friends and family assured. "Little boys always talk later than girls. Just give him time and before you know it he'll be talking up a storm." The words reverberated in my mind like a familiar song.

For a moment I pictured him sitting on my lap. His big, brown, saucer-shaped eyes continently staring into mine, whispering, "I love you daddy." If I could have a wish, this would be my birthday present, on today, his third birthday.

We had a special day planned. First, his annual evaluation with child psychologist Dr. Mary Cunningham, then off to join my wife, Joan, and his sister, Ashley, for a trip to the zoo capped off with a night in our log cabin. It was to be the perfect family weekend.

Pulling up to Dr. Cunningham's office, I cut the engine and sat in the lot, surveying the perfectly kept landscape of shrubs and flowers that trimmed the manicured lawn. I liked this time of year. There was always a myriad of azaleas, rhodies and bachelor buttons in full bloom. Making the otherwise typical office building look like a page out of Better Homes & Gardens with the big, fluffy, white and pink blossoms blending with yellow and orange circles of the bachelor buttons.

My thoughts shifted to my reason for being there. There was a lot riding on today's evaluation. I hoped Preston would be able to continue his twice-daily speech classes for another year. He needed it. While most toddlers his age had a vocabulary of several dozen words, Preston struggled to grunt out one or two. "Speech delayed." The social worker had informed us a year earlier at his last evaluation and yet in the last twelve months he'd shown little progress. I looked at his face; his expression was neutral. Did he have any idea? I unstrapped him from the car seat and proceeded into the office.

A few minutes later the receptionist, a tall blonde woman wearing an emerald green dress, appeared and led us down the long hallway that took us to Dr. Cunningham's office. I could feel my stomach growing tight after she left. As I waited, I surveyed the office. I began to peruse the titles of books crammed on her four bookshelves, one neatly centered against each wall. Most of her books were either on child psychology or child development. Sandwiched next to the shelf by the only window in the office was a row of plaques denoting her professional accomplishments, and in the corner behind her credenza, a box full of toys. Tools, I thought.

Preston was being his regular self; expressing his displeasure by making a series of high pitch screams and grunts while simultaneously pounding his head with a closed right fist. Such behavior had become the norm.

Dr. Cunningham had a lofty reputation. She'd been a child psychologist for more than 30 years. She entered looking stiff and professional, wearing her mahogany hair in an early 70's style beehive. Her dimly lit office, an archive of history, was musty and grim. They were a perfect match.

"Mr. Davis, I'm going to begin this assessment using a series of standardized Bailey Scales and Vineyard Development tests. This will allow me to further analyze your son's advancements in the last year, and give us a look at his mental capabilities," she said as her hazel eyes politely met mine with that professional gaze familiar to so many psychologists. The gaze that said they saw you, but weren't really seeing you. Then she brought out a medium-sized wooden chest filled with a variety of blocks, beads, and puzzles.

"Mr. Davis, you can take a seat in the waiting room, I will let you know when we are finished with the testing."

Forty-five minutes later she emerged looking even more rigid than before. I took a seat in front of her desk and eased back into the chair. I knew that look. The news was not going to be good. I could feel the tension creeping into my face as I braced myself. Preston ran to me, climbed on my lap and threw his arms tightly around my neck. It was obvious he didn't want to be there anymore than I did. She returned to her seat behind the desk shuffling through her papers as if stalling, looking uncomfortable.

"Mr. Davis," she said hesitantly clearing her throat. "I'm afraid I have some bad news." Her face was stoic. My stomach did a somersault. I could feel my heartbeat. What came next was not going to be anything I wanted to hear.

"I have totaled the scores from the various tests." She paused again. An emotionless stare in my direction, perhaps searching for words that wouldn't hurt. "And in evaluating your son's progress over the last year he appears to be significantly delayed." Her eyes avoided mine, she focused on the scores holding a piece of paper in her hands.

"Whaat…what do you mean…What are you saying?" I asked in a whisper struggling to get the words out. Already the term, "significantly delayed" was burning a hole through my heart.

"What I mean, Mr. Davis, is that your son Preston is significantly delayed and functioning in the moderate to severe level of mental retardation. I'm truly sorry," she said looking away.

My world came to a crashing stop. Mental retardation? Time suspended. Silence entered the room like a negative force. I didn't want to deal with this. Preston's arms drew tighter around my neck. Did something within him understand what she had said?

"Exactly, what do you mean?" I asked, needing to know.

"As I said," she began.

"Well say it again dammit!" I snapped. Her eyes met mine. I knew it wasn't her fault, but I was angry. This couldn't be happening. How could she be so calm? Because it wasn't her child, it was mine.

"Your son has an IQ of 40-60. Unfortunately he will never be like other children. He will grow but it will be at a much slower pace than others his age. As he gets older, his shortcomings will become more and more evident and pronounced," she replied just as calmly.

My eyes focused and defocused. I was numb. Once again I felt life had pushed me off a cliff and the sky was falling down on top of me. I bent over in the chair, elbows on my knees, and ran my hands through my thinning blond hair. Why God, why this? I heard the words over and over in my mind. I'm sorry Mr. Davis, but your son is mild to severely retarded." How could God be so cruel?

My thoughts went back to my father and his forced sterilization in exchange for freedom. Being labeled feebleminded, retarded, defective. But it had all been a lie. He was simply a troubled youth running from the hands of an abusive father and stepfather and had been too introverted to defend himself. What a huge price he'd paid for their arrogance and ignorance.

It was a harsh reminder. If he'd been misdiagnosed, couldn't Preston's diagnosis be wrong too?

Silver pearls welled in my eyes and rolled silently down my cheeks spilling onto the floor. I grasped my son tightly. I knew my son had experienced some delays, but to impose this sentence on a 3-year-old child and a 46-year-old father. I thought of my wife. What would I say to her? How would I find the words? Another journey in my life was about to begin. A repetition of my past, one more hurdle of which I had no control.

I quickly gathered Preston and his diaper bag and left Dr. Cunningham's office. I wanted to scream at the top of my lungs until I had no screams left. I wanted to hit something, someone, anything to give myself relief. But there was no sanctuary; this was it. I left knowing I had only one choice. I had to face it. This was not the first time that reality had raped my emotions. I was a survivor and I was determined to make it thorough this crisis.

The drive home seemed like an eternity. I fixed my rear view mirror so I could watch Preston fumble through his books. He loved books but was more fixated on licking his index finger or giving imaginary baths to their characters.

Then for reasons unknown, he would suddenly rip pages and throw them on the floor, screaming in some intrinsic agony as they left his reach. I knew it was unusual behavior. Perhaps I'd always known. His little differences were growing daily. But he was my son. It was easy to pretend.

Finally we arrived home. The house seemed unusually quiet. I carried Preston downstairs to the playroom and put on a Barney video to entertain him. I needed to go into my office, close the door and cry. But when I opened the door I was greeted by twenty parents and a dozen screaming children. It shattered my hope for silence.

"Happy Birthday to you, Happy Birthday to you, Happy Birthday dear Preston, Happy Birthday to you." The words flowed, filling the room with an iridescent happiness. Bright red, blue and green mylar balloons billowed against the shiny colorful packages cluttered everywhere. Children were playing, running and screaming. How carefree they appeared. It made me feel a twinge of envy. Why couldn't Preston have that?

Joan emerged from the crowd, wearing a color coordinated birthday hat blowing on a kazoo. She noticed my din.

"What's wrong honey?" I could see it in her caring blue eyes, she knew something was wrong. "Everything O.K.?" I felt another knot in my stomach. How could I begin to tell her. She'd tackled more than her share of struggles too.

"Yes, everything is great." I replied trying to hide behind my smile. The lie hurt. I needed to talk about it.

This was Preston's moment. I would not ruin it. I watched him, sitting in the corner, his back to the crowd, his mind in some far off place, oblivious to his surroundings. I quietly slipped out of the room. I needed silence.

Over the last year Joan had witnessed Preston's lack of advancement and behavior too. She shared the dream of all parents who wanted only a happy and healthy child. Not this. Not her child.

But then you eventually accept, as all those before you who have had to deal with similar plights have accepted, it did happen. It is reality. You learn to play the hand life has dealt you or allow it to bury you in ruin. We were not quitters. That I knew.

For the next two hours I put on my party face. I would be the dad for Preston that Harry had been for me. No matter what obstacles lay ahead, I would be there for him.

During those hours I realized Dr. Cunningham had been correct in at least a few of her initial observations. Preston didn't act like other children his age. His behavior was not only unpredictable, but lacked the normal excitement of typical toddlers experiencing their third birthday.

He had over twenty presents and wasn't interested in the contents of even one. A sadness enveloped me; he couldn't even communicate to tell us why.

I decided not to tell my wife what had happened earlier. There was no point in her sharing the pain. The sorrow would be there waiting for another day. I dodged her questions.

"Oh, they just did some testing. We should have the results some time next week," I said, carefully avoiding eye contact. If she'd seen my eyes, she would have known. Already there was a hint in her voice, but I couldn't deal with it.

Not yet, not now. Maybe I was being selfish or weak, but I needed some time to just let myself absorb the words.

As night fell, Ashley developed a slight fever. She laid listless on the couch, curled in a ball. Like her brother, she had big brown eyes, usually they were dazzling, but tonight they lacked their normal luster.

"Don't think we will be going to the cabin tonight. Why don't you and Preston go? You can have a father and son evening." My wife suggested. I looked at her lovingly, her habit of such thoughtfulness never failed to move me. I looked at Ashley, like Preston, her face was flawless, a porcelain doll baby.

"Yes. That would be nice," I replied. And maybe God would perform a miracle and heal him if I prayed hard enough, then I wouldn't have to lie, I thought. Holding in my despair was taking its toll; I could feel myself getting more and more distraught. If I stayed much longer, Joan would know. I was glad to be leaving. Alas, I would have my time.

We loaded up the Expedition with two back packs that held clothes and miscellaneous supplies, then took off for the cabin. The trip was unusually quiet. Preston slipped into a nap as we rolled over the rocky terrain that led to our family cabin. An expanse of pine trees and underbrush filled the land that crept along the rough road. The last flecks of sunlight died as embers of a campfire behind the mountains and darkness set in. Two hours later we arrived.

Pine Flats was our private getaway. A sanctuary rich in history. No running water. No electricity. A 100-year-old log cabin on an old mining claim in the middle of nowhere. Just me, Preston and God. Now I needed them more than ever.

God had been my favorite playmate most of my life, yet He was also my fair weather God. When life was good, I didn't have the time to talk. When life was bad, I would come crawling back on hands and knees. Tonight I'd be crawling.

As I unpacked, I took a deep breath of clean mountain air. This was what I needed. I carried Preston's sleeping body inside. The silence was loud and deafening. Even the mice were quiet. I could see my breath crystallized in the cold mountain air. A light snow had begun to fall through the densely crowded pines. A peacefulness began to fill me.

I laid beside Preston on the rackety tick bed and drew the goose down comforter made by my late mother around us, shutting out the gritty, cold night air. It had been knitted over a decade ago for a little grandson that she would never meet. Memories from another time, gone now. A thought came to mind; would she have loved him? Before I could answer, sleep covered me as gently as the snow covered our Pine Flats.

I never realized how important family was to her until I realized how important family was to me. Tonight, I would find that truth.

5

Courting Reality

I awoke to Preston yanking my arm, big brown eyes ablaze with mischief. I stared at his toddler face, full of innocence, so untethered by all that had happened the day before. To be so carefree; I felt a twinge of envy. His insistence to get me up was wearing me down; I had to smile.

"Hey buddy, how is Preston today?"

"Daddddddddy, git upp," he persisted, enunciating his words with difficulty.

I watched his eyes roll, his focus clearly somewhere else. He abandoned his efforts and left me still lying in bed. Sunshine brightened the room in slivers through the partially closed shades.

I heard a car door shut. Then I heard the front door. I knew Preston couldn't manage the door alone. It had to be Joan and Ashley.

She sauntered into the bedroom wearing jeans and a light sweater. She was dressed appropriately for the chilly morning air at Pine Flats. Her eyes surveyed the situation lightheartedly.

"Working hard?" she said chuckling.

"Definitely," I returned her serve. "How's Ashley?"

"See for yourself sleepy head," she instructed before heading to the kitchen.

The smell of fresh coffee brewing brought my appetite to life. I lumbered into the kitchen to see Ashley struggling to eat a bowl of cereal and Preston just playing with his. For a moment I studied him. "What is it?" Joan noticed my introspection.

It was time to talk. I needed to tell her the truth.

"The other day?"

"At the doctor?" she finished for me.

"Yes," I said sheepishly. "Well, I left out a few details."

"I know." We looked at each other. To my surprise, there was no anger in her eyes. Guilt washed over me. The words were in my mouth but she raised a hand, pressed a finger to my lips. "It doesn't matter. Tell me now," she said softly. Once again, she had succeeded in filling me with great emotion. I swallowed, trying to compose myself.

"Dr. Cunningham said he's…" I hesitated looking at him.

"He won't understand you," she answered the question I'd been stumbling over in my mind.

"His tests indicate that he's mildly to severely retarded," I swallowed again. This time the tears came.

"Honey," she said coming to me. She held me. Me. Mr. Macho was falling apart, crying like a baby.

Preston slipped off his chair and ran to me.

"Daddddy," he stuttered hugging me.

"That's right, that's right," I choked out, barely able to see but holding him tightly, none-the-less. "She could be wrong," I heard myself say. My voice sounded small and distant.

"Listen to me," Joan said, turning my face to her. "We're going to get through this," she told me.

Preston wiggled out of my arms. I let him go, watching him tear into a box of toys. There was no rhyme or reason to his actions. He was just being who he was.

"Hey," she whispered. I refocused, seeing her eyes looking at me so lovingly. "We will. I promise."

"It's not fair,"

"Life's not fair Scott. What are you going to do about it? Let it conquer you?" she challenged. She had a point, but it was not one I wanted to see. Yet, I knew I didn't have a choice. If I denied it, I would be denying him. Whatever else I fought with, that was not something that was open to debate. I would not do that to him. He didn't ask to be autistic anymore than my father had asked to be sterilized.

"Let's take them out. It's a beautiful day. Too beautiful to stay inside. Come on," Joan suggested.

"You go ahead, I'll be there shortly, okay?"

She looked at me, her eyes searching mine. I could see the worry in her eyes.

"I promise," I said softly, composing myself. She moved back, squeezed my shoulder.

"Okay," she said then turned away from me to face the kids. "Okay you two, let's go outside," she suggested. I watched Preston protesting and how well Joan managed to distract his already easily distractible mind.

Ashley came forward quickly. They left me to my thoughts. I sat there for a few minutes spying on them from inside, the kids playing. They seemed happy. Ashley tossing a ball with Joan and Preston playing with his fire engine. Throwing it around as much as he rolled it. I let out the sigh I'd been holding.

"Can you hear me dad?" I whispered.

Before I realized I was thinking about him again. Thinking about his world, how it all started. My mind took me back. I had to smile at my father. He truly was a shy man.

My father had shown up at the drugstore two hours before the lunch crowd. Blushing, he handed my mom a bouquet of flowers he'd picked from a neighbor's garden. She tried to accept them as if such attentions were an everyday occurrence. Frank just grinned, trying to get a better peek at Barbara's mystery man by peering over the counter.

"Hi," Harry said.

"Hi," she replied. They both stood caught in their awkwardness.

Harry swallowed hard. It was now or never, he told himself.

"I sure enjoyed dancing with you last night," he said.

Barbara nodded; shyly she glanced over her shoulder. She caught Frank watching.

"Me too."

"I mean, I liked talking to you too," Harry quickly added, not wanting to give the wrong impression.

"Me too," Barbara said. Then realizing how that sounded, added, "I mean, I didn't mean I liked talking to me, I meant I liked talking to you," she said as her face began to blister with embarrassment.

Harry laughed. She giggled in spite of herself.

"I kinda hoped that's what you meant."

Barbara smiled, hiding her teeth behind her hand. Her inhibitions of the previous night had vanished. The ungainly waitress had returned. Harry took her smile as a good sign and pressed on.

"Do you think I could see you after you get off work?"

"I don't get off 'til five."

"That's okay, I'll just wait," he said blushing. "That is, if you don't mind," Harry said, trying to appear nonchalant, even though he felt like shouting his feelings from the sidewalk. I got a girl!

"Don't you have to work?"

"Oh," Harry panicked. She's gonna think I'm some sort of bum. Good thing I looked for a job this morning, he thought. After all, a man with a girl has to have some spending money. "I just got a new job, over at the depot washing buses. It starts tomorrow."

Barbara's silence bothered him. Was she disappointed?

"It isn't much, but it's a start and it's honest," he finished weakly, fearing his first romance might be over before it began.

"I think that's fine," she said. "Who knows, maybe you'll end up running that ol' depot one of these days." She smiled sweetly. Harry grinned.

"I just might," he said, suddenly feeling like he could conquer anything. It was a new feeling. It made him feel good in a way he had never known before.

He took the same seat in the corner booth where he and his friend had sat only the day before. Today it had new meaning. This was the booth where he'd first noticed his girl. Thinking about the events over the last twenty-four hours made him giddy.

He stayed there for hours, looking out the window some of the time, watching the bustle of customers coming and going, but mostly watching Barbara as she hustled behind the lunch counter. Watching her made him happy.

Barbara noticed him studying her. She prayed he wouldn't notice her weight or horrible dentures. She had her own little disappoints, wishing he could have magically grown an inch or two overnight. But hearing her dad's voice hissing in the back of her mind never satisfied helped her dismiss her qualms.

Finally the last customer shuffled out, leaving Harry, Barbara and Frank the only people left. Frank shot a look at Harry, then back at Barbara. Watching them fumbling, so eager to impress each other brought back memories of his own courtship. He smiled at Barbara in a knowing way.

"Guess you best not be keeping your young fellah waiting any longer," he told her.

"Thanks Frank," she giggled rushing away to the stock room to change.

When she returned, Harry was up fidgeting by his table. He looked like a little boy who was suddenly afraid that his mother had abandoned him in the super-market. But when he saw her standing in the satin-like green dress, the worry disappeared from his face. Immediately he straightened, taken back. A big smile curled his lips.

Barbara smiled back. He might be a tad short and a trifle uneducated, she thought, but she had to love that smile. The best part for her was the way he seemed so absolutely taken with her. She'd never have to worry about him straying, she told herself.

They spent the evening walking through the park, talking and laughing. Like many new couples, they delighted in each nuance and gesture. Even simple swinging was special and new; she sat while he pushed. Finally it came time to escort her to the bus. His eyes flicked at her. He debated, should he or shouldn't he? They were nearly to the bus stop before he got his courage up. Awkwardly he stole a kiss, it left them both blushing.

Then, realizing there were other people around, he quickly composed himself. An elderly couple, both bent like weeping willows, smiled at them. Harry smiled back. The man, a tall reed of a man with sparse wisps of gray hair, was helping his wife, considerably smaller, but equally gray and fragile, onto the bus. Harry looked at Barbara. That will be us someday, he thought.

The courtship progressed quickly. After only one month Harry proposed. They became inseparable, spending nearly all their free time together, much of it just walking. Barbara knew Harry didn't have much money so she salvaged his pride by saying, "I like to walk" or "I need to lose some of this weight."

Being both relieved and appreciative, Harry would add, "You look just right to me."

Harry was a perfect gentleman. Nothing like her landlord's son. She found his reserve and thoughtfulness refreshing. Yet they both were aware it was becoming increasingly more difficult to be proper. Too many passionate kisses shared beneath too many moonlight nights. They wanted more.

The morning after Harry proposed, Barbara wrote to her father asking for his permission. It was necessary since she was only 19 and unable to marry legally in Kansas without parental consent. Her quick acceptance to marry had surprised Harry. They set the date to tie the knot in two weeks.

But Barbara's father, Bernard, didn't share their joy. He refused permission. Instead, he wanted answers. Who was this fellow? What did she really know about him? Why the big rush?

"I'm in love, daddy," Barbara would say. "If you won't give me permission, then we'll run off to Kansas where I'm of legal age."

Realizing the couple was determined, he relented. But things continued to unravel. Harry's nemesis, Ed Foster, got wind of the pending ceremony and wrote Barbara's parents hoping to sabotage their plans. His words were nothing more than outright character assassination.

Harry Davis was good for nothing, he told them. In fact, he had spent a number of years in the Beatrice State Home because of trouble with the authorities. But he left one thing out; he was unaware of the price Harry had paid for his freedom.

Again Bernard called. This time relentless, he absolutely forbade her from going through with the ceremony. He continued to hammer questions at her. Did she know where her fiancé had been? What kind of man he really was?

"Yes I do. As a matter of fact, Harry told me himself," she insisted. But her father was a dog working on a meaty bone.

"You'll regret this for the rest of your life. I raised you better than this. Why are you falling for the first chump off the train?" he pressed. Barbara felt anger and defensiveness curdling inside her.

She had to admit she had questions too, but she still believed in him, no matter what. She had wondered herself recalling a time they had been at his sister's place. Barbara had casually remarked about Harry's supposed Navy career.

Puzzled, Ed Harris, his brother-in-law had said, "Harry was never in the Navy."

"But he told me," Barbara had started to ask. Clearly uncomfortable, Ed abruptly discontinued the conversation under the pretext he needed to run an errand for his wife. It had only served to increase her suspicions.

In response Barbara confronted Harry. She wanted the truth.

"Why'd you tell me you were in the Navy when you weren't?" she countered.

Harry blushed a crimson red. Caught. She'd caught him in a lie. Finally the words spilled from his being; the words he'd desperately wanted to share but hadn't out of fear.

"I was afraid you wouldn't want to see me again if you knew where I'd been," he confessed. His voice unsteady, he told her about his nightmare existence at Beatrice.

This time it was his turn to omit the fact that he had been sterilized. Fear gripped him like a tight band around his soul. He couldn't breathe. He couldn't tell her. Not that. He couldn't. He'd lose her for sure.

"Why Harry," she said when he finished, "that's terrible what they did to you. But you didn't have to lie to me. You don't have to be ashamed; you aren't crazy or dumb. You were just a troubled kid, and there's plenty of them that never get caught," she told him.

They were both crying now. Harry offered his handkerchief and Barbara had gladly taken it. While she blew her nose she began to thank God for sending her such a good man. Such a loving man. It humbled her. Finally she cleared her throat.

"I think you've turned out fine, and I love you just the way you are," she said this time dabbing away his tears. His sweet brown eyes held a sadness almost unbearable to Barbara, she never wanted to see that look again.

Well, maybe not just the way I am, Harry thought. Sharing just that much had been emotionally draining to both of them. He knew it would be awhile before he broached the last detail.

A deep sadness welled within; his whole life had been about abuse and isolation. All he ever wanted was a family to love and care for. He'd love and care for Barbara, and somehow he'd find a way around his inability to give her a baby to make it turn out all right. After all he'd been through, he deserved at least that much.

Bernard made one finally attempt to curtail the wedding. He played his trump card, Harry had been in Beatrice, unaware she already knew. Undaunted, she was more determined than ever. She would marry him and have his babies come hell or high water.

Against the odds and her family's wishes, at last their plans rolled forward. On a clear day in June, while sunshine peaked through maple trees across the grounds, they stood beneath the tree closest to the chapel facing each other. There was only the couple, the minister and Harry's sister and brother in-law gathered. Yet the pristine grounds of Pine Crest made a beautiful backdrop for the wedding.

Because it was an afternoon ceremony, the sunshine had removed the chill of the morning, making the day pleasant and warm. Harry stood nervously in the same oversized jacket he'd worn on the first night they'd met. Barbara wore a plain white dress. She had no money for a traditional gown. At first, it had made her distraught, but once she realized that Harry didn't care, she adopted his attitude. Happy to finally be marrying the man she loved.

They had no money for a honeymoon, so they went to the Capitol Beach Amusement Park and then to the Starlite Ballroom where their love first took root. They proudly showed off their gold wedding bands and danced as if the band played only for them.

They slept together that night for the first time. Awkward fumblings, nervous releases, enjoying a new world between them.

The following morning, Harry put on his hard hat and proudly went to work. Already he was anxious about returning home to his new bride.

Barbara's parents were slow to accept him as their son-in-law. Her father even considered going to court for an annulment.

But Harry had a way of warming people to his easy-going style and all-around nice-guy attitude. They began to overlook his past and shortcomings. He was no genius, but they respected his earnest work ethic and the extra construction job he took to earn more money. Money they promptly spent. Harry was dedicated to making Barbara happy.

On it went, with each new hurdle he'd find a solution. That's how they added a house and furniture. Piece by piece, day by day. But with each new thing, the responsibilities, grew along with his hours to accommodate the new growth.

As month's passed into years, even Barbara's most skeptical family members and friends had to concede that marriage certainly seemed to agree with her. She even had money to get her teeth fixed. The ugly duckling farm girl emerged as a beautiful swan, lithe and glowing.

Harry was as content as a pig in warm mud. Almost. He had a pretty wife, a nice home, more friends than he could shake a stick at, and he was free. What the heck if Barbara had champagne tastes on their beer budget? As long as he was healthy, he could work it off.

But there was still that looming secret that no amount of hard work could erase or cold cash buy. Every time one of Harry's friends would have a baby or Barbara got invited to a shower, he'd cringe. His day of reckoning was approaching. What would he do?

It was particularly aggravating when their next-door neighbors, Roger and Peggy, had first one child and then the next. Harry had known Roger for years, ever since they had both been residents of the Beatrice State Home. But he was puzzled. He couldn't have kids and watched with envy as Roger played with his. How was it possible that Roger had escaped their barbarism?

When Barbara mentioned Peggy was pregnant again, Harry grew silent. Barbara began to grow restless and discouraged. Why couldn't she get pregnant? Harry just kept his secret, afraid of losing the one person he loved above anything else.

But the pressure continued to mount. This was the 1950s, a caricature of American life the way life was supposed to be. A home for every working man, a car in every garage, and four children in every household. It was positively un-American not to have children.

Instead, for four years, Harry's secret threatened the very structure of love that held their marriage together. Every once in awhile her frustration would surface in the form of arguments. Money woes and Harry's failing as a provider became staples. But in all that time, they never talked about the real reason—their inability to have children.

Ashamed of the lie he was living and too frightened to confess, Harry took Barbara's bitter tongue-lashings. Well-intentioned remarks from friends only compounded the problem.

"Hey, Harry, when are you and Barbara gonna drop a few babies?" they would tease. "You've been married four years, what's the problem?"

"There isn't no problem," Harry would shoot back defensively, feeling his face growing hot and red. His embarrassment only made his friends laugh all the more.

Sometimes, Harry would catch Barbara watching him. It made him wonder if she suspected. Yet Barbara was convinced that Harry blamed her for their lack of children. Her own uncertainty made her lash out all the more.

Had she married the right man? Initially it had been so easy to love Harry. His pleasant demeanor and kindness had won her over. But nothing seemed to please her anymore.

In her heart, she knew she still loved him. They were best friends, easy to talk to and laugh with. If we only had a baby, she thought, a baby would bring us closer together again.

Finally Barbara had decided enough was enough and without explaining anything to her husband, made a doctor's appointment. If there was something wrong, she'd rather face it than be buried in a pack of fears and doubts.

Harry picked her up at the office. Right away he could tell she was upset. Suddenly afraid, he grew quiet. They drove home in silence. Then, just as he was pulling into the drive to their tiny house, Barbara bursts into tears. He swallowed, staring at their shabby home with the sagging porch and chipped blue paint. He didn't know what to say to comfort her, but he knew he needed to try. It took her a few minutes to regain control.

She opened her purse and pulled out a cigarette. Her hands shook as she lit it. He watched her exhale with a sob.

"Oh Harry, I want a baby so bad," she said. "It's not fair that everyone has a family but us." Harry stared ahead over the steering wheel. Barbara continued, "I just went to the doctor, and he says there's no reason I can't get pregnant. I'm healthy. I'm young."

Barbara began to cry again. For the first time, Harry looked at his wife and gingerly placed a hand on her shaking shoulder. It was time. He had to tell her. Fear rose in his throat, threatening to choke his words. He knew the words he was about to say could cost him the most important person in his life, but he loved her too much to see her suffer anymore.

Gently pulling her to him, he took a breath for courage and began.

"Barbara, there's something I have to tell you," he said softly, "I should have told you a long time ago. If, after I tell you, you don't love me anymore, I'll understand," he said. His words made her stop crying, she stared at him, confused.

Then Harry told her every last sickening detail about the Beatrice State Home and the horrible price he'd paid for his freedom. "You are the only thing good that's ever happened to me," he said once he'd finished. "I didn't want to lose you. I love you so much," he choked. It was his turn to cry.

"Oh my God, Harry. You've been carrying that around all this time," she muttered as she stroked his hair. "It's okay. It's better to know the truth. Now we can decide what to do from here. Maybe we could adopt."

Harry lifted his head to see her face. A seed of hope sprang to life. He knew at that moment he had never loved anyone so much. "You mean?" he began as Barbara touched his cheek.

"How could you think I wouldn't love you? Don't you know you're the only man for me Harry Davis?" she said, her eyes searching his. "And we'll still have a family. Somehow, God will help us find a way."

That night when they went to bed, they slept tightly coiled in each other's arms. However, despite Barbara's optimism, their relationship continued to decline as agency after agency told them that they didn't qualify. It was the same scourge: You barely have enough money to make ends meet. How are you going to provide for a baby?

No amount of tears or pleading seemed to matter. They were too poor.

Out of sheer frustration, Barbara increasingly took it out on Harry. It became one barrage of insults after another. He didn't bring home enough money despite working for a pipe-laying company 60 hours a week. He'd never amount to anything. Why couldn't he pick up his clothes? Why did he have to sleep on the couch when he came home from work? What was the matter with him?

Nothing he did was good enough. She would take his paycheck the moment he arrived home. If he was lucky, he'd have enough to buy cigarettes. Everything went towards paying bills. Even with the extra hours, they were a sinking ship.

Occasionally his own frustrations would well up and Harry snarled back. He grew tired of feeling like a junkyard dog that had been kicked too many times.

But then the tide inexplicably shifted. Barbara excitedly told Harry about an article she'd read in a mystery magazine. It spoke of artificial insemination. So desperate for good news, she'd even gone to her doctor, Dr. Wayne Thurber, to consult with him about it. Finally they'd caught a break. Thurber not only knew about the procedure, he'd also performed hundreds of such operations.

"The doctor wants to talk to both of us," she said excitedly. But Harry was dubious. Could it really work? Could this be their miracle?

A few days later, they sat impatiently waiting for Dr. Thurber. It was an office like so many others. Four sparse, plain white walls with just a token picture and his credentials hanging on two of the walls. There were two rows of chairs behind the desk where the receptionist sat typing. A plump, nervous brunette slouched in her chair, occasionally peeking up at the patients.

Barbara, however, was perched on the edge of her chair. Her eyes twinkled with excitement, while Harry sat slumped against the back of his. He wasn't sold on this idea. After all, it wouldn't really be his child. But if this was what Barbara wanted, he'd go along.

Thurber was a tall, thin man with a pleasant smile. He emerged from the back office to greet them with a firm handshake.

"Right this way," he said ushering them into his office. There was an examining table in the midst of the room and two chairs. Immediately Harry felt queasy, remembering his past. He squeezed Barbara's hand. She just looked at him, puzzled.

Thurber began to explain details. He had delivered his first baby in 1936, but he took a special interest in the cases of infertile couples. He saw their plight as a true tragedy. With the help of God and science, he could give them what they desired most—a baby.

His voice was soft and comforting as he explained the procedure. It was really pretty simple, he assured. Because Harry could not produce sperm to fertilize Barbara's eggs, a sperm donor would be necessary. The donors he used were only the best and brightest, Thurber boasted.

"Many of them are already successful professionals or graduate students from the University of Kansas," he said proudly. He noticed Harry's quiescence, speculating he needed some convincing, he continued. "And, of course, we do our best to match the characteristics of the donor with the birth father." His last sentence sparked interest from Harry, he leaned forward in a conspiratorial whisper and added, "No one need ever know."

"In fact," he said, looking from Barbara to Harry and back again, "You must never tell anyone. Not your families, not your friends, and certainly never the child. The news could be extremely damaging."

Thurber extracted promises from the young couple that they would keep this their secret. Barbara wondered about Thurber's insistence. Could it be that artificial insemination was illegal? But Thurber convinced her that the secrecy was only to protect the child and themselves.

"No one will ever know," he said again as they stood to leave. "No one but me and the two of you," he promised.

Assured, the couple went home, gushing excitedly about the baby they would soon have. Barbara babbled about the baby items they would need to buy now. Even Harry got in the spirit. No one would ever know the child wasn't his.

Suddenly, it seemed that the dreams that had carried him through those dark days at Beatrice were alas coming true. He had a home, a wife he loved, and now, a child. Their troubles would be healed with a child. They had found their miracle.

6

A Ray of Hope

Dr. Thurber's words resonated a wellspring of hope within the young couple. Suddenly, the day to day mundane seemed easier to endure. Everything was going to be okay now, Harry thought. A son, he would catch himself envisioning before adding, "it really wouldn't matter if it were a boy or a girl, So long as it's healthy."

The anticipation of a baby helped to ease the pain of his past. They would be a family, he told himself. He couldn't have been happier.

The romance that had waned between them was suddenly back and thriving in their marriage. He was all smiles and giddy as he brought her flowers. She, in turn, would dress nice and prepared special meals for him. Each night she greeted him with a smile or a welcoming kiss as he came through the door. It was a blissful time for them. They felt like newlyweds again.

They both agreed privately that her pregnancy had been the saving grace for their marriage. Instead of demanding or being impatient with him, she'd become too busy preparing the baby's room. Other days were spent shopping for the new arrival. That he wasn't really the father was their little secret, a secret that bound them closer than ever.

One evening Harry arrived to find Barbara sitting on the porch steps. Since the behavior was so atypical for his wife, he stopped in front of her studying her face. If there was something wrong, he wanted to brace himself for the news. To his dismay her eyes were like fireflies in a container, all aglow.

"Honey?" He made it a question as he sat beside her. Immediately she cuddled against him. He wrapped an arm around her. "What is it?" he asked, treading softly.

"I'm pregnant!" she exclaimed clutching his arm. Immediately she began to sob. Harry felt himself spiraling, ecstatic. He moved back. Could it be true? After all the time they'd wanted a baby?

"You sure?" he asked, she nodded. "Thank you God!" he shouted, slapping his knees. "Oh honey, I am so happy!" he cried, embracing her as tears escaped down his face. "I love you so much," he said feathering kisses all over her face.

"I love you too!" she confessed kissing him back. He pulled her close, then scooped her into his arms and carried her into the house.

Joyous giggles and laughter filled the bedroom where he laid his wife down on the bed. That night they made love with a renewed passion, as if the forthcoming child was indeed the product of both their biologic histories. The pretense helped Harry get over what few reservations still lingered.

After that night they began walking again, excitedly waving to friends as they passed each neighborhood block. Harry would puff up proudly when greeted by well-wishers who noticed Barbara's expanding belly. Barbara took to pregnancy as a cowboy takes to horses. She not only loved shopping, but thrived on the envious looks of other women. She remembered what it had been like to feel such envy. But now, she was a whole woman.

It was only at night, while Harry peacefully snored by her side and hearing the clock ticking loudly in the dark, that she would place her hands on her stomach and wonder. Who are you? She asked of the unknown father. Are you a good man? Are you smart? Are you healthy?

Sometimes her uncertainly would lead to fear, but it always seemed to disappear with the morning sun. She dismissed such thoughts as normal motherhood worries.

Summer was coming. Trees were green, lawns were full, flowers in bloom. Being expectant seemed like a natural progression. She delighted that she would be having their baby while the world blossomed and the season smiled upon them.

Alas, at 4 a.m., on the auspicious Wednesday morning of June 8th, 1955 while Harry snored and Barbara lay awake, she sensed something. She looked at her husband lovingly. You're such a good man, she thought, I'm so lucky. Thank you, God, thank you.

Suddenly, Barbara's quiet musing were interrupted by a jab of pain in her abdomen. She gasped crying out. Pain and fear clutched her violently.

What's going on? She asked herself, panic flooding her heart. I'm not due for another ten days. A clammy dampness enveloped her. Oh God, please don't let me lose my baby! Unable to control her fear any longer, she released a long wail that echoed through the tiny house.

Immediately Harry bolted upright in bed. He wouldn't have moved any faster if someone had shouted "Fire!" Unlike his wife, he was not afraid. Contrarily he was elated. Instinctively he began to gather things as they had rehearsed.

"It's time!" he shouted after one look at Barbara's face. "Okay," he said more to himself trying to remember details. He wrapped his sobbing wife in blankets and carried her to the car, placing her atop two pillows he had been keeping in the back seat for just this occasion.

It was all Harry could do to avoid racing to the hospital as his wife cried out in the back seat. The early morning stoplights seemed to be against him as they shone red while he impatiently waited. "Come on," he hammered the steering wheel. Finally, with his horn blaring and Barbara wailing, he careened up to the entrance at St. Elizabeth Hospital. The car came to a screeching halt.

Nurses and doctors huddled around Barbara. Everyone seemed to be talking to her all at once. "When did the labor start? How far apart were the contractions? How was she feeling?" Through the harsh glare of the evening lights and her own pain, Barbara could hardly focus.

Soon they whisked her away, leaving Harry deserted in the waiting room. In his excitement, he hadn't noticed Barbara's fear. But now, with time on his hands, fear found him. Women died in childbirth, didn't they? What would he do if he lost Barbara or the baby? Without them, his life had no purpose.

Harry became distraught with worries while Barbara successfully delivered a son. Unbeknownst to Mrs. Davis, Dr. Thurber was one of the pioneers in Lamaze natural child-birthing, so she was awake to hear her baby's first cries.

Tears flowed freely from her eyes. A son. She had a son. A healthy, happy baby boy. At that moment, life seemed perfect.

"Would you like to hold him," a squat, but friendly-faced nurse asked. Barbara smiled at the woman holding her child. She was happy and content, if not a little too tired to do much, but nodded all the same.

In the waiting room, minutes ticked by in slow motion. At last, a nurse beckoned for Harry.

"You can see her now," she instructed. Harry followed the short nurse to Barbara's room. Harry poked his head in the door. His wife lay on the bed very still with her eyes closed. A whoosh of terror seized him, immediately he remembered another hospital, another bed. Seeing the sheet pulled up close around Barbara's face overwhelmed him. The baby, he thought, what happened to the baby? As if she could read his mind, the nurse said, "You have a beautiful, healthy baby boy. He's in the nursery."

His internal tremors subsided. It was 1955, he told himself, over and over.

Barbara opened her eyes. She smiled at him. Harry rushed to her side, then stood awkwardly, unsure of what he should do. Somehow everything had changed. She held out her arms. He bent to hug her, tears dribbling from his eyes. For a few moments they cried together. They were the only ones that knew how much this baby's arrival meant.

The same nurse returned with their baby. She offered the bundle to Harry. Hesitantly he took the child and looked at his face. Did he look like him?

"Do you, do you think he looks like me?" Harry asked Barbara after the nurse left. She nodded. Actually, the baby looked like it had been squeezed out of a garden hose; but his hair was dark, even if his skin was pink and fair.

"Sure, sure he does," she comforted.

But the illusion was short-lived. It wasn't long after the little family was settled in before neighbors began to comment on how fair their child, Scott, was. His hair was definitely going to be blond and his eyes would remain blue.

Women would coo "he has your eyes" or "he has Harry's nose." To which Barbara would just smile or nod. Of course he looked like her, why wouldn't he? But there were times while she nursed that she would look into his eyes and still wonder: "Who are you? What does your real father look like?"

7

Humble Beginnings

"Scott; come home," I heard my mother calling. I was twelve years old that year and hanging out with my best friend Kelly in what we referred to as our clubhouse. In earnest, we'd built it from scrap pieces of plywood, discarded metal siding and burlap sacks. It was maybe all of four feet wide by six feet in length, but it served us well.

Hearing my mother's voice always got my attention. Immediately I hid the old Playboy with worn, frayed edges we'd been looking at under a piece of ratty carpet. Then I crawled out of our clubhouse and started for the house.

"God dammit," I cursed. Profanity was becoming a common occurrence at home. "It's my mom," I said sulking as I looked at Kelly. Unlike me, Kelly had dark hair and curious blue eyes that almost seemed translucent at times. We were pretty close in stature and size.

Actually, I never liked swearing just for the heck of it, but I did have to admit it made me feel important around my friends. They might not have been impressed but I certainly was. Still, I could hear my mother's words like a familiar record, you shouldn't use the Lord's name in vain. Then she would give me the lowdown on Christianity. If you were good and prayed real hard, you'd get what you want, she promised. Or, even if you mess up, tell a lie or commit some other sin, the Lord would forgive you and you'd still get what you wanted.

At times it confused me. If I could get what ever I wanted either way, why did I have to be a good boy? It was so much easier to be bad.

"See ya tomorrow," Kelly said. I collected my two mutts, Blondie and Fritz. They'd been patiently waiting outside the clubhouse. Blondie looked like a blond wolf hound. Fritz, on the other hand, was black and white and about the size of a cocker spaniel. Together they resembled the canine version of Mutt and Jeff.

Immediately Kelly hopped on his gold Schwinn and veered off to the right as we both tossed our cigarettes. Cache from my mother's stock. If she ever found out my back side was going to be a blister red.

Sometimes I was envious of that bike. At twelve, it looked like a Porsche to me. With shiny chrome spokes and a rod that ran along the back of the bike with multi-colored tassels that streamed behind Kelly as he caught the wind.

It was a nice bike. I watched it become a blur in the distance before I went inside.

When my parents got me one for my twelfth birthday, I burst into tears. I knew they couldn't afford it, but my father was so proud the day he wheeled it out into the living room from their bedroom. I'd suspected I'd be getting a bike that year, but until that moment, hadn't been sure.

I looked at both of them, unable to express the emotions welling up in me. That was the way they were. We might have been poor, but they always doted on me and got me nice gifts. It made me feel a tremendous amount of guilt.

Should a child be so adored? I wondered as they recorded every special occasion with a photograph. I can still see some of those pictures. At four, standing proudly in front of my folks' house decked out in an expensive cowboy outfit, complete with chaps, vest, hat and a pair of six shooters.

And if that wasn't enough, my folks cluttered every wall with pictures of me from infancy to the present. One, in particular, always stands out. I was in front of a model wood house, almost as big as my parent's first home.

Just the payment on that thing was a struggle, leaving scarcely any money for food.

But food was never a big draw to me. It seemed like we survived on a steady diet of hamburger; the one meat we were able to afford. And my mother knew at least 100 ways to prepare it.

Meatloaf. I knew that smell.

I was less than enthusiast as I came through the door that evening. I saw my father fast asleep on the couch. His socks and work boots lay in a heap in the center of the living room. I moved them to the front closet before my mother spotted them. It would have been fodder for another argument.

I spent a lot of time during my childhood anticipating and trying to stave off potential arguments, but I hated the discord between them. Anything I could do to minimize it was a necessity.

My father's head was cocked back, his mouth hung open. It was then that I could see his stained and dirty teeth. It made me feel sorry for him, but it also made me curious. Why didn't he take care of them?

He looked so old and tired as he took deep, heavy breaths, like that of a coal miner. His snoring was hard and laborious. He was putting in over seventy hours a week.

Was that any kind of life? Sometimes I feared the work would kill him.

He'd drag himself home with his stained tee shirt and grimy clothes to take his spot on the couch. I remember him being planted there like a permanent fixture. He was too exhausted to notice small details like fresh flowers my mother had placed in a vase in the middle of the kitchen table.

It seemed he was only awake long enough to wolf down the night's hamburger dish, mopping up every last bit of grease with his bread before he'd crawl off to bed. Being with my father at times made me feel like I lived with a mole.

I knew it wasn't his fault, but I missed him. Missed having time to interact with him.

Month after month, I watched my parents and the dissension between them growing. If my mother couldn't buy me or herself something she wanted, she would blame him, growing impatient with our poverty.

It mattered not that we were always one step ahead of the bill collectors. Nor whether or not we could afford another item for the house or whatever was her latest complaint, she'd get it anyway. I grew to hate credit. I saw it murdering my father and deteriorating my mother.

Weekends were our salvation. They were the only days that afforded us any father and son time. I lived for the weekends. Those brief moments when my father was more than just a laborer. He became my dad once again as we went to the park, played games, or just spent time together.

But the older I got, the more distance seemed to separate us. I increasingly blamed my mother for belittling and riding him so hard. Moreover, the striking differences between us grew more and more derisive. Why was he so dark while I was so fair?

It wasn't just his physical characteristics that bothered me, it was also his personal habits. My father was disorganized and messy, while I was fastidious. I carefully categorized my comic book and coin collections. I even ironed my money and cleaned my room. I did not like clutter of any kind, and the fact that my father seemed to thrive in such an environment bothered me.

Soon it became all too obvious that I was also smarter than my father. A part of me was thrilled, enjoying my bombastic moment in the sun, while another part of me was losing respect for him.

In fact, my teachers had excitedly called my parents to inform them that I had tested within the genius level on the national IQ test. That information was withheld from me for years, but still I outshone my father without even trying.

I still remember an occasion one Sunday morning at church. I had asked my father why he never sang. His retort, "I don't have a good singing voice," was all he said, but it seemed odd. Why did he even bother to open the hymnal?

Suddenly I pieced it together; all the times I had thought my father was reading the paper, he was actually just looking at the pictures. It sent a chill through me. He couldn't read. A grown man who was virtually illiterate. Now I realized why he would never be more than a common laborer; you had to be able to read a blueprint to be a foreman. I felt a prick of shame.

It took me months to broach the subject. Then one evening, while my mother was ironing and my father was finishing his dinner, the moment seemed right.

"Dad," I said. My father looked up from his plate, scooping the last bit of gravy onto his bread.

"What is it Scott?" His soft brown eyes looked at me. I swallowed, afraid of hurting him.

"Dad, can you read?" I finally choked out.

Immediately my father's face turned red. He pushed away from the table and looked at my mother who had stopped ironing. She looked at him, then me, suspended.

"I never went farther than the third grade, but I'm a damned good worker," he said.

"I could teach you," I offered. He bolted from the table.

"Don't you have homework?" he shot back. It was the last time we ever discussed it.

In an odd sort of way, he wore his illiteracy like a badge of honor. As long as he could say he was a good worker, a hard worker, he was "alright" in his book.

But something changed between us that day. At times I regretted ever bringing up the subject, but it bothered me the way my father just allowed my mother to bully him. A seed of resentment continued to grow in me.

Then one day my mother decided public school wasn't good enough for me. It was, of course, just one more thing that we could not afford. She wanted more for me than Harry's life. She had aspirations of me becoming a doctor or a lawyer. Anything but a common laborer.

But what I secretly craved she couldn't provide. I wanted a brother or a sister and preferably both. Seeing the large families within our neighborhood just compounded my feelings. I didn't like being an only child.

Even as a toddler I felt the deficit, expressing to my mother a need for a sibling; but my mother just bought me a doll so I invented an imaginary friend, Knockie, to ease the pain. Why was my mother so reluctant?

I knew babies had something to do with the funny feeling I got while Kelly and I looked at the women's bodies in Playboy. Like all kids, I acquired some general knowledge from older schoolmates. Basically, it boiled down to one man and woman. In realizing that, I was stumped about my folks. Why couldn't they supply me with a sibling?

That night as with so many evenings, my father was asleep on the couch. That left mother. I found her at the sink washing dishes. She smiled at me as I walked into the kitchen. I was on a mission.

"Hi honey," she said. "Go wash up and wake up your dad; dinner will be ready soon."

"Okay," I said, unmoving. I wasn't ready to give up my directive.

"What's the matter Scott?" My mother asked, noticing my reticence.

"Mom, where do babies come from?" I asked earnestly. Instantly, I watched my mother start fumbling with the dishes, turning three shades of crimson. This made me all the more eager, figuring it had to be something big indeed.

"Well, ah, when a man and woman love each other, they get together and the woman gets pregnant." She said it so quickly I could hardly understand her. "Babies come out of a mommy's tummy. Just like you," she added in a sugary tone. It left me perplexed. Somehow I knew there was more to it than that.

"Do you and daddy love each other?" I pressed.

My mother looked flabbergasted. She dried her hands on her apron then faced me. Her expression very serious.

"Of course we do; now do as I told you" she finished before making a dismissing gesture.

"Then why don't you have another baby?" I asked, needing to know.

"Well," she stuttered, "We just haven't had time. Maybe someday. Now please, go wash up," she instructed. Slowly I obeyed, still bewildered. It didn't seem to me that they loved each other. I had actually been surprised to hear her acknowledge it.

When I failed to return a few minutes later, my mother went looking for us. She found us both asleep; I was curled up next to my dad. Something within had made me want to be close to him.

She looked at us as tears pooled in her eyes. She knew the time for truths to be revealed would be coming. Already there were unmistakable differences between us. She knew we had both noticed; one day it would be addressed.

Soon I would no longer be a boy, and her simple answers would not placate me. But for the moment, I had let it slide. There would be time.

8

Growing Pains

At twelve, my world was evolving. I was growing and exploring almost faster than my senses could comprehend. I was also clashing with my parents frequently. During those turbulent years, I am certain I gave my parents more than a few gray hairs as I learned to stretch my wings. But you have to understand, I was a bright, active preadolescent that was constantly on the go.

Physically I was busting out too. Nearly to my mother's shoulder, I knew it wouldn't be long before I would be able to face her at eye level. Perhaps one of my greatest challenges was keeping pace with my mother who had a large gait. For all my growth, it was still a struggle to keep up.

I discovered this while we were at Chicago's O'Hare International Airport. I could see my mother's black coat billowing out around her as she zoomed down the busy concourse. Between the milieu of people greeting loved ones or bustling for their own flights, it was hard to stay focused. But I did, none-the-less, fearing that if I lost sight of my mother, we might never find each other again.

I wanted to yell: slow down! But my mother was on auto-pilot. Her legs carried her as if they had wings. Along the way I heard her speaking in a shrill, panicky voice: "My baby, I've got to find my baby."

For a moment, fear fluttered inside me, I thought my mother's cognitive abilities had finally been vanquished by insanity. After all, I was her baby. But that morning my mother was oblivious to me.

She was preoccupied a lot these days. Ever since she'd seen a special news clip on television about adopting babies from Korea. Miraculously I hadn't made the connection, not even when she asked me if I'd like a baby sister.

Just that morning we'd hopped a small commuter plane in Lincoln. Since it was my first plane ride, I was excited and full of questions. It had been a weird, yet wonderfully emancipating feeling, seeing Kansas City from the sky. At that altitude, it just looked like a toy model. Unreal. And it didn't hold the same stifling existence from the air that I felt living there.

Once again, our stark finances precluded us from adoption. It stung. I wanted a sibling so bad I told myself I was prepared to surrender to a life of crime to finance it. Instead, I listened through the walls of my bedroom as my parents argued.

"We'll never get anywhere is this damned dust bowl!" I heard my mother shout, followed by a deadly silence. Briefly I fretted my mother had left. Eventually I heard the familiar rustle of pots and pans coming from the kitchen. My mother was washing dishes as she often did when her own frustration got the better of her.

I wondered where my father was. Probably sulking on the couch, feeling sorry for his lot in life. His total inability to satisfy his wife. Twinges of anger poked at me. I lay awake on my bed staring up at the peeling plaster of the ceiling, feeling resentful and helpless. Equally, anger stirred inside; I was mad at my father. Once again, my mother had successfully emasculated him. Why didn't he stand up to her?

As a result, we started taking in foster kids. Poor, frightened children that had no place to call home. They shared a look of desperation and uncertainty. Each child's almond-shaped eyes reflected a fear and sadness that never went away. No matter how much love we tried to give them, it remained. I wondered about their world. How would I have felt?

Each time when they left, my mother would cry. I learned to distance myself. It made me suspicious and cynical. Why couldn't my parents have another child? They'd managed to have me. Unbeknownst to me, my mother had tried over and over again for another visit from the stork. But none of her efforts with artificial insemination paid off.

A gnawing desperation took hold of my mother. It replaced the loving tender woman I'd seen her be with one that held a distance and dissatisfaction in her eyes. I was growing up, hardly her cuddly little boy anymore. I knew she loved me, but I also knew her maternal ache for more children burned in her soul.

On some days my mother would still look at me and wonder: Who are you? Really? Temporarily caught in that hushed chasm of a stealthy underworld she never spoke of.

She knew that the constant discord that defined our household was eating away at me, but she couldn't contain her own disillusions from spilling over and causing more arguments. There were times when I was tempted to retaliate for my father. More and more, I was beginning to feel like the man of the house.

When it finally became obvious that my parents weren't going to be able to conceive again, the subject was dropped. They never discussed their secret; it just loomed like some undefined blight in their lives. A cruel reminder of days long forgotten.

Our home became a war zone. I began to dread any conversation, fearing where it would lead. It seemed everything was fair game, my father's lack of initiative, money or sloppiness. Take your pick. While my mother screamed at him, my father just recoiled. He took her tongue lashings like a broken man. And maybe that was what he was. Unable to defend himself against the harsh truth that he was sterile. He could never give her the babies my mother needed.

In turn, my mother felt betrayed. My father had not lived up to her expectations. But each and every argument on their disposition was really a rouse. A fact I wouldn't come to appreciate for many years. All would have been forgiven, tolerable, if he had just been able to give her babies.

My mother's need to be a parent was larger than life. In her day, being a prolific mommy defined a good and successful wife. She'd never forgive Harry for denying her that.

Just when I was sure my parent's were headed for divorce court, another news bulletin seemed like our salvation. Media appealed for families that could adopt Korean orphans. Without even bothering to consult my dad, Barbara sent for the information and when she got it, immediately sent it in.

In the interim, her disposition once again improved. An old spark had been rekindled between them. I knew my father had no grasp of her sudden change of heart. But he embraced it eagerly.

Arguments had been replaced with kisses or humming as she cleaned the house and prepared meals. My mother had traded her drab life for a brighter, more prosperous one in her mind. She convinced herself that soon she'd have a little girl to dress up, dote on, send to ballet, and take to piano lessons.

Her ideal world wasn't without flaws. She was aware that even though I had been very enthusiastic about having a sibling, I was also used to ruling the roost alone. I'd never had to share anything, especially my parents. She worried.

My father continued his silent protest, but he would never challenge my mother. If adopting another child would make her happy and keep the bickering at bay, it was worth it. He relinquished all of the child-rearing decisions to her.

There was another upside to the situation. The new baby wouldn't be anymore her genes than his. Alas, he wouldn't feel so ostracized within his own family circle. For that reason, he welcomed it.

One cloudy afternoon in spring my mother beckoned me into the living room. I had just gotten home from school so I placed my books on the coffee table and took a seat. Right away I could see we were going to have one of my mother's talks. Her face was rigid. I'd grown accustomed to her way of approaching serious subjects.

"Scott, I need to talk to you," she began, fidgeting with her fingers. She'd raise them into a steeple, and then fold them out, over and over, as she prepared herself. I was intrigued with her gestures, figuring that whatever she wanted to talk to me about was probably more of an issue for her than it would be to me.

"What's wrong mom?"

"Well honey? Scotty, would you mind having a little sister that wasn't?" she searched for the words. "Wasn't white like us, or looked a little different?" Her eyebrows pinched in worry while she waited on my response.

"Jesus loves all children mom, no matter what color they are," I told her and shrugged.

That merited a big hug as she clutched me tightly. Slowly she released me, moved back. She was more than smiling. She was beaming.

"You're such a good boy," she said, patting my shoulder.

"When?" I asked wondering if this one would truly be staying.

"A couple of weeks," she said folding her hands. I wondered if it was the truth or if my mother was prevailing to God. I decided not to worry; I'd know soon enough.

Of course, my mother probably wouldn't have been glowing so brightly if she'd been aware of my sordid activities, specifically lying, pornography and stealing. It was beyond her to acknowledge that I was anything but her studious, cheerful boy. For that, I was grateful.

Ironically, my father had caught me smoking, but his response only fed the wedge already growing between us. Unlike my mother, he would venture out to my clubhouse, and on one beautifully warm and sunny summer day, he pulled back the flap of burlap that was my make shift door to discover me with a cigarette in my mouth. He just stood looking as smoke curled around me.

It hurt more that he didn't discipline me. Something I never entirely reconciled. Why hadn't he? Instead he just said: "So long as you don't tell your mom; she'd be very upset with you."

It left me perplexed. Did that mean he wasn't upset? From that day forth it became our secret and he supplied me with a steady stash.

Preparing for a new family member took an unexpected twist. Mother insisted that Blondie and Fritz had to go. Dogs couldn't be around the baby. They might hurt her. No amount of pleading made a dent. It was the first time I actually cursed my soon-to-be sibling.

I'd even visited our local humane society, but I didn't go in. I knew they wouldn't be there anymore. Because both of them were so lovable, finding them a new owner would be easy. And if by chance they weren't so lucky, I knew what the incinerator around the back was for.

I was careful to take the back roads home. No one would see me cry.

Several months later, there we were, running around haphazardly through the airport trying to get to gate 57 where international flight 205 from Korea had landed. Finally, my mother slowed down to a human pace and I caught up. It was a welcomed reprieve. I could actually breathe again!

We got in line behind a cluster of people awaiting the passengers of flight 205 to disembark. Most of them were couples or families. Seeing a man with his wife and two sons standing in front of us made me miss my father. How I wished he'd been able afford a ticket. I felt he needed to be there. This was a family event.

The man's boys were both dark-haired. A family resemblance obvious in their faces, stature and characteristics. I felt a stab of envy. Again I questioned why my dad and I didn't look alike?

Suddenly the plane door opened, the ramp unfolded and out spilled a blur of crying children either being carried or dragged along by their caretakers. After the twenty-two hour flight, nobody looked happy. But the children that all seemed alike to me, looked the least happy. All of them had black shiny hair, almond eyes and copper skin.

Inexplicably I began singing; "Jesus loves all the little children. All the children of the world. Red and yellow, black or white. They are precious in his sight."

My mother looked embarrassed but the family in front of us just smiled. I decided I liked their response better and continued singing.

Each child had a number pinned to their clothing. But it was still bedlam as anxious parents cried out rushing from child to child in search of the number to match the one stamped on the forms in their hands.

My mother followed suit. Carefully she screened each new face, looking for her number.

"Where's my baby?" she cried over and over becoming increasingly frantic.

I tried to be of assistance but the complete pandemonium overwhelmed me. It was hard not to be intimated by a crowd of children and adults all hastily shoving and scurrying about.

"There she is! Lisa, Lisa!" I heard my mother wailing joyfully. But the child didn't have the right number so my mother went back to waiting impatiently, staring at each new child that came forth.

At last, nine-month-old Lisa came as a crying bundle hand delivered by her caretaker as she emerged among the confusion on the walkway. Immediately my mom was there. She snatched the baby from the elderly lady holding her as if she had just caught the football for the final touch down in a close game. I bobbed up and down trying to get a peek at my new sister. Alas our eyes met; it was love at first sight. Something inside my very being leapt for joy, an unspoken bond had been created. Did she feel my love? Have any idea how much we wanted her?

Harry was worse than me, gawking at Lisa. He showered her with kisses before bestowing a series upon my mom's tear-stained face. I just soaked it all in, happy to see them so happy.

My parents might have doted on her but I topped that; I'd become obsessed. Each day I would grow impatient as the clock at school was approaching three o'clock. Soon I would be rushing home to gather Lisa into the baby carriage just so I could take her around the block. I was so proud of her, ecstatic to have a sibling at last. Someone to share with, play with, confide in.

Occasionally, we would encounter a few rude strangers who noticed our striking differences. And it didn't help that the Vietnam War was in full swing and Mid-Westerners didn't trust anyone who even remotely looked like they came from "over there." Their ignorant remarks and glares only served to make me more protective of my new sister. Sometimes I would get fed up and declare, "She is my sister!"

Lisa's arrival seemed to be the quintessential band-aid my parent's marriage needed. But as with all band-aids, they are only a temporary fix and my hope for a peaceful home life soon vanished as easily as the novelty of Lisa's arrival.

Ironically, my mother began pushing to adopt another child. Lisa was hardly settled in before she became fixated with the notion. As usual, my father found himself bucking her defiance. All he said was: "We can't afford it." But my mother was quick to rebut that she would find a way. I wondered how, since I knew our finances were stretched to the limit already and their paltry savings exhausted. How?

It made me wonder about my mother and her profound need to be maternal. Finally I understood her need exceeded everyone else's, and she didn't seem to be even remotely aware of how demanding or unreasonable she really was.

I feared my father would surely die from the overload. He was already stumbling in exhausted, just to collapse on the couch. Some nights he didn't even finish his dinner. He would fall asleep during the middle of a bite and I'd find him either slumped in his chair elbows on his plate or the food on the floor.

As before, I'd clean up any mess quickly. If my mother saw it, she'd explode. The poor man was totally depleted; he didn't need to be yelled at too.

Day after day, I watched his steady decline. It made me feel bitter towards my mother that she would drive him so hard. I began to wonder if she secretly wished he were dead.

At night I would be on my knees. I begged Jesus to stop the fights and restore happiness to our humble home. But the fighting continued; in turn it shook my faith. If there was a God, why didn't he hear me?

Already a petty thief, I would go to church and wait for my opportunity to steal loose change from the collection plate. If God wouldn't help us, I would. It was easy to justify my actions by deciding we were entitled to the money since God did not intervene on our behalf.

Within a year, Jodi became the newest member of the Davis household. Now I had two baby sisters.

My father was totally tapped out, physically incapable of doing anymore. Guilt and repressed anger reinforced old feelings...God had abandoned us. I was the man of the house now. Which meant, more stealing. I began to concentrate on bigger heists. My nightly routine of prayers ceased. I told myself I was alone. I would find a way to turn things around. My family needed me.

9

New Faces to Love

My mother had gotten her two girls. The hearth was still a mangled semblance of normalcy, but at least some of my mother's energy was directed towards rearing the girls instead of being expressly vented at my father. For that much, I was grateful.

Lisa and Jodi filled our home with a hope it had been lacking for years. Of course, much of that hope I attributed to their innocence of youth. But I welcomed the change, no matter the reasons. We were a sinking ship; anything that helped patch our intrinsic potholes was okay in my book.

At thirteen, I got a paper route. Still feeling pressure to alleviate my family's financial troubles I could take comfort in the fact that at least it wasn't illegal, stealthy or something I needed to be ashamed of. Of course it didn't fix our money woes, but it did give me money and a means to do things that kept me away.

Family pictures no longer displayed a happy face. Instead, they reflected a serious, troubled youth with long blond hair and distant, sad blue eyes.

I was learning the route and replacing Roger Carmichael, who was moving on to bigger and better things. He would be working at one of the local burger joints soon.

One afternoon while we were folding papers for delivery, the headlines caught my attention. We were at war with Vietnam, fighting a country whose people had features like Jodi and Lisa. Another article talked about protesters and debunking the establishment. At thirteen I had no concept what that term really meant, but I did know that in five years I would more than likely be facing the draft. Already I had decided that if that day came, I would run away to Canada. It would be my silent protest. I loved my sisters dearly and would not support a war that killed people who looked like them.

A pang of sadness ran through me. I realized they would never know their parents. It made me sympathetic to how they must have felt coming to a strange country, knowing no one, being rejected by many just because they looked like people we were at war with. The cruelty and inequity of such a harsh truth struck me.

Suddenly I was catapulted back to reality. Roger hurt his finger and for his trouble was generous with the profanity.

"Fuck!" he exclaimed, stuffing it into his mouth.

"Roger, don't say that," I scolded. I watched him suck on it briefly then began to smile. It was a mischievous smile.

"Fuck! Fuck! Fuck! Poor little Scotty," he taunted. "I bet you don't even know what fuck means. Well, fucking is how your parent's had you," he sassed. I could feel my fists balling up. I contemplated pasting him as he proceeded to elaborate, letting his imagination fill in the details where he lacked in facts.

The explanation shocked me. I knew it took a man and a woman to make a baby, but he knew scantly more. Naively I still fostered the notion that it had something to do with stork deliveries.

Roger went into his house. I waited outside with my stack of newspapers dumbfounded by his sudden departure. A moment later he returned with something obviously concealed beneath his shirt. It made the front of his tee bow outward. He motioned me to follow him behind the house. When I did he pulled out the magazine he'd been hiding. In it were pictures of naked men and women doing things my Playboy's hadn't even suggested.

Enjoying my surprise Roger continued. His eyes sparkled with covert happiness. He was obviously delighted to be my mentor.

"Haven't you ever jacked off?" He finally asked incredulous.

Just the thought of it made me blush. I knew how the pictures in my Playboy's had made me feel but I'd never explored nor conceived where those feelings could lead. Roger, however, wasn't a bit shy. He proceeded to explain this wondrous discovery to me too. For a few minutes I half expected him to demonstrate. When he didn't, I was relieved. But the details stayed with me.

I went home feeling very confused. I saw my father in a whole new light, even though there was nothing extraordinary about the way he was sleeping on the couch. He looked the same as he always did. I smelled the aroma of frying meat and heard the familiar sizzling that meant food was cooking. My mother was busy frying hamburgers. As with my father, I felt like a light had gone on, yet she looked as she always did, standing in front of the stove, wearing a purple dress and apron. She noticed me and smiled.

"Mom, what does fuck mean?"

I watched the color drain from her face as she dropped the spatula she'd been using. Her face suddenly grew harsh as she stared at me.

"Scott! Don't ever use that word again!" she snapped.

"But what does it mean?" I persisted. She looked as if she were caught between impulses to thrash me or bolt. Surprisingly she did neither; realizing it was once again my innate curiosity requiring straight answers.

She knew the day for explaining the facts of life had come. I watched her smooth back her hair and purse her lips. She seemed to be contemplating on how to approach it. Finally she cleared her throat and with a half smile began. We sat at the kitchen table and she pulled me to her.

"When a man and woman love each other, they come together in holy matrimony, and God blesses them with children. Like you," she began. My confusion must have shown because my mother continued, this time getting a bit more technical. "It's like this honey, men and women are..." she paused, "physically different. What boys have," she swallowed then pressed on. "Is what makes a baby in what girls have. Understand?" she asked.

Roger's pictures were worth a thousand words. In my mother's case, probably two thousand. But it was enough. I saw in my mother's eyes that she was hoping her sketchy explanation had been sufficient. I wouldn't shatter that hope.

"Sure, thanks mom." I said.

"That's quite all right. Now wash up for dinner and wake your father please," she asked.

"Okay," I said softly. As I nudged my dad, my thoughts were consumed with this new world. I wanted to know more. Sex was fascinating to me.

My collection of pornography continued to grow, but rather than hiding it, I simple forbade anyone in my room. Whenever anyone challenged my warning I would become very angry. Mostly it was my sisters who wandered in. I would scold them before I shooed them away. Not sure if any of it was really sinking in, but still feeling the need to assert myself. This was MY turf. My private domain.

Over the months, my father continually digressed into a pool of selflessness. He was a withdrawn shadow that cast a sad pall wherever he was. But I was too involved with my own world to consider his much. I was fourteen now, as big as him with broader shoulders. The gap between us cut a deeper groove daily.

We didn't do much together anymore and talked less. The worn out rebuttal to my inquiry about our startling differences remained the same, but my cynicism was growing. Supposedly, I looked like my dad's sister, but nobody ever managed to find a photograph which only served to fuel my suspicions. Did she even exist?

It lead to deeper scrutiny. Finally, one evening as I watched him sleeping, I noticed his second toes seem to curl a little funny like mine. It was a slim similarity but I wanted, needed something. Anything.

This was not a topic to approach my dad with. As usual I turned to my mother who was in the kitchen. I strolled in, watching her stack plates in the rack. Taking courage in hand I proceeded.

"Mom, am I adopted?" I blurted out. My mother's hand stopped, a dish suspended in her hand. She released it into the pool of murky water. Then she faced me but she didn't look me in the eye.

"No, you weren't adopted, I gave birth to you. Why would you ask such a thing?" she asked as her eyes met mine. It was my turn to look away.

I wasn't convinced. It just didn't add up. Of course I wasn't aware then of how often my mother had searched her own soul wondering about my biological father. I just knew something was wrong.

When my mother turned away from me to resume washing the dishes I knew the conversation was finished. At least in her mind. But her indifference to discuss it just made me more determined to know. I knew she was lying. But I couldn't figure out why. Or what the lie was entirely. Why not be honest?

Frustrated and angry, I stomped out. Usually I was careful to close the front door quietly but this time I didn't care. I let it slam, thinking that if they were going to lie to me I didn't owe them better.

"Scott!" I heard my mother yelling from the kitchen.

I climbed on my bike and began pedaling furiously. The whole world was a lie. The government, my mother, everything. I pedaled so hard that my chest heaved to breathe. Finally I skidded to a stop beneath a large oak in Madison Park.

Madison Park was about five miles from my home. Whenever I needed to clear my head I'd go there. I rested looking out over the park. It was not a large park, mostly yard with a smattering of trees, playground equipment and a baseball diamond. There were a couple of kids playing on the baseball diamond, two boys alternately pitching and hitting. They looked younger than myself. I guessed eleven or twelve.

Watching them helped me to calm down. Paradoxically, believing I was adopted also seemed to help. It abated my qualms that I would turn out like my father, a common laborer, prematurely aged and straddled with a bitch for a wife.

The fantasy allowed me to believe my real parents were some happy, wealthy couple living in a big house somewhere. I made my father a doctor and my mother a socialite who, for reasons unknown, had tragically been forced to give up their baby boy.

Unfortunately, all my fantasies were short-lived and couldn't mask the anger that reality brought. More and more I was lashing out. If the world was lying to me, I would lie too. It also helped to curb any previous guilt over stealing.

Family arguments were suddenly taking second chair to my acting out. One evening, out of sheer desperation, my mother threw up her arms. I'd just slammed the door for the tenth time and she'd had it. She glared at me as I headed to my room.

"You know, I love you, but it doesn't mean I have to like you," she snapped.

"Good, because I don't like you either," I sneered back. Briefly our eyes met. I was not about to back down but neither was my mother. That was the end of our conversation.

Lucky for us, Jodi broke the tension. She stumbled in, dragging a doll that was mangled along with her. Her soft brown eyes looked at both of us. My mother scooped her up. Had she ever been so loving with me?

I left them in the living room as I closed my bedroom door. The words hurt us both, mostly for the elements of truth contained within them than anything else. In turn, my rampage for destruction continued. Whatever I was searching for, I hadn't found.

I graduated to lighting fields on fire, then high tailing it at the first screech of a fire engine. I pushed the envelope with my shoplifting too, daring the world to catch me. Hoping in a strange way that it would force my father to punish me without asking for my mother's almighty permission.

Ironically I had no fear of God's wrath. It was my opinion that He had already punished us with the enmity between us. I hated God. I hated him more the day I came home from school to learn the bank was foreclosing on the house and we had to move—again. An acidic bitterness curdled within my being. I hated everybody and everything. As far as I was concerned, the whole world was one giant cesspool.

The girls had cost a lot to adopt. Payments had been missed to the point where there weren't any being made. All the dance and music lessons combined with my mother's out of control spending sprees had finally caught up to them. My father couldn't work enough to keep up, and he was slowing down. All the years of double shifts and overtime were catching up to him too. His hair was going gray and his hands shook more.

He was slower to move, requiring more rest on his few days off. I saw more of his back side then I did his face, awake and cognitive. His job had him more than we did. It made me bitter.

My world came to a crashing halt. It was all her fault. Not that our neighborhood was anything to brag about, but I knew this neighborhood, had my friends here, knew the schools.

The new house was actually better than the old one. More spacious, better design, more modern and in a nicer neighborhood. Before long, in spite of my previous declarations, I was adjusting to my new home. My new friends spoke my anti-establishment language, were resentful of authority and had long hair.

Part of that adjustment consisted of cranking up my stereo to the max so that all my family and our immediate neighbors could hear a steady diet of the The Doors, The Who and any other group I wanted to listen to. I'm not sure the neighborhood enjoyed my selections but if I could tune out my family's fighting, I was happy.

We all agreed, you couldn't trust anyone over thirty. Our anthem became: Live fast, die young, and rock and roll forever. It was a reckless concept, but it fueled our passion. We might not have been original, but we were a good fit. They bolstered my ego and I did my best to bolster theirs.

One day one of my older friends mentioned he had a motorcycle that he was looking to sell. I quickly jumped on the bandwagon. As usual my father said nothing. The same however could not be said about my mother. Immediately she tried to get me to return it. Ranting on that it would be the death of me.

Eventually she caved in just as she relented to my going to public school. I wanted to be there because public was where my friends were. My mother allowed it because we could no longer afford parochial school. It was one of the few moments that I was actually glad we were poor.

For awhile, life was actually starting to seem pretty good but then, as I was accustomed, another bump in the road of my life occurred. My mother assembled everybody into the family room one evening and while my dad slept and the girls listened, I stood fiddling around with my pocket knife waiting for the news.

It seems my mother had once again overextended the family budget and now we were going to be evicted. Evicted! I let the word roll over my tongue. I was so angry that I momentarily couldn't speak. Jodi and Lisa looked scared. My mother just looked as she always did, as if it were something that was beyond her control, as if she hadn't had a hand in it.

"But we have nothing to worry about," she said, trying to look cheerful. "I found us a little house in Greenwood."

I could feel the anger rising in me like mercury. Greenwood was a tiny, insignificant farm town eighteen miles from Lincoln and my life. This time I exploded.

"God Damn, why can't you two get your act together?" I screamed. I saw the shock on my mother's face. My reaction had even gotten my father's attention. He sat up. "Why do my parents have to be such losers!" I screamed again, this time ending on the word "losers" in a shrill crescendo. "I can't fucking believe it!" I yelled.

"Scott?" my father started. I glowered at him amazed.

"What you actually have a voice? All these years I didn't think you even knew how to talk!" I quipped. As soon as the words left my mouth I regretted it. The pain I saw in my father's eyes was a haunting sorrow I will never forget. I wanted to take it back but I couldn't. I had to be a man. Didn't I?

"Scott you apologize to your father!" My mother fumed. As usual we faced off. I stared down at her angry eyes. If there had been any chance, it was gone now.

"No. And I'm not going either. If you want to go, you can, but you're not ruining my life, no more!" I said defiantly.

It was the first time in a long time that I saw tears running down my mother's face. She didn't say another word. A part of me actually wished she had. But it was too late to undo it. Before anyone else could speak, I was gone now.

I didn't know where to go or what to do, but I had to get away. I knew I couldn't afford being emancipated but I hated my options. Still after an evening of roaming the streets and feeling homeless, depressed and angry, I climbed into my bedroom window knowing I was sunk. Not only did I end up going to Greenwood, but it turned out to be every bit the hell I imagined.

Farm communities, I soon discovered, are like one big happy family. Nonconformists were not appreciated nor tolerated by the dominant redneck majority, and with my long hair and "hippish" style, I was challenged daily to fight. Not being much of a fighter, I kept my mouth shut, my pride buried and stayed miserable. I tried to tell myself that I could get through it. Making friends with a few straggler outcasts helped a little, but the rejection cut and I found myself feeling even more cynical and resentful about my lot in life.

Before long, I joined the leagues of teens working for burger joints. Mine was working at Mc Donald's and I was desperately saving my pennies, planning my escape. As soon as I was able to scramble together enough money I bought a car, never mind that I didn't have a driver's license. It was my ticket to salvation. At least I could visit the old neighborhood and see some of my friends.

At night I would drive the rolling, twisting back roads of rural Nebraska with the lights off. I'd push the old Buick to go as fast as it would. It was a game to see how long I could cruise before the tires would grab a soft shoulder. That was my clue to yank it back before plunging into the depths of oblivion.

But as time passed a miraculous thing happened. I was beginning to like Greenwood. It surprised even me. Yet there was something about the fresh air and small town friendliness that was helping to soothe my anger. Eventually, even the rednecks grew tired of pestering me. Perhaps they figured that if the hippie was staying they might as well get used to him.

Sex continued to intrigue me, but I didn't have a girlfriend. I was self conscious about my teeth that were stained and rotting. Thanks to my poor dental hygiene and one too many candy binges, I hid my smile. It was a strange twist of fate, I was indeed my mother's son, hiding my smile too.

As a result it left me shy and awkward around girls. I seldom talked to female classmates. My only knowledge of women was what I gleaned from my mother, sisters and the glossy bodies in my pornography magazines. It was definitely a lonesome, unfulfilling existence.

Then fate seemed to smile on me. One Sunday while sitting in church I noticed the face of a pretty girl just a few pews in front of us. I watched her looking around wondering what she was looking for. Suddenly she turned around and our eyes met. I could feel my heart pounding. To my delight she smiled at me.

She had lovely blond hair that ran half way down her back off set by a pair of almost emerald green eyes. She was pretty and slender. Instantly I was enamored and smiled back.

After services I mustered the courage to walk up to her. She looked up at me with a bashful smile. My eyes ran the length of her body and settled on her face.

"Hi, I'm Scott," I offered my hand. She looked at my extended hand then me, for a moment she seemed unsure, but then she shook my hand. It was not a firm handshake, rather it was soft and delicate like she seemed to be.

"Nice to meet you. I'm Connie Henderson. That's my mom," she said gesturing to a short woman with short blond hair. They shared a pug nose and blond hair but little else. Her mother was stocky with deep set midnight blue eyes.

"My mom's behind your mother," I said pointing. She looked at my mother busy talking to a couple of her friends while Lisa and Jodi dutifully flocked around her. Connie nodded in acknowledgment.

From that day forth I looked forward to church. Before summer's end Connie became my girlfriend. We were inseparable. Together we discovered sex, drinking and pot.

One night after finishing up at McDonald's we found ourselves out cruising the back roads like we did so often just for something to do. Passing the fields of shocked hay and pumpkins, we decided to visit a friend of her older sister who lived with some biker named Bear. His name made me curious. What sort of man would be called Bear?

We pulled into a trailer park and rolled down a rough gravel road littered with potholes. Then parked in front of a double wide. It was an older model with tan trim that was faded and bent in places. An older two tone black and white pick up truck was parked under the car port. On both sides of the carport were shelves. They were cluttered with miscellaneous tools and knickknacks. The front yard was overgrown, but had a rough dirt path that led to the front porch. It was a makeshift porch of three rickety wooden steps.

We got out slowly. I was absorbing every detail. With all the tools, I wondered if he was a mechanic.

We hardly knocked before the door creaked opened. A big burly man with tattoos over every visible part of his body except his face, stood in the frame. Only his baby face and warm blue eyes destroyed the image my mind had conjured.

"Come on in," he instructed, stepping aside. "How about a cherry vodka?"

Before I could answer he was gone. But when he returned he carried two pink tumblers with ice. He handed each of us a drink.

Beer cans lay scattered around a coffee table in front of the television. More empty cans were on the floor. A tall cylinder stood centered on the coffee table, it was a bong. He noticed my focus and smiled, deep circles around his eyes.

"Have you ever smoked pot?" he asked.

"That stuff's bad for you," I said. He laughed, looking at me then Connie.

"Hey little brother, I guarantee, it'll make you feel good."

I watched him carefully light a funny-looking cigarette he'd extracted from a pack of Marlboros on the coffee table. It looked like a self-rolled ciggie but smaller and darker. He inhaled deeply, held it and slowly exhaled. Smoke poured from his nostrils and mouth. He offered it to me.

My mind was remembering all our school lectures on the evils of marijuana, but health warnings clashed with the disillusions I felt towards my world, living in Greenwood, my family's unending chaos and the Vietnam War. Why shouldn't I feel better?

I placed my lips over the joint and took a long drag. A moment later I was coughing while Bear slapped my back in an uproar of laughter.

"Take a little less next time, you Bogart!" he exclaimed between chuckles. My head felt fuzzy as the dense smoke loomed in the air.

I took Bear's advice. My next drag was smaller. In turn my lungs didn't hurt so bad. And I could feel something happening. Something I liked. I was getting a buzz. Before I knew it, I was twisting Connie's arm into trying it. Soon we were all laughing and giggling at the least little thing.

When that joint was expired Bear simply got another. This time when he lit it, I felt anxious. Eager to get another buzz.

"You sure I won't get addicted?" I asked half-heartedly. He chortled shaking his head.

"Nah, it's just pot man." Then he handed me the joint.

It was the first of many journeys I would have with weed. Without realizing it, I'd just taken another step towards a life-long struggle. Unfortunately, I was too busy feeling good to notice.

10

The Beginning of the End

"I don't care what you say. I am not going back to school!" I shouted defiantly at my mother. She looked like a wet dish rag, tears streaming down her face, clutching her apron contorted into a mass of sobbing. I almost felt sorry for her.

But at sixteen, I felt like I knew better than my parents. It was the summer of 1971 and I decided I was old enough to determine my own life's path. School of which, was not to be a part.

School was for losers. The nauseating, so-called good little boys and girls who bought into all the that establishment crap and the great American dream. They could follow their fantasy life of college and careers and happily ever after, but it was not for me. I was self reliant, or at least determined to become such.

"Scott?" my mother said, extending her arms as if she could stop me. But I just stomped out, leaving her to deal with it and my dad, once again. It never even occurred to me what kind an example I was setting for my younger siblings.

Later that week, I calmly walked into the kitchen and stood peering at my family eating at the dining room table. All eyes were focused on me but nobody was talking.

"I found a full-time job, I want to start paying rent and help out," I announced. It was my backhanded attempt to appease my parents. Hoping that if I helped ease their financial woes, they might overlook the fact that I wasn't in school.

"That's a big decision son." My father said. Our eyes met. There was something intangible in that look. Did he relate? Did it remind him of his own wayward youth? "I'm proud of you for working, helping out," he looked down. I knew it bothered him that he couldn't adequately provide for his family, but I wondered of any man could appease my mother unless he was rich.

"But you still need an education," my mother said softer than usual. Perhaps she'd grown tired of fighting about it. I looked at her, astonished. Those were the only words she said that night. It was so strange to see my mother actually backing down. It made me feel invincible and a bit pompous.

But it wasn't enough. One month later, after dropping out of school, I came home to find an empty house. Without telling me, my parents had filed for bankruptcy. Everything was gone. The creditors had repossessed everything.

To make matters worse, my father had been laid off and our only dependable vehicle was gone, leaving a rattle trap that worked when it wanted. And the house had been sold. We were homeless.

I stood amongst the emptiness letting it all sink in. My mind reeling, disbelieving. It was just too much. How many times were we doomed to start over? It was unfair.

"I don't believe this!" I said, kicking a piece of debris across the floor. My father sat on a wooden box staring at the floor, too ashamed to look me in the eyes. I wasn't sure which one of us I felt worse for.

My mother and sisters were a collection of sobs sitting in the corner of what used to be our living room. A little while later, she seemed to pull herself together as she looked up.

"It'll be okay," my mother started to say, but she stopped in mid thought as we exchanged looks. I was making a concerted effort not to explode. Once again feeling betrayed, deceived, and irrepressibly angry. I took a deep breath.

"You must have known?," I said sounding more curt than I'd intended.

"Yes. And I'm sorry Scott, but I really thought I could handle it," she said quietly.

"Like you've handled it before, mother?" I said more to myself. Her eyes looked into mine. I knew she'd heard but I was too hurt to apologize.

"Bob is a Realtor, and he's promised me we won't be homeless," she said sheepishly.

I just looked at her speechless. Did she really believe that? If there was anything remarkable about my mother it was definitely her way of having hope when by all rights, one should have had none. My mother was the original Molly Brown.

We were homeless. Maybe things would turn around but I was looking at an empty house with five deserted souls searching for security amongst the for sale sign. It was too overwhelming. I walked outside.

I let the cool air kiss my face. The air smelled of rain. It was a comfort against the terribly oppressive and suffocating atmosphere inside. I couldn't face any of their sad, forlorn faces. If I had felt like my life was crumbling before, it seemed in shambles now.

In a strange way I felt a stronger alliance with my father, understanding what he must have felt being the man of the house but still unable to provide and protect his family. I felt the same helplessness wash over me. I didn't feel much like a man at that moment but rather a broken little boy. I hadn't saved them as my imagination fancied. We were still a sinking ship.

My mother did have a strong conviction even if she couldn't balance a checkbook to save her life. She'd managed to talk Bob into helping us. Even though we had nothing to offer, and most certainly nothing of any value. Perhaps he had just taken pity on us.

He told my mother about a placed he'd purchased over in Havelock mostly for the land. He said he couldn't promise the place was even inhabitable but we were desperate. So my mother agreed, gladly. And thus we had a new home.

I fully expected to be facing a junk pile. But the neighborhood wasn't so bad, it actually had nicely kept lawns upon which older, small wood houses sat. Our house was two story, boarded up complete with a sign that stated uninhabitable until the furnace was up to code.

The roof sagged like an old horse. I cautiously stepped onto the porch, wondering if it would collapse at any minute. But it was sturdier than I guessed, it only creaked as I pried the one by fours off over the entrance.

The interior was composed of musty smelling walls with huge patches of mold growing under the windows and terribly worn and scratched wood floors. There was a pile of litter that had been pushed off to one side of the living room.

Lovely, I thought wandering into the kitchen. Orange crates had been nailed to the wall for cabinets. Immediately I began planning on improvements. The tacky cabinets would be one of the first.

It was a good thing that no one in my family was overweight, otherwise the single, tiny bathroom would have been a struggle. It was a challenge enough just to close the door without hitting my knees.

My mother gave the girls a bedroom and one to me. Both of our rooms were upstairs. My parents hung a sheet across the large entrance to the living room that would suffice for their room until my father had time to make a wall.

After the initial shock, I wasn't entirely unhappy. The distance between my parents and me guaranteed I wouldn't be hearing their arguments. That in and of itself almost made our horrible situation palatable.

We had gone full circle. I was now close to my old friends once again, something I heartily embraced. Even the distance from Connie didn't bother me. Greenwood was close, I could pick her up easily.

The move had an odd healing affect on the entire family. My father returned to the cement factory as if he'd never left. While my mother worked tediously on refurbishing our very modest home. No easy task without the privilege of credit. But the huge task of making a home at least kept her busy and too preoccupied to fight much.

It was my own fear of turning out like my father that brought me back to school. Besides, I had to admit, it would feel good to be among friends again.

Summer was ending. Leaves were falling and the weather was becoming more breezy as the New Year started. On opening day, I stopped on the sidewalk, watching the steady stream of students filing in. It was my final year of high school. I was more than ready to be through.

We were asked to stand for the pledge of allegiance in my first period class. As I stood up my eyes saw her. Her name was Belinda Johnson, a curvaceous brunette that definitely had my attention.

She was wearing a red polka-dotted dress but I was fixated on her breasts. She noticed me staring and smiled. I smiled back, giving her my best come hither look.

Before long we were passing notes. Eventually I mustered the courage to ask her out. I almost forgot about Connie, occasionally feeling a twinge of guilt. When alas I did call her to break it off, I could hear her crying but emotionally I felt numb. I told myself relationships didn't last and it was the last time I allowed myself to think about it.

I was more concerned with getting into Belinda's pants. We did everything together. School, parties, sex. Often while my parents were home. I even convinced her to pose for me. It gave me more photos for my stack of porn.

Her nature made her feel pressure to please me. Whatever I wanted, she'd do. I knew her home life wasn't much better than mine. It was easy to take advantage of her and play with her emotions.

The school year was passing quickly. We were rapidly approaching the Thanksgiving holiday. Turkey day decorations lined the halls. I hated holidays. They meant more family time and down time from my girlfriend and friends. But I was as happy as I'd been in a long time, getting all the sex, pot and fun I wanted.

Using at least three joints a day, I had finally become mellow. I knew my folks had noticed the difference but they never brought up the change and neither did I. It helped me stomach their bickering, which I considered a good thing.

I began to wonder about my future and for the first time I thought about what I would do once I graduated. Finally the world felt like my oyster.

When my dealer, a street-smart eighteen year old suggested I work for him, I eagerly agreed. Steve Schaefer had been dealing for over half his life. He knew his way around the thriving underworld of drugs and dealing. He was a thin, wiry looking man with bad skin, empty almost black eyes, a nervous demeanor and curly brown hair. He fit the stereotype.

It seemed like the logical choice since I was frequenting him so much and it would be a way to pay for my own use. I wondered if people would think I looked like a dealer too.

The perks were an intoxication. In a single night I could make what took me a month to make at McDonald's. Immediately my popularity soared and I suddenly had money to burn. It was the most liberating feeling I'd felt in my seventeen years. To finally not be groveling or struggling. I even had money to fix my teeth.

If my parent's wondered about the late night traffic visiting me, they never expressed it. Ignorance was bliss.

I began to buy myself things, acquiring a few precious belongings. It felt incredibly good to be able to buy whatever I wanted, whenever I wanted.

Soon I purchased a better stereo system and black lights for my room. Next I got another car, and another motorcycle. And while my family sweltered in the tiny house I kept cool in my air conditioned room. I was still too angry at them to share my wealth.

Communication between me and my parents all but ceased to exist. What was there to say? I considered them and their lifestyle one for losers. I had absolutely no sympathy for them as I saw the house decked out with an assortment of fans and their red faces looking languished on my way to and from my room.

My sisters, however, were another matter. They, as much as myself, were victims of circumstance. I took them out for rides or to the movies quite often. It made me curious, did they feel as lost in that household as I did?

More than ever I was convinced that I was adopted. Or if that wasn't the truth, that my mother had had an affair. I still loved my father, but I was certain we were not related. All my anger became directed towards my mother. I told myself everything was all her fault. I began to group my father and I together, seeing us both as bullied and henpecked victims of my mother.

Dealing drugs not only afforded me the luxuries I had missed throughout my young life, it was an ideal way to thumb my nose at my mother and the establishment that I regarded as being equally awful. I knew of course that jail was always a possibility, but like so many things back then, I chose not to think about it. And like most teens, had my fair share of cockiness going. Feeling like I was invincible and one step ahead of the law.

Then one day while a friend named Paul was visiting, the conversation took a sinister turn. Sunshine spilled in through my open window, highlighting my cramped, but now, nicely furnished room.

Paul was a senior like myself. He had long dark hair that ran just beyond his shoulders and an athletic build. Like myself, he was pretty anti-government but was a lot less vocal about it.

"Did you sell some pot to Steve Schaefer a few weeks back?" he asked.

I'd been standing in front of the window but suddenly moved away and sat on the opposite side of my bed. I looked at him curiously.

I'd been buying my pot from another supplier for awhile and had lost contact with Steve. I realized I had had a transaction with him a couple weeks earlier when he had purchased the same ounce I'd originally purchased from him.

"Yeah, why?" I asked, wondering where this was going.

"Well, I heard he got busted and that now he's a narc, turning in everybody so he can get out of trouble," he said matter of factly.

"No way," I shot back. "Steve would never turn me in," I said.

But the rumor stayed with me. I began to wonder how loyal Steve truly was. My trepidation, however, wasn't enough to stop me from carrying on business as usual. I assured myself that us "hippies" stuck together; no one would rat me out to one of the establishment pigs.

Weeks passed and the rumors became a distant blur, but then came my day of reckoning. As I laid on my bed on the night of January 9th, 1973, I heard a car pull up outside. I could see from my window that it was a black Chevy Impala; an unmarked police car.

"Fuck, I'm busted," I muttered to myself contemplating about the two pounds of pot I had hidden in a panel in the ceiling. I was inordinately calm as I waited for the inevitable knock.

Perhaps I had been waiting to be caught. I knew I'd been dancing along on that razor's edge for quite some time, feeling invincible, above the law, indifferent to the world around me. But as with all games, the odds eventually change and suddenly you're not winning, happy-go-lucky any more.

A minute later I heard it, followed by my father's voice.

"Scott!" I heard my father yelling. "Come down here!"

I got to my feet slowly. A gnawing ache of shame ate at me as I shuffled downstairs. Two detectives watched me.

Both were big men, over six feet and broad shouldered. One had dark, almost coal black hair and a bushy mustache. The other was blond. Both men were stoic.

The detective with the mustache stepped forward.

"Scott, I'm Detective Henson and this is Detective Truit. We have a warrant for your arrest for dealing a controlled substance. Turn around please and lean against the wall," he instructed calmly.

I could feel blood coursing into my face. The detectives were all business but my mother's eyes were welling with tears. Jodi and Lisa looked frightened but my father looked disappointed. I swallowed back my own tears, chastising myself for being so foolish. Suddenly my father blurted.

"Why did you do it son?" he asked, his eyes searching mine as Detective Henson snapped the cuffs on.

I stared at him. What was with the sudden tone of authority? Was he playing concerned daddy in front of the police? Disdain curdled in my stomach. I had nothing to say to him or any of them.

I knew I should have been afraid and perhaps I might have been if I hadn't been so incredibly angry. Angry at my parents, at Steve for selling me out and especially angry at God. In my estimation, he had once again forsaken me.

From the station I called Belinda, waiting anxiously between a throng of other inmates to be released. I told her where to get the money I needed for bail.

Two hours later I was back on the street, defiantly selling pot. Infused by a new righteous anger, I decided I didn't give a damn about anything. Fuck the police. Fuck the establishment. Fuck the whole damned world, I thought.

I strolled the wet Lincoln streets, remnants of a fresh winter rain. It gave me a renewed rush. Nobody was going to bring me down. I was tougher than they were. It made me view my world differently. Viewing myself as a single entity against the world.

Ironically, my arrest and tough-guy reaction had made me a hero among my friends. I felt like James Dean in A Rebel Without a Cause. And I was more than willing to play the unruly delinquent.

At my court appearance I was accompanied by a lawyer I paid for with my drug money. A burly, older man that looked as worn as his gray flannel suit.

His name was Wiring, and he had a solo practice in one of the brick builds in the older part of downtown Kansas City. He instructed me to act remorseful and be respectful in front of the judge. But with Belinda looking on, I would have none of that. I'd rather she thought of me as a tough criminal than a wimpy nice guy.

I fancied myself a young maverick facing down the forces of evil. I wore my John Lennon-like wire rim glasses, a rock and roll tee shirt that pictured the Beatles' Abbey Road album cover on the front and my bell bottom jeans. They were badges of my disdain for an unfair system.

Judge Bower was a frumpy, dried up specimen of a man who peered out over his gavel at me with contempt. A heavy frown drew between his brows. Immediately I felt like he'd been on the bench way too long.

"Remove your glasses Mr. Davis," he said sounding impatient. In turn I snatched my specs and cocked back my head, glaring back at him. "You, Mr. Davis, have a severe attitude problem," he said dryly.

In response I just rolled my eyes which made him all the more angrier.

"It's obvious to me that you haven't learned a thing. Often, as a first time offender, I'd give probation; especially since you're only seventeen. But since you insist on acting like such a tough guy, we'll see how tough you really are," he continued.

Now I was afraid. My bravado evaporated quickly. This wasn't what I'd envisioned.

"That means a felony conviction on your record. Do you understand? It will follow you around for the rest of your life. If you even know what your constitutional rights are," he scoffed, "you've just lost yours. Which means, you can never be a lawyer or a doctor. You'll never be able to vote or hold a liquor license. And you cannot join the military.

"I hope it was worth it to you Mr. Davis. I am not going to send you to prison, but I could. I think a stiff fine is appropriate and if I ever see you again, mark my words, it'll be twice as bad. And you will regret it," he said. Then he slammed the gavel down. "Next case!"

I struggled to maintain my mask of defiance. If Belinda hadn't been there, I probably would have left to be alone.

As I left the courtroom she joined me. I locked my arm in hers, feeling the hatred rising within. Over and over I head it in my mind like a mantra: Fuck you judge. Fuck you. Your family. Everything about you, you old red-necked asshole. Fuck you all!

11

Spiraling Out of Control

No sooner had I been dismissed from court than I was back out on the street dealing again. It was my way of thumbing my nose at the establishment, law enforcement, my family and my life. I was determined that nobody was going to tell me what to do.

Occasionally cops would drop by the school to harass me. Each time they came I felt a renewed vigilance to my anti-establishment convictions. I wore my righteous indignation like a coat I wanted to show off. Who were they to tell me what was right from wrong?

The country was in conflict too. Vice President Agnew had resigned amidst the rumors of criminal investigation. It made me chuckle, every man was out for themselves. They weren't any models of virtue, so why should anyone clip me for my petty dealing? Everyone knew Nixon was lying about Watergate.

I found it curious how they all invoked God as their witness to their innocence, thinking they should have proclaimed just the opposite. But it mattered not, they were still liars. The whole lot of them, just as God was a lie.

Our country was indeed in turmoil. Torn between the politics of pro and anti war advocates that rallied around every major capital to voice their feelings or outrage. And then there was me, the fallen prodigal son. Under the scrutiny now of local law enforcement.

It was a twisted time in my life, feeling caught between the chords of familial loyalties and national loyalties and yet feeling (and believing at times) that I was a force to be reckoned with. Of course, I was but a cog in the vast configuration of life's wheel, but being embroiled in my problems, it was hard for me to acknowledge that fact.

One Friday afternoon in spring while the sunshine flecked through the trees across the school grounds, I hooked up with Belinda. We joined Joey and Jane, another couple that we sometimes partied with.

Joey and Jane looked like matching strung out book ends. Both were tall, wiry reeds with long stringy dishwater blond hair. Jane had braces and Joey had acne, perhaps the only two distinguishing characteristics between them.

On a whim we opted to go camping and headed to Lavaland State Park; a known hang out for the area's young people. I hoped we could score some pot there since both of my regular suppliers were out.

At times I had actually considered quitting. I knew I wasn't getting the buzz I once got and actually felt more tired and drained than anything else. But it afforded me a pause from my life that I needed, so I stayed hooked.

Luckily, Joey had some speed. I hoped that the speed along with the beer we'd just bought at the local convenience store would be enough. It made me relax a bit more. If I couldn't find any pot, I could just get drunk. Anything to numb my senses. Thinking that if I couldn't feel it, I didn't have to deal with it.

We settled into one of the campsites and made a fire. As evening fell, I was happy about our choice to camp. It never occurred to me to tell my parents. I figured they wouldn't miss me anyway.

We were huddled around the fire, Joey and Jane on one side and me and Belinda on the other. I lit a cigarette and offered a puff to her.

She took it and sucked in deeply. She coughed a little before handing it back. Then we heard a loud crack in darkness of the woods behind us.

"What was that?" Joey asked.

"Ah, it's nothing," I said. But Belinda and Jane were anxiously peering at the darkness behind us. "You're just being paranoid," I told him.

Hardly a moment later we were suddenly encased in the spotlights of a dozen flashlights. I shielded my eyes as I realized it was local and state law enforcement officers who had us surrounded.

Then a state trooper who recognized me from Lincoln stepped forward.

"Well, hello Scott," he said in mock surprise. There was more than a hint of laughter to his voice. I could feel steam rising in my soul. Sabotage. "What are you doing here? You wouldn't happen to have any drugs on you, would you?"

My mind began to race. They obviously had followed us. I knew we didn't have any pot but my mind got fuzzy, where was the rest of the speed. My heart was slamming against my chest but I was straining to appear calm.

"No. You know I can't get into any more trouble or I'll go to jail," I said softly.

The officer shifted his weight to his other leg as he stared at me. He was a big man with a pronounced beer belly. His eyes were laughing as he focused on each of us then back to me.

"That's right Scott. But do you mind if we check your stuff?" he pressed. I glanced at Joey and our backpacks. I didn't want him to look. But I didn't want to appear guilty so I nodded.

"Sure, go ahead."

We watched them proceed, pulling out everything carefully. They found nothing in my pack. I felt myself releasing an intrinsic sigh. But one of the other officers quickly found the vile of speed in Joey's pack.

"Well, what have we here?" the first cop said smiling at me. It was clear he intended to nail me but one of his colleagues tapped his shoulder. It made him straighten up. "Well?" he slurred the word slowly. "It appears we can't bust you because we didn't ask your friend here for permission to do a search," he said gruffly, obviously disappointed.

I felt my heart leap. I'd caught a lucky break. I needed one.

"Of course," the cop began. I looked up. Our eyes met. I could see passion burning within his eyes. He'd love to bust me just on principle. I swallowed looking away. A deep seated fear settled in my stomach. "We could always make it look like we'd found it among your stuff," he said tossing the vile so it landed on my pack.

We exchanged looks. I hated him at that moment. I hated everything. All I could think about was my fear of jail and how I couldn't face it. Suddenly my tough guy facade crumbled and I started bawling uncontrollably.

"Why are you guys picking on me?" I managed to whimper out. He shifted legs, staring down at me.

"Because the judge wants you to clean up your act Scott," he said curtly. "Personally, I don't think you can. But it looks like you're going to get another chance. Just remember," he pointed a finger in my face, "I'll be watching you."

With that he stepped back and they collectively left. We were all visibly shaken but as time passed and we retold the story, suddenly the fear and my tears were absent. Instead I started mocking them: They'd just blown an easy bust.

"Fuck the cops," I snarled while collecting firewood. "They probably would have framed me if there hadn't been witnesses. They lie just like everybody else." I told myself.

Belinda half heard me muttering, she looked up as if to say what, but I gestured it was nothing. I'd keep my rage to myself.

Conveniently, I convinced myself that my initial bust had just been a fluke. It wouldn't happen again because I wouldn't pick unreliable friends anymore. Besides, I was smarter than the cops. What did they know? In my estimation, they were nothing more than a bunch of ignorant rednecks with badges.

I decided it was time for me to expand my horizons and began selling LSD with Joey. After awhile, we opted to eliminate the middle man by driving to Boulder ourselves.

Boulder was five hundred miles to the west. Home of the University of Colorado, a hotbed of revolution since the flower-power days of the Sixties. There was no doubt it was the drug capital of the Rocky Mountains.

Immediately I found a source who would sell me a thousand doses for $500, which in turn I would sell for two dollars a piece. Once again I was in the money and able to get a lot of expensive toys. My latest being a 56 Chevy Blair Coup. I loved that car, waxing it till it gleamed.

The admonition from the state trooper was hardly a whisper in my brain now. Once again, arrogance prevailed and instead of heeding the warning I had lost my fear. I respected no one and nothing except money and a good "fix".

One evening as I found myself comfortably trying to get high with a friend of mine, I grew discouraged. Usually one hit was enough for me to get my buzz, but after waiting two hours, I started to believe my latest buy was junk. So I took another dose, this time twice the amount. Big mistake.

Five minutes later I was on the floor, screaming and striking out. Everywhere I saw demons. I closed my eyes and opened them again only to see their grotesque figures and faces lurking around me. Their clawed hands reaching for me.

Terror seized me like a seizure. I swung aimlessly trying to keep them at bay. This was not the peaceful, wonderful ride I had envisioned. No, it was the stuff that nightmares were made of and I was hideously a part of it.

Nothing I did seemed to make a difference. Vaguely I was aware of my friend Joey's presence even though I couldn't seem to clear my head enough to be lucid. It was a dragon I'd just have to ride.

My bad trip suddenly gave me an acute conscience. Was I subjecting unsuspecting friends to similar torture? What kind of demons were on their doorsteps trying to get in? Guilt wrapped me tightly in its grip. I felt overcome with emotions, none of which were very nice.

As I would feel one wave of hallucinations passing, another would begin. I began to fear what my outcome would be. Something inside my being made me pray. On my knees and with tears streaming down my face, I prayed over and over, begging the God I'd denied for mercy. "God, if you get me through this, I'll never have anything to do with LSD again," I promised mumbling inaudibly.

Slowly the ilk of my bad trip began to subside. My world was coming back to me in bits and pieces and I was thankful, clutching desperately to each and every one.

In the days to follow I kept my promise, but I didn't stay on the straight and narrow. I concluded that LSD was evil but pot was harmless. I continued to deal, justifying my actions by placating myself. It made people feel good, it didn't hurt them. Besides, it wasn't addictive like LSD.

My own usage grew daily. I was using it from morning till night, with every other time becoming a blur. But as long as there were no demons on my back, I could skate along with the fantasy.

Eventually the status quo became boring and banal and I allowed myself to start using methamphetamines. Again I justified my drug use; it was just speed. It helped me get through my daily activities, so why not? Never mind that I wouldn't eat or sleep for days. If it wasn't hurting anyone, it was okay.

At times the face I saw in my mirror seemed like another man. I began to feel like I was living my life in a bubble. That Scott was a persona of someone else. A man who lived fast, died young, just like my own mantra. It was as close to introspection as I'd allow myself to get. I wasn't ready for the truth. Not yet.

After graduation I was eager to move out. I quickly found a comfortable apartment on the outskirts of Kansas City. The distance helped me sort out my twisted family life. I had grown to hate my mother. I needed to separate myself from the trademark fighting that had eroded the health of my family and my inner being. Now I could be my own man.

Inside my heart, a part of me knew she was actually a very sick woman. Plagued with depression and vices. It was not unusual to find my mother nervously chain smoking or drinking cup after cup of coffee at the kitchen table. The only things that seemed to help bring her out of her moods, no matter how fleeting, were my sisters or fighting with my father. It didn't seem like much of a life to me, but she probably thought the same of my existence.

On I went into my spiral of downward living. Careless driving and too many accidents had cost me my license. It left Belinda to chauffeur me around to which I took full advantage. I'd even make fun of her and all women behind her back to my friends. Claiming women were only good for cleaning, doing dishes and sex. The only females I treated decently were my sisters.

Regardless of her loyalty, I remained convinced that Belinda would eventually abandon me. Deliberately I'd test her, driving a wedge between us until alas after a big fight she left the apartment in tears. I let her go, confused with my behavior but not willing to acknowledge my blame in the demise of our relationship.

Belinda took solace in the arms of my good friend, John Galliger. John was a handsome man with wavy, light-brown hair. It was no secret that he liked her. Our fight provided the perfect venue for him to move in.

Quickly he told her I'd been stepping out on her. Perhaps out of spite or hurt, she believed him. As much as I tried to pretend I was unaffected, I was actually devastated.

Like before, I soon buried my pain in more drugs, more meaningless sexual relationships and more denial; telling myself I didn't need anyone.

As before, I soon got busted and with a strange twist of fate, it was while selling a $10 bag of pot to an undercover cop. It was an unspoken rule: never sell to strangers. And I wouldn't have if the detective hadn't been with a regular contact. I had no idea at the time that my friend had already been busted in what would eventually be recorded as one of the biggest drug sweeps in Lancaster County history.

Still feeling pretty confident during those days, I walked into court thinking the sentence wouldn't be too bad; it was after all, just a ten dollar bag. Others assembled were being popped for selling coke or morphine. I reflected on the words the judge had told me: If you get caught again, it will be twice as bad. Foolishly I thought that just meant twice the fine, which would make it $1000. I could pay that, no sweat.

This time, however, I had no drug money lawyer, only a public defender. He looked more nervous than me. Wearing a sky blue suit that was a size to small, his tie and collar seemed to be strangling him. As a result, his eyes bulged and his face was flushed. He dabbed perspiration from his forehead with a handkerchief.

"Just plead guilty. You'll get probation, one to three years, tops," he waved his hand in a dismissive gesture.

I surveyed the courtroom. It was filled with about a dozen drug dealers and their public defender lawyers. Most of them looked pompous or nervous. It made me wonder if I looked the same way.

Before I could decide I suddenly noticed the judge. It was not someone I recognized by face, but the name on the plate made my stomach tight. It was the honorable judge Richard Farmbrook. The same of which was legendary for presiding over the Charles Starkweather trial of the Fifties.

Starkweather had only been a teenager when he'd suddenly gone on a murderous rampage that resulted in nine deaths. Farmbrook had coolly sentenced him to death.

Clearly he was older, but still the stern, righteous jurist of days gone by. I looked at the tall, wisp figure with glasses and snowy white hair. His reputation had definitely proceeded him.

When I glanced at my lawyer, I could see fear in his eyes. It was looking more grim as the day went on. He patted my hand. But I wondered if it was to console me or himself.

"It'll be okay," he said, dabbing his forehead again.

Again I wondered if he was trying to convince me or himself. Finally my time to rise came.

"Scott Davis versus the State of Kansas," the judge's voice boomed. He cocked his head back, staring, his face stoic. "You got anything to say for yourself?" he demanded sharply. I could feel the room getting small. My heart squeezing the blood out of my chest. Sweat rolled down my face.

I shrugged only because words failed me. I was too scared to speak. Finally the words came out in a muffled dribble. I told him I was sorry.

"Your honor, I know I made a mistake," I said softly.

Suddenly he slapped one of his bony hands on the podium. I grew quiet. He shook his head. In my mind I could hear my inner voice screaming: I'm cooked.

"Well Mr. Davis, this is the second time in two years that you've been before this court for the same offense," he said harshly. "And I don't think you've learned a damn thing. In fact, it is the opinion of this court that a little prison time would do you good," he finished dryly.

As the judge continued to talk the room began to spin. Images of prison rotated through my mind. I envisioned being stuck in a tiny cell and being at the mercy of some huge, hairy ape being fucked in the ass. Murderers, rapists and bank robbers belonged in prison. Not petty dealers and mixed up kids like me.

All because of one lousy ten dollar bag of pot! I couldn't believe it. My mind was reeling. I could feel my world shrinking as his words floated through my brain: In my opinion, you should serve three to five years in the Kansas State Penitentiary.

If there was anything more, I didn't hear it. Suddenly darkness covered me like a sheath. I'd blacked out.

I opened my eyes to see my mother standing over me with a worried look on her face. Once I got my bearings back, I realized I was in her bed.

I prayed for it all to be a dream, but knew it was real. I was going to prison. Luck had abandoned me. Shame washed over me.

Hot tears cascaded down my face. My mother tried to comfort me in her fashion but it was useless. All I could see was the doom that lay ahead for me. I clutched the sheets to my face and wept bitterly.

I cried so hard that my head began to pound making the room spin. At that moment I didn't care if I blacked out, or even if I died. I was actually hoping I would. Just so I wouldn't have to deal with it.

A thousand bits of memories, past misdeeds and idle promises seemed to flash through my mind. Repeatedly I cursed myself, how could I have been so stupid and foolish?

I could scantly feel my mother stroking my head as she tried to comfort me. My father was just a silent shadow who stood in the background. Did they regret having me? Perhaps there was some comfort in believing I was adopted; at least my waywardness couldn't be their fault.

"Mom," I said sitting up. I knew what I needed to do. "Please call the minister," I said. She nodded and soon he came.

But Reverend Farley was an man from the old school and he had no clue on how to help me. He looked like a pickle that had been out in the sun too long. He had no miraculous solution; in fact his only suggestion was prayer. It didn't feel like enough.

I tried to pray but debauch images haunted my thoughts. I couldn't shake the fear of prison initiation and the ideation of grimy inmate faces grinning while they watched me being brutalized.

Suddenly I bolted. I fled the disquieting scenario. Not sure what I was really thinking or doing as I hopped on my motorcycle, only that I needed to get away.

I revved the engine, twisting the throttle higher and higher as I tore down the residential streets of Lincoln; not concerned about anything but escaping.

The faster I went, the more reckless my driving became. Until alas I failed to negotiate a corner and went over a curb, abruptly I was thrown some thirty feet, ending my escape efforts.

Suddenly I was face down in dirt, gravel and grass motionless. Someone called for an ambulance and I was whisked away to the hospital. Miraculously I hadn't been killed and even more striking, had few real injuries.

After the initial evaluation, the hospital quickly put me on a suicide watch. I was confined to a small hospital room with restraints on my arms and legs. Once again I began to cry. Nothing was going right for me.

I began to curse God for letting me live. Was it some cruel joke that I would survive only to face rape and abuse? It made me shudder.

The next day a squirrelly looking man with coke-bottom thick glasses came in. He wasn't more than five feet four inches. Nervously he adjusted his glasses while he spoke.

"I'm Dr. Randel," he said offering his hand. Then he saw the restraints. It made him blush. "Sorry," he muttered.

He sat in the only chair in the room. It was placed at the bottom of the bed. He moved it so he could look at me while he talked and took notes in his notebook.

"I can't go to prison," I whimpered before another avalanche of tears overtook me. Doctor Randel sat quietly as I sobbed. Finally he set his notebook down.

"Scott, I will help you, but let's take it one day at a time, huh? First I need to ask you some questions, okay?" he asked, I nodded. How could anybody help me?

The questions were pretty standard covering a wide array of subjects that touched on my home life, career and personal relationships. To my surprise, I enjoyed talking to him. It felt good to be getting some of my anger and frustration out.

After a long while he put his pen down and looked at me. He pushed up his glasses and blinked. The sunlight of the day was slipping away as water draining from a bathe.

"I'm going to give you something. Let's see if we can get you feeling better, then perhaps you'll feel more able to conquer your other problems, okay?" he asked. Thinking I had nothing to lose, I agreed.

Randel prescribed an anti-anxiety medication. After just the first dose, a new world seemed to open. Immediately my downcast heart seemed lighter. Ever my pending sentence seemed less foreboding.

My head cleared enough for me to realize I had been impetuous. Again I instructed my mother to summon our minister. Perhaps I hadn't given God a fair chance.

A younger man arrived in Farley's place. He was tall, blonde, broad-shoulder and intelligent, not unlike the portrait I'd painted of my imaginary father.

This time, upon the suggestion of prayer, I had a focus and calm that before I could only attribute to pot. As the young preacher stood to leave he gave me a note card with a religious inscription on it. Turn your eyes upon Jesus and look into his wonderful face, and all the problems of the earth will grow strangely dim as you look on his love and grace. Immediately I knew those words were God's message to me.

I neatly put the small card into my wallet. Already I could feel a difference.

"I'll see you tomorrow Scott," he said with a kind smile.

"I'll be looking forward to it Pastor," I answered.

With that, he was gone. I knew I was experiencing a revelation. Reflecting on the night before and how it had seemed so long and full of anguish. Minutes had seemed slower than normal as the light of day took it's sweet time in arriving. There were desperate moments of longing for death and darkness. But as shadows began to creep into the room that night; contrarily I felt no fear, only a tranquility that had eluded me for so long.

Pastor Ryan kept his word about returning. And with his visit he had a wonderful idea. He said to get my friends and family to write the judge. Character references couldn't hurt.

"I'll go to bat for you Scott. But in the meantime, you know what you need to do." He raised a brow.

"Okay," I said.

To my astonishment Farmbrook was a member of his church. Maybe I did have a chance. I began to feel optimistic as I called everyone I could think of that might be willing to write a letter.

Something must have worked because Farmbrook relented. When I reappeared in court, he said he'd had a change of heart. I would not have to go to prison.

I felt euphoric hearing the words I thought were incredulous. Something inside made me say a silent prayer. God had listened. He had helped me.

"None-the-less, I am going to give you three years of the strictest probation I can order," he said. Then pointing a long, skinny finger at he me he spoke firmly, "No drugs, no alcohol, and stay away from drug dealers and anyone you know who has a felony. You're to report to your probation officer once a month. And just to give you a taste of what you'll get if I see you in here again, you'll spend every Friday evening to Monday morning in the county jail for the entire summer. Mess up again and you'll go straight to prison. That's all!" He slammed down his gavel.

I hardly heard his last admonition. I was too overcome with relief and emotion.

As I left the courthouse, I was promising to swear off drugs. For a moment I stood in the sunlight, basking in the radiant warmth of the sun. It felt good. I remained for a moment longer watching people coming and going from the courthouse.

I wanted to remember that feeling of freedom. My demons are in the past, I told myself. I'm a new man, a better man.

For the next few weeks I actually managed to keep my promise. But then, just as New Year's resolutions fade, so did my good intentions. I found jail to be a quagmire of contradictions. I might have been confined, but there was an unending supply of drugs and other illegal paraphernalia. It made going straight a very difficult path.

Perhaps showing my naiveté, I asked a few fellow inmates about it. Both were in on drug charges also. They invited me to have a joint with them.

"But how?" I asked a shaggy looking man. He was a scruffy looking fellow with a beard and mustache. He looked as if he hadn't bathed in a month and smelled as bad. He chortled, displaying yellow and missing teeth.

"Shit. You can get anything you want in here. Heroin. Hash. You name it. The guards will even bring it in for a price," he cautioned. I wondered about the price. I didn't know if I wanted to find out.

Frightened and uncertain of my new roommates. I decided it was healthier to acquiesce than defy them. Surely God would understand. Besides, being in jail I was denied my medication and the pot did help calm my nerves.

I found the jail house rules obliging until a couple of my roomies aptly informed me that I was expected to supply them with next week's stash. Instantly I felt ill. The idea of countering any of my inmates was less than appealing. Not only was I grossly outnumbered, but most of them were bigger and tougher looking than me.

"How can I do that?" I stuttered. Everyone laughed. Then the scruffy one stepped closer.

"It's easy. You put the stuff in a condom and then shove it up your ass!" he began to cackle. His cohorts joined in, making me more alarmed. What was I to do?

The weekend came and I returned to my jail sentence without my token package. But I was too afraid of messing up. And found since I had essentially dropped pot from my daily life, I actually felt better.

My inmates were not sympathetic however. Immediately two big galoots shoved me up against the wall. While I strained to breathe the meanest one drew closer until his face was but a few inches from mine. His blood shot eyes gave him a whacked out look. He could have easily passed for a hell's angel, complete with tattoos and dirty, stringy hair.

"You better bring it next time or you'll be a dead man," he snarled in my face. It was nearly enough to make me pee myself. Fear permeated my being, I knew he meant it. Finally he backed off. I slid down the wall and wiggled over to the farthest corner where I stayed trying to figure out what to do.

Once Monday morning rolled around my first stop was my probation officer. Since it was Monday, Sandy Hillflicker was inundated with calls. I could tell from the way her hazel eyes were shooting me daggers that she was not happy to see me. She pivoted around in her chair so she could face me.

She was not a large woman. She was actually on the small side and seemed too feminine to be a probation officer, but none-the-less could be very strict when she needed to be.

Carefully and hesitantly I explained my situation. When I finished I looked up. I'd been wringing my hands so tightly my fingers had temporarily lost all color.

"So you see, I can't go back. They'll kill me if I don't," I said.

She dropped the pencil she'd been taking notes with on her notepad. Then she leaned back in her chair. She folded her arms behind her head as she peered at me.

"You're in a rather tight spot it seems," she said coolly.

"Exactly, so what am I supposed to do? How can I get out of this? You need to protect me," I told her. Could she sense how scared I really was?

"I'll take care of it. There's going to be some ass kicking tonight," she said with authority. Relief swept over me.

As I left, I began to thank God for once again saving my neck. But as Friday approached without a call from Hillflicker, I grew more and more anxious. Where was the cavalry? When was she going to start kicking some ass?

As I reported to the jail I felt like I was moving in slow motion; afraid once the guards put me in my cell I would breathe my last breath. I soon discovered that the entire population was on lock down.

All the jeers and glaring eyes let me know they were aware I was the snitch. On the way to my cell one of the inmates spat on me and hissed: "I'll get you Davis.

Your ass is mine!" The guard accompanying me didn't even raise an eyebrow. I knew then that I was completely on my own.

The guards were obviously just as pissed. I knew it reflected badly on them, but I was stuck. Forsake my future or come forward. It had been a painful but revealing lesson. No one cared about the inmates. No one. If I lived, it would only be by the grace of God and my wits.

At least they didn't put me in the general population, thank God. Surely someone would have killed me. But the guards made their feelings known too. The next lunch time, my plate arrived as usual but in lieu of a hotdog, a fresh lump of human feces had been placed on the bun with a sign that said simply: Enjoy!

After that, I refused to eat any of the meals. I would wait till Monday, then I'd eat my fill. And to help me get through the remaining weekends, I would sow a double dose of my medication into my waist band. Then once inside I'd swallow the pills and essentially sleep the entire weekend. Thus became my routine.

12

Selling Out and Breaking Up

In September 1977, the summer was coming to an end but seemed to be holding on for at least one more day. As the temperature soared and sunshine was resplendently abundant, I was taking full advantage by hanging around the pool draped over a lounge chair. Being lazy was a luxury I didn't often afford myself, but the moment seemed right, so I remained, watching other tenants coming or going after a swim.

She made me sit up and take notice. I did a double take at the young woman walking into the apartment complex. Who was she? It wasn't just that she was beautiful and had a body that could put some of Playboy's centerfolds to shame, there was something else. A presence about her.

It was perhaps an affinity. That if I had a biological sister, this woman epitomized what I would envision her to look like. Blond, a wide-face off set by pale, blue eyes. We even shared the same quirky smile. It made me wonder for the one thousandth time, who was my real family?

For some reason, thoughts of my jail days came to mind. I was thankful for my freedom and the distance from the whole jailhouse mindset. Finally, it seemed like my life was going in the right direction.

I'd found my niche as a used car salesman and I was good at it. In fact, hardly any potential customers escaped my pitch. Most of the time when they left, they were leaving as buyers.

The money was good. And for the first time I bought a brand new Trans Am with money I had earned legitimately. There was a wonderful sense of accomplishment, unlike the internal struggles I'd wrangled with while dealing. My new job became my new life style. I wasn't smoking anything stronger than pot these days, and even my consumption of that was down.

Floundering relationships however, had remained. Initially my elevated income had attracted a class of women who were only interested in high finances and perks. The abundant sex had been welcomed but eventually I started feeling the void, wondering if this was all I'd ever have or if I could someday have a lasting relationship. I wasn't through with being cynical but when I was alone it was hard to contest the truth, I wanted someone special.

The beautiful blonde's name was Laurie. Like myself she had tasted disappointment in relationships too. In fact, she'd just split up with her boyfriend and was now searching for someone better.

But she was a native of Iowa and would be leaving soon. The similarities we shared were almost spooky, we even seemed to like or dislike the same things. Frequently we'd finish each other's sentences or come up with the same idea for doing things. It was unreal.

At times we'd just sit staring at each other. The strange closeness and affinity was unsettling but hypnotic.

When it came time for Laurie to leave, I appealed to her to stay. We belong together, I pleaded. Perhaps feeling as confused and enamored, she decided to move in. At last I felt like I knew true love.

One afternoon in June while Laurie napped, I sat on the recliner watching her, studying her features, thinking about us. We were a good fit, I told myself.

Suddenly the phone rang. Reluctantly I picked it up. Immediately I could hear my mother's frantic voice. She was ranting on about my father. It took me a few minutes to realize what she was saying.

Then it sunk in. She'd divorced him. All the times she'd threatened to, perhaps a part of me prayed she wouldn't truly do it. Yet, not only had she done it but apparently she couldn't seem to get my father to leave. It was not the type of situation that I wanted to be pulled into, but who else would she call?

"He refuses to leave Scott. If you don't come and get him the sheriff will be taking him out soon. I've already called them," she warned. Resentment flushed my body in hot waves. I felt outrage. How could she do that to Dad?

Before I could defend him, my mother had hung up. Instantly I slammed the phone back against it's cradle.

"Dammit!" I shouted stirring Laurie. She looked at me bewildered. Her blue eyes read my visible anguish. Quickly she came to me.

"What's wrong honey?" she asked stroking my back.

"My Mom! That fucking bitch!" I spat angrily. "She's throwing my Dad out!" I shouted. Hatred coiled inside me. I wanted to lash out.

"I'm so sorry. What are you going to do?" she asked. I moved away from her. It was too much to be so close. I knew she was trying to help but I didn't trust myself not to verbally strike out at her just because she was close and female. An assortment of negative thoughts clouded my thinking.

"I've got to get him," I said finally.

"I'm coming with you," she said. Laurie was well aware of the long standing feuding between my parents. She'd always been kind to my father and had been quite vocal on his behalf numerous times.

I just nodded. We got into my car without speaking. It was hard not to succumb to the urge to speed.

Long before we reached the house, I saw my father. There he was, sitting on the same cement bench he'd originally brought home for my mother, his few earthly possessions surrounding him. But it was the battered old lunch box that struck me. With it's myriad of dings and scratches, it had endured. Just like him.

His eyes were pools of sadness that reflected a look of total despair. A stoic man by nature, I could see him straining not to cry. Seeing him so pathetic made me angrier. I helped my father to his feet. He shuffled like the bent limb he was, clearly in pain, as he slowly got into my car.

I glanced up to see the blinds of the living room moving. Did you see it all mother? I resisted the urge to kick in the front door and pummel her. What good would it do? If she hadn't softened after all these years, nothing would change her.

"You bitch! Are you happy now mother? How could you do this?" I screamed at the closed front door. I saw the curtains move again. "I know you're in there mother!" I yelled. The door remained closed.

It took everything I had to face my father. Here was an honest, hard-working soul, who had damned-near worked himself to death just to provide for us and still it wasn't enough. Sometimes my mother astounded me. I secretly wondered if she would have preferred if he'd died.

"Where are you going to go Dad?" I asked him softly, still feeling incensed.

"I don't know," he shrugged. He turned his hands out, palms up and looked at them as if they held an answer.

I decided to take him home with us. For the time being it would do; then I'd find a place. If the apartment had been bigger, I would have kept him there.

The apartment was small and sparsely furnished but it was still in Havelock so my Dad could be close to the girls. I knew it was tearing him up not being able to be there for them. A new infusion of anger coursed through me. I would never understand my mother.

I left him in the new apartment with streaks of sunlight fading from the dirty curtainless windows and my father clutching his radio. Walking away from him that night was harder than serving all my jail days combined.

"I'll be okay son," he tried to assure me. "Thanks for everything," he added.

I managed to nod. If I spoke, I knew I would break down. No sooner had I closed the door than the tears began to fall freely. Being the oldest had its downside.

A month later, my mother called again. I hadn't spoken to her since she had evicted my father and wouldn't have then, but as I listened to the message I realized I needed to. Something had happened to my Dad.

"Mom?" I picked up the phone.

"Oh Scott?," I could hear the tears in her voice. "I'm so sorry but your father was lying on the curb this morning when his ride came. He's had a stroke Scott. He's at the hospital," she said between sobs. I fought the urge to say something cruel.

Immediately I was out the door. I floored it all the way to the hospital praying my father would be okay. I couldn't imagine my life without him in it. Fortunately the stroke hadn't been as bad as I'd feared. More than anything it had left my father weak and disoriented. I found myself saying a silent prayer and aware I had again, appealed to God.

A short, stubby man bristled into my father's room holding a medical clipboard. He had salt and pepper hair and small eyes that peered out over his glasses. He looked at the monitors around my Dad and went to him. I stood watching.

"I'm Doctor Hale," he offered while pulling back the sheet that covered my father's chest. He made no effort to comfort me. He pressed a stethoscope against my father's chest and along the veins of his neck, then he scribbled information onto the chart as he headed for the door. I was flabbergasted.

"Excuse me," I said just before he managed to make his great escape. Doctor Hale stopped abruptly. He looked up as if acknowledging me was annoying him. How did he ever get to be a doctor? "How is he?" I pointed a thumb at my Dad.

"He's fine," he said quickly, then closed the flap of the chart. I glowered at him. Perhaps it was my steely stare that prompted him to retract his former statement.

"Well," he paused clearing his throat. "He's not fine. He's had a stroke, but you knew that," he looked at me. "But with time he'll be almost as good as new. I'm sending him home tomorrow," he said dryly.

"Tomorrow?" I swallowed and glanced at my father. My mind was racing. Could he be alone after this? Should he be going home so soon? I stared down at the runt of a man who was irritating me more by the minute.

"Yes," he repeated.

"But he's had a stroke for Christ's sakes," I explained. Doctor Hale looked at me as if I were some insignificant parasite he needed to be rid of. He pushed up his glasses and briefly faced me.

"There's nothing we can do for him that we haven't already done. Your father is going to need lots of rest and physical therapy. I wrote the order. Just make sure he keeps taking his medicine and doesn't overdo it," he finished.

"But what if he has another?" I asked.

"Let's just take a wait and see approach, okay? We don't know he'll have another one," he informed me.

None of his answers were very convincing but I was no doctor. What could I do except take him home? I knew he wouldn't be able to care for himself for awhile. I began to speculate how Laurie and I could care for him without even thinking if it would be okay with her.

Doctor Hale left and the very next day I was loading my father into my car. I'd had all night to break the news to Laurie, but somehow had dodged the bullet each time the subject came up.

"Dad, you need help. You're going to stay with us for awhile," I said observing Laurie's response from the corner of my eye. I knew she was mulling it over but she didn't say anything. My father however, did.

"No Scott, you have your own family now," he said smiling at Laurie. She looked relieved but was polite enough not to say so.

We helped him into the tiny apartment. I opened a few windows to allow some cross ventilation. The apartment was stuffy and with no fan or air conditioning it tended to hold the heat like an uncomfortable presence.

"I don't have it so bad Scott," he told me as he adjusted himself to be comfortable on the old recliner. "I got me a job. A place to stay, you for a son and my two girls. Many men don't have that much. I'm really quite a lucky guy," he said. For several minutes I remained, torn between emotions. But then, despite my reservations, I left.

Over the next few months I spent all of my free time with my father. I rediscovered his sense of humor and gentle demeanor. We were growing very close while Laurie and I were drifting farther and farther apart.

Guilt pricked my senses. I was glad we didn't share genes. It scared me to think that I could have a stroke too or wind up dying from diabetes as two of his brothers had. But as much I was comforted, I was disquieted. That ever present whisper kept reminding me: I didn't know where I belonged or to whom.

I kept my qualms to myself. I didn't have the heart to share it with my father. He was holding on by a thread, clutching to the illusion of me as his son. How could I tell him otherwise? And what did I really know?

My suspicion of relationships, particularly women, continued to grow. It gnawed at me. You couldn't trust anyone over thirty, nor the government, and especially not women. I vowed to myself it would never happen to me.

Laurie was feeling the shift, but as was her way, she continued to be loving and supportive throughout. Perhaps thinking that it was just stress causing me to be so aloof. In turn, I had convinced myself she would get around to dumping me eventually.

Thus, while she visited her grandmother, I took the opportunity to move my things out. I left no note, no explanation. I knew she would be hurt, but I just kept telling myself it was self protection.

The following day I started having second thoughts. Why was I running away from the perfect woman? What was wrong with me? Why was I sabotaging myself?

I saw her car parked at the curb and decided to go in. I found her crying in the middle of the living room. Her eyes were puffy and red. She looked up as I entered the room, then hid her face behind her hands. It was then that I realized I had made the biggest mistake of my life.

"Why? What did I ever do to deserve this?" she demanded between sobs. I was numb. There was no apt answer. I was a shuck. She knew it and I knew it.

"It just wasn't working," I started to say then stopped. It was too lame. And it was a lie. It had been working beautifully. In fact, Laurie had added a richness and stability to my life that had been lacking between Belinda and I. "It's just that I'm under a lot of pressure with my Dad," I left the sentence hanging.

Laurie rose. She dried her eyes on her sleeve. She looked at me for a moment more, then disappeared through the front door. Immediately I wanted to tear after her and beg her forgiveness. Instead I began to sulk.

That night sleep eluded me. Fears and worries drummed down on my head with a vengeance. How could I have been so foolish?

The next morning I awoke determined to plead for forgiveness. Perhaps I could get her to forgive me, give us another chance. But Laurie was resistant.

"No Scott, you'd do it again. I just can't go through this," she told me. "I could never forgive you for this. You could have talked to me, but you didn't. You decided alone, now you can be alone," her voice held an edge. Suddenly I heard the dial tone.

I could feel the walls closing in on me. I was standing against one wall. I let myself slide downward. Then I wept. Gut wrenching tears pored out of me. The sounds echoed through my small apartment.

"Fucking loser!" I yelled at my own reflection in the glass panels. I threw a shoe across the room at my reflection. There were times I hated the man in the mirror. This was definitely one of those times.

Staying true to form, I took the opportunity to entrench myself in more abuse and bad mouthed Laurie every chance I got. Sometimes I hated myself for spreading such vile lies, but the demon inside just continued to grow and laugh at me.

Through the grapevine I heard Laurie had run off with another of my friends and moved east to Oklahoma. I cursed her name and cried.

As if that wasn't enough, I continued my trek into the dismal abyss by quitting my job. All out of money, I spent my first New Year's Eve broke, alone and plugged in to the Playboy channel.

The lithe bodies dancing across the screen were beautiful, but they didn't elicit any emotion. I began to fear I would never find love again. Could anything be more sad or pitiful than that?

13

Bringing Dad Home

The following Spring I started a lawn care business. I knew I needed a change and somehow being out in the weather amongst the sunshine and the elements was helping me mend my broken heart. Never mind that the heartache had mostly been my fault. I wasn't ready to cope with the truth. It was hard enough just managing day to day. There was something nebulous and soothing about complacency. If I didn't have to think about it, I didn't have to accept it existed.

It was a few weeks after I had my business up and running when I received a cryptic message that took my breath away. It was left by my dad's employer. I heard the words then pressed the repeat button on my machine. My dad had suffered another stroke.

I let myself fall into my desk chair. My hands held my head as the tears and violent emotions came. Anger and fear fed off each other as a thousand different scenarios and thoughts plagued my mind. Why was this happening?

A part of me cursed the cement factory for hiring him. Harry had no business working anymore. He was an old, failing man. And yet I couldn't deny that I knew he needed something to keep him going. It stung my senses knowing that I couldn't take care of him. But business was new and I was just getting on my feet and dealing with my own demons. I couldn't heal an old man, not even if that man was my father.

I hurried to the hospital, afraid I wouldn't make it in time. The message had been urgent, so I drove with the same kind of urgency not really concerned with the stoplights and stop signs I'd ran. If I'd been caught, I really don't know what I would have done or how I would have dealt with it.

Once inside the hospital doors I waited impatiently behind a Hispanic family of four, two girls and a mother and father, as they got directions to their son's room. Briefly I wondered why he was there. Then they moved and my thoughts shifted. I stepped up to the desk.

An elderly lady clad in pink smiled at me. She was a small woman, her face wrinkled like my fingers after a swim.

"Hi. I need to know which room my father is in," I said.

"His name?"

"Harry Davis," I said looking around the lobby and watching a steady stream of people milling around. Some waiting on loved ones, some waiting for news of loved ones.

"He's in room 215 in Intensive Care. Do you know where that is?" She asked, her kindly face pinched with concern. I nodded.

"Thank you," I said hustling for the elevator. My mind played with it, Intensive Care. That wasn't a good sign. It scared me. Would I find him dying or dead?

I found the room easily. My father was lying on a bed under a ventilation tent. Right away I felt my heart beating faster, my mood sinking. It looked worse than I thought. Two nurses bustled about performing routine services. Tubes ran up my father's nose while the ventilator hissed and his heart monitor beeped steadily.

At that moment my father opened his eyes. We exchanged looks. For the first time in a very long time, I watched my father's eyes fill with tears. I swallowed hard, biting back my own emotions. He struggled to speak but I raised my hand to silence him.

"Dad, don't try to speak," I said but my father persisted. I leaned closer to hear him.

"I want to go back to work," he said sadly. "I have to get back to work." He told me. I swallowed again. Tears splashed my father's cheeks. Immediately I began to cry along side him.

It hurt me tremendously to see him struggling just to breathe and yet wanting to go to work. He'd lost his home, his wife and what was left of his family. It was tragic to realize his paltry job sweeping floors was all he had left.

I placed my hand on his arm. In as much as it mystified me, I also understood. Being a hard worker had always been the one thing my father could count on, have pride in. He was a better man than most, and that included me.

"That's going to have to wait for awhile," I told him gently. My father turned his face away from me. I knew he'd heard me, but he was still crying. I felt conflicted knowing I really shouldn't encourage him, but understanding his need. And yet there was a very real possibility that my father would not be able to return to work. So much would depend on the damage that had happened to his body and how well he recuperated.

Sadly, my father was not to be a whole man again. The stroke had caused considerable damage to his right side and speech. He'd become childlike and walked with a shuffle only able to slur words. Almost overnight my dad's hair turned a snow white. The contrast from his dark locks was shocking.

It took me awhile to concede that my father's doctors were right. I needed to place him in a nursing home. Just the thought of it made me depressed, but I knew there was no way that I could care for him. Attempting to do that though was another matter.

The minute my father realized I was leaving him at Pine Woods he switched as if he'd stepped into a character role. He was utterly horrified. Why? It left me perplexed. Was his reaction more remnants of his years at Beatrice? Did they have any idea how much they had traumatized him? Ruined his life?

Not that I didn't understand at least part of his reaction. Seeing baby puke yellow walls filled with shuffling people, many of whom were dazed and or speaking to themselves while aimlessly wandering, would have been disheartening to anyone. To say nothing about the ever present smell of urine overlapping with disinfectant. And for the really hopeless, a few rooms reserved for the screamers. I'd want to leave too, but what choice did I have?

After several hours of consoling and convincing my father it wasn't as bad as it looked, I left. It was one of the defining moments of my life and I'd failed. I'd left him there in that hellhole. He was obviously terrified and I'd deserted him.

It was only because I'd promised to visit him the next day that I finally managed to leave. But that look on his face, of a broken man holding on by a thread, will haunt me till I die.

Early next morning I awoke to the irritating squawk of the phone. I'd fallen asleep in the recliner so I was stiff. Slowly I came to life, working on massaging a kink out of my neck as I answered the phone.

"Hello?"

"Scott," it was my father's voice and he was whispering. I straightened up.

"Dad?"

"Scott, please, please. I have to get out of here, I can't take it. I'll go crazy. Please son, won't you help me?" I couldn't handle hearing my father pleading so pitifully, knowing how terribly frightened he was to be there. I broke down.

"Okay dad. I'll do whatever you want me to," I told him.

"Come get me. Hurry," he said, already sounding better. To hell with the doctors, I knew him better than they did. And I knew if he stayed there, he'd most certainly be dead within the year. He'd give up. After everything he'd done for me, he deserved better than that.

I found my father waiting on the curb, his bag in hand. I gently helped him into the car, then I parked. That had been the easy part, now came the tricky part; convincing the administrator that my father leaving was actually in his best interest.

I marched up to the receptionist's desk where a middle-aged woman commanded the post. I jingled change in my pockets nervously.

"I need to talk to the administrator," I said. She looked me up and down.

"Who are you?" she asked.

"I'm Scott Davis and I want to take my father, Harry Davis, home with me," I told her. Her eyes narrowed suspiciously.

"That's against policy," she said smugly. I wanted to slap her. He was my father; nothing was going to prevent me from taking him home even if I had to make the great escape with him. Realizing, of course, that belligerence probably was not the best way to handle this, I smiled and repeated myself.

"I'm not leaving until I've spoken to Mr. Wilcox," I called her bluff. Her arrogant smile vanished. Obviously confrontation was not something she'd counted on. Immediately she buzzed the appropriate number.

Ten minutes later a slightly frazzled Mr. Wilcox appeared. His light-green three piece suit was mildly rumpled, a thought crossed my mind that he was either having a rough day or he'd slept in it. It reminded me of days where I had done the same having been too hung over from the night before.

"What seems to be the problem?" he asked anxiously.

"I want to take my father home and Ms. Ratchet, err, Ms. Stall, says I can't," I said staring at her. The scowl on her face told me she hadn't appreciated the negative reference.

"She's right," he said but before I could talk he had his hand up, then he waved me to follow him. He moved out of ear shot from Ms. Stoll. "I understand Scott, but if he leaves, he'll be considered as having escaped and an APB will be put out on him," he informed me.

I ran fingers threw my hair contemplating. Why did it have to be so complicated?

"Unless," Mr. Wilcox added. I looked up. "He is signed out by a guardian," he told me.

"Okay," I acknowledged. It was the least I could do. I knew my father would do it for me. It was an easy choice to make; handling his care would be the struggle. But I told myself I didn't need to jump the fence yet, I'd deal with whatever came along as it became a concern, for now, dad would be coming home with me.

It took a few days to square things legally, but alas all the t's were crossed and all the i's dotted and I was his guardian. But what to do?

Suddenly one evening it came to me while I stood looking at the glorious horizon of pageant reds and oranges. I needed a fresh start and Boulder was just the place. My probation period had finally ended; it would be the perfect time. Besides I had an old connection in Boulder and my little business wasn't going to support both of us.

I loaded up my second hand and sputtering dolphin blue Dodge truck and pulled away. I was more than ready for the change, but my father, sadly was not. I knew he'd miss the girls and his estranged wife too. Love does funny things to people. In my heart I knew dad would always hope to win Barbara back. But I equally was aware his chances were remote. It was a tired cliché, one partner had moved on but the other could not. For them, it would always be my father.

I caught my dad looking wistfully out my rearview mirror as we drove away. Out of nowhere a surge of anger erupted within me. Impulsively I wrenched the mirror off the windshield and tossed it out the window.

"Dammit dad," I said as I saw him watching the mirror bouncing down the highway. "What's behind us doesn't matter anymore. You need to stop looking back. It's just you and me now," I told him.

But in his eyes I saw confusion and sorrow. Kansas was all he'd ever known. I knew it frightened him to leave, but I also knew I couldn't provide for us there. I prayed he'd adapt.

"It's going to be okay dad," I told him as I squeezed his arm. He looked at me, his eyes full of uncertainty but yet a slow smile emerged.

"Thanks for getting me out," he said, his eyes flicking where the rearview mirror had been. Only time would tell if I'd made the right decision.

14

The Dark Christmas

Boulder was everything my old dealer buddy had said it would be. It was the land of milk and honey, and after enduring a financial drought with my landscaping business, I was anxious for abundance again.

Once I attended to the basics of renting an apartment for the two of us, I immediately dove right into the party lifestyle. This was living!

Most mornings it was a struggle to keep my glassy, bloodshot eyeballs open. Never mind trying to recall the name of the female in bed next to me. Dragons of shame would snap at me with their trough of fire, but as long as I stayed in denial, I kept them at bay.

Then the fateful day of December 8th, 1980 arrived. Just as I was in route to yet another party the radio announcer interrupted the music to broadcast that John Lennon had just been shot.

That was one party I didn't make it to. Instead I detoured to the Broken Drum to have my own little party. The place was a dive with a flashing neon arrow pointing to the small building. There were no parking spaces; only gravel where cars parked every which way. Inside it was just as tacky and stale, tables and beer signs made up the ambiance. But it fit my mood, so I spent the evening making imaginary toasts to the legendary rock and roll icon. I'm doing better than him, I thought. At least I'm alive.

But my sobering moment was fleeting. I went through such a heavy spree of bar hopping that I came close to losing my roommate location service. Working drunk or hung over eventually begins to take a toll. People expect you to be responsible, and during those days I was anything but responsible.

I was also making a name for myself as the shuffleboard king since I spent so much time perfecting the game. I was the local hero. At one point I even pondered if it was my purpose in life. Dragging my poor father night after night to each dump I frequented.

Christmas Eve was nearly upon us, and once again we were at the Broken Drum. But for a change I noticed the crowd around my father. He wasn't playing shuffleboard or drinking himself blind, he was just telling stories of the old days. From the looks on his audience's faces, I could see they were totally engrossed. It never ceased to amaze me how easily my father made friends. People just naturally migrated his way, like dirt being sucked by a vacuum.

Inexplicably my thoughts drifted towards my mother. We still weren't talking. Ironically I had no interest in repairing the relationship, but it still bothered me to think about the way she'd treated my dad. Secretly I blamed her for his demise and my own.

And yet the last few months spent with my father were the best we'd had since my youth. We frequently drove to the mountains or played Frisbee in the park. We talked about everything; girls, memories, life, whatever we wanted. It was a side of him I hadn't known existed. It made me view our relationship differently.

I always knew when I'd hit a nerve or gotten too close to something my father chose not to recall because he'd quickly withdraw, suddenly sullen and quiet.

My father noticed my attention. He smiled at me, then pointed my way. A group of faces turned in unison.

"That's my son, Scott. He's the best son," he told them. The words made me blush. I quickly waved them off and went back to my beer.

A young man from my father's entourage had detached himself to join me at the bar. He introduced himself. I raised my stein.

"Hey, would you like a little snort?" he asked. I sized up the stranger. He was smaller than myself, but thin. His sky blue eyes blinked tentatively. I knew he was referring to cocaine; something I hadn't tried up to that point. I hesitated. Hadn't I heard it was supposed to increase a person's confidence and make them feel good about themselves? I could go for that.

"Sure," I said. We walked silently through the cluster of people and smoke and clamored to the men's room. I eagerly watched him pull a small vile from his shirt pocket. Popping the lid he dipped a small spoon inside and withdrew a tiny mound of sparkling white powder.

I leaned over the spoon, plugged one nostril and inhaled. Immediately the jolt made me want to sneeze followed by a feeling of euphoria. I repeated the gesture with my other nostril.

My first thought was that the stuff was far better than its media hype. My mind caught on threads of a Newsweek article referring to "coke mania" sweeping the nation. I understood the calling. It seemed to be a veritable cure for the blues and like pot, was nonaddicting. That was as good as it gets. Able to get high without worrying about flashbacks or getting hooked.

I walked out of the bathroom feeling inordinately cocky. I caught my father's stare but I was too buzzed to be concerned.

"Hiya Harry!" I yelled across the bar. In my father's eyes I could see worry. He knew I was different, but none-the-less smiled and wave back at me.

The interior of the bar seemed to be swirling as I found myself lost in a world of joy to all humanity, smiling at everyone, obvious to anything but the wonderfully liberating feeling.

People playing pool seemed to be smiling more and laughing louder. Faces were distorted, but gleeful. The world was my oyster.

After about an hour, the room seemed to be coming more into focus and the joy ride was over. I wasn't ready for my good time to be done so soon, so I sought out the same young man and purchased a couple more snorts.

In no time at all I found a connection locally and began purchasing it by the gram, which only lasted two or three days. A slew of nameless strangers continued to parade through my apartment as my world once again got lopsided. I knew my father and I were drifting apart, but I was too absorbed with my own high to be paying attention to his woes.

Even one of my Kansas pals noticed the shift. Thinking perhaps he was doing me a favor, he took it upon himself to bring that fact to my attention. He was aware not only of the cocaine, but the subsequent drinking I'd do to offset my buzz. Little did he know how explosive I'd get. My reaction surprised both of us and scared me a little. Where was Scott Davis?

"Hey Scott, you know I know it's none of my business man, but you've really been hitting the sauce lately," said James softly.

James was a pal from the old days. He'd definitely seen me at my worst before, so his remarks caught me off guard. Was I really doing that bad? Still, they were not words I wanted to hear.

Physically he was a human teddy bear. Shaggy, curly auburn hair fell past his shoulders. His round face and soft, brown eyes gave him a nice-guy look.

"What the fuck are you talking about?" I screamed defensively.

"Jesus Scott, I'm your friend; I just don't want to see you hurt yourself, that's all," he replied, backing away. Seeing him withdraw made me take notice. Something was happening to me and it wasn't good. Shame hissed at me. What had made me lash out like that?

I left him sitting at the bar while I hit the bathroom. Under the pretext of trying to get my perspective back, I once again took another snort. Concluding it was just stress pushing me to excess then, I returned to the bar and promptly apologized. But James was not impressed. He knew I was high again.

"James, thanks man but I really do have it under control," I said placing a hand on his arm. It was then I noticed the pity and disgust in his eyes.

"Sure you do. Get real Scott, you've lost your control," he said shaking free and walking away. The words hurt me, and like any good, wounded soldier I did another round. It was amazing that I managed to drive myself home, but truthfully, no one but a police officer arresting me could have stopped me.

As before, days blew by in succession without distinction. I was so enmeshed with the pursuit of staying high that scarcely anything else seemed to matter or get my time. Only those things I needed done to survive were attended to. Everything else got ignored, including my father.

As a result I returned home one evening in April to find my father once again sitting on the curb. It brought back previous memories of him at the nursing home and my mother's place. His focus was East as if he was expecting someone. Was he?

"Dad, what are you doing?" I asked.

"Scott," my father said pensively. "I want to go back to Kansas City. I want to go home," he finished, then looked away.

Once again, someone was deserting me. My world suddenly got fuzzy. Rage was clouding my thinking. All I could think of was how I'd rescued him. What I had done for him. It never occurred to me that while I was experiencing one prolonged high after another, he was probably very lonesome, stuck in an apartment in a city he didn't know, with no one to talk to.

From the corner of my eyes I saw a single tear on my father's cheek. Immediately I began to feel like a son of a bitch for ignoring him and being angry. I realized then that Boulder would never be home to him, but rather just another reminder of his captivity.

Kansas City, for all its warts, was the only place where my father had been happy once. I couldn't give my father his family back, but I could take him home and love him. That much I could do.

"Okay dad, I'll see what I can do," I said softly hiding my own tears. Gently I lead him back inside. My father was my anchor and my moral fiber. Even if my actions seemed contrary, his presence gave me a sense of hope and purpose that I knew I would sorely miss.

As luck would have it, a former high school friend was visiting from Kansas City. Unlike myself, Jayne had her act together. There wasn't anything exceptional about her appearance except for her brilliant smile. She could light up Shay stadium in the dark with her gregarious, bubbly nature.

Ironically, Jayne would approach me a couple days later to inform me how much my father missed Kansas. The timing seemed perfect. I couldn't take him home, but Jayne could.

While the night stars of the twilight flickered, Jayne stood on the steps in front of my apartment telling me about my dad while gazing up at them. Occasionally she'd glance my way. Was she expecting me to be mad?

"He really needs to go home," she told me, holding my gaze.

"I know," I said looking at the night sky. The vastness struck me as it had before. There was something about the stars that made me feel philosophical. But realizing this wasn't the best time for it, I nodded. "I don't know what to do Jayne. He can't take care of himself, but I can't give him what he needs," I confessed, suddenly feeling very inept. Why couldn't I do it? Was it just selfishness?

"I know that Scott. That's what I wanted to talk to you about. He's welcome to come back with me and stay with my roommate and I. There's plenty of room and I'm sure you could use the break," she said quietly. Jayne was being true to form, thinking of others first again. Why couldn't I?

The look in her eyes made me feel that it was the right decision. There was no question that my father would be happier. But as always, a certain amount of guilt started to rise inside me.

"Thanks Jayne, I'll let him know. I'm sure he'll be tickled," I said retreating inside. A part of me felt rude but a bigger part felt defeated, so I did what I always do. I ran.

Two days later I was waving at them driving away. I could still hear my father's words, I love you son. We'll see you soon. Tell everyone at the Broken Drum goodbye.

Naturally their departure gave me a reason to have a snort. I chopped up a line on the hand mirror and pinched one nostril closed before I inhaled deeply.

With my father gone, my conscience evaporated. My routine took a nose dive to existing just to get high. Eventually I sold the roommate business just so I could hang out with my friends around the clock. Nothing seemed to matter but that next party, that next fix; hoping it would exceed the previous.

By summer's end I was frustrated and broke. All the fruits of my hard labor were gone; leaving me with only one option. I needed to go back to work. Although I wasn't particularly keen on the idea, I knew I could have a job anytime I wanted dealing cars.

The time I'd put in working for Weird Wally, who expected honest employees and good work ethics, had guaranteed that. Just like before, I didn't disappoint.

Coke kept me fired up like a perpetual ball of energy. Combine that with my high pressure sales pitches and friendly face and it made me unstoppable.

Within three weeks I had succeeded to being the top seller. Unlike the reputable policies of my former boss, nothing mattered at the new dealership except sales.

It got to the point where I could spot an easy mark seventy yards away. There were very few I couldn't manipulate into buying more car than they could afford or a policy they didn't need. All under the guise that it was an excellent deal, when in reality the one getting the excellent deal was myself. For each additional bonus, it meant a fatter check for me.

At the time the lies and deception were a way of life that seemed as normal as breathing. All I saw was the bottom line: Money.

Every couple of months I'd make my way back to Kansas City. I'm not sure if it was more from guilt or love, but I'd stay just long enough to check up on my father. Then I'd leave.

That November during one of my regular visits, my sisters cornered me. They arranged to stop by Jayne's at the same time so they could see my dad and me together.

I looked at Lisa and Jodi, the changes in them striking. They had blossomed into beautiful young women. Lisa smiled at me across the living room. She was tucked away in a recliner and Jodi was sitting next to her on the arm of the chair, leaning against it.

"Come on Scott," Jodi said. She was trying to talk me into spending Christmas in Lincoln. Selfishly I thought about the extravagant party I'd miss. Thinking of the coke I'd miss out on hurt more than anything else.

"Well," I said with the party scenario running through my mind. Would I be able to handle myself around my mother? "What about mom?" I made it a question.

"She'd love it if you'd come," Lisa said. Considering my mother getting excited about seeing me seemed dubious. My cynical nature won.

"Lisa," I said firmly. She and Jodi looked at me simultaneously.

"Please," she said. I could feel myself caving.

"Okay," I said. And that's how I left it.

It was Christmas Eve when I got into Kansas City. Temperatures were in the teens with two feet of snow on the ground. I parked the rental car in front of the small house. I sat there watching the girls busy in the kitchen and dining room. That house held so many memories. Seeing them brought it to the surface.

The aroma of roasted turkey curled around my nose as I climbed the steps. I had a bag full of presents for the family. I'd even acquiesced to getting one for my mother.

I knocked. It seemed odd to be so formal but I no longer felt comfortable with just entering my mother's house. Jodi opened the door; her lips were wide with a happy smile. Immediately she threw her arms around me.

"It's Scott!" she hollered over her shoulder. Suddenly my mother and Lisa were there. I stepped in pushing the door closed. Heat wrapped around my frozen limbs slowly starting to thaw them. It felt good.

Lisa gave me a hug. I watched my mother standing off to the side, reserved. I looked past all of them, searching for my father. I'd invited him earlier but it appeared now that my father was probably not going to come. Would the girls be upset? Would my mother get mad?

It was Christmas. He deserved a little slice of happiness too, whether my mother agreed or not. Jodi handed my mother the bag full of gifts to put under the tree as she whisked me away into the kitchen.

I was bombarded by all the glorious scents of food wafting through the house. Dinner mixed with pasties and confections, many of which I spied samples of throughout the kitchen.

"You've got to try this," Jodi gushed shoving a plate of fudge my way. I took a couple of pieces.

"You make this?" I asked sinking my teeth into some of the best fudge I've ever had. Her eyes sparkled.

"Yes," she answered. It had been a long time since I'd feasted on so many delicious homemade treats. It made me ache for family. Why couldn't we be normal?

"It's good," I told her just before we heard someone knocking. Immediately my mother looked at me. My sisters exchanged surprised looks. Suddenly all eyes were upon me as I opened the door.

There stood my father wearing his best dress slacks and shirt. His hair neatly combed, with a look of anticipation, like the face of a child waiting for his presents.

"Hi dad," I said pleasantly. Hesitantly he stepped just inside the door. A huge smile formed on his face as his eyes took in all the seasonal decorations inside the house he'd once called home.

"Dad!" Jodi and Lisa said in unison. Jodi dropped the garland she'd been draping over the tree. Lisa stood up from the dining table. Just as they were nearly to him, we heard our mother's voice boom over the clamor of Christmas music and conversation.

"What's he doing here?" she barked. I spun around on my heels. There stood my mother looking indignant and huffy, hands on hips glowering at dad. Anger coursed through me, with balled fists I stepped in front of her. It was his holiday too.

"It's Christmas, I invited him," I told her as calmly as I could.

Mom was in the midst of another bout of depression. Consequently her emotions were unstable and often manifested itself as anger. Not surprisingly, her coffee consumption was through the roof again and she'd digressed to chain smoking once more.

Usually she'd regret her outbursts once she was thinking clearly again. Unfortunately she never managed to contain them while in the throes of her anger. She stood wagging a finger at him, shaking her head.

"No! I want him out of here," she demanded. My dad opened the door but I stopped him. His eyes met mine with that same resignation I'd seen so many times. It only served to infuse my rage.

"It's okay Scott," he tried to comfort me. Then he squeezed past me outside. I faced my mother, my heart racing, infuriated. Why couldn't she have just swallowed her stubborn pride for a few hours?

"He's still our father. God forbid that you should show him any kindness. You fucking bitch, you can go straight to hell! I'm out of here," I shouted.

Already my mother was falling apart. Lisa and Jodi had run to comfort her. I ran out to the car so quickly I skidded on the snow and ice and nearly fell under the car before I managed to regain my balance.

"Come on Dad, I'll take you home," I opened the door for him. He shuffled slowly and painfully to the open door. "I'm sorry dad," I said swallowing the lump in my throat.

I banged my hands on the wheel, trying to contain my anger. Profanity and slurs against my mother came out in rush. I felt my father squeeze my arm. I glanced at him.

"Scott," he said softly. "Please don't talk about your mother that way. She's a very unhappy woman and some of that is because of me," he said softly, but I couldn't listen. I couldn't hear him once again taking all the blame, being withdrawn, subdued, placating my mother.

Out of respect, I kept the cutting remarks to myself. But I knew this wasn't the last of it. After I left my father off I returned to my mother's, still fuming with visions of squeezing the life out of her whirling around in my brain.

Knowing I was out of control, I took a snort of coke and followed it up with a joint. Anything to help quell my pain.

By the time I actually went inside, I felt almost human. I gave my sisters a good-bye hug. Both of them had tears in their eyes. They were obviously disappointed too.

The image of my mother sitting at the kitchen table with her coffee in one hand and a cigarette in the other, remained in my head for many miles. When I wasn't angry at her, I could almost feel sorry for her. She was a sad, lonesome old woman. What did she really have?

Still, it was hard not to blame her; hard not to let anger get the better of me. And perhaps among the list of wrong doings, the way she had foiled my plans for a merry Christmas. As much for my father and my sisters as for myself. Mostly I survived on cynicism anyway, but the girls didn't. That went double for my father, a man whose time was running out. Surely, he deserved at least one more Merry Christmas.

15

My Twenty-Eighth Birthday: Defining Moments

My twenty-eighth birthday would prove to be a benchmark in my life. Little did I know just how much my world would change from that moment on. That morning I awoke, aware of a difference. In the back of my mind I was toying with a few ideas on celebrating it. I stood at my open window peering out across the grounds. Inhaling the scent of freshly-mowed grass through the mild breeze caressing my face.

The warmth and brilliance of the sunlight made me feel chipper. I was prepared for a great day.

In the midst of my reflection I was suddenly disrupted by a thundering, demanding knock at the door. I turned, surveying the Spartan fixtures within the small dormitory room. Home was temporarily a drug rehabilitation center. Ironically I was not depressed about my circumstances as much as I felt I'd been given a great opportunity to turn my life around. Lord knows, I needed it.

It had been a year and a half since I'd stormed out of my mother's house on that less than memorable Christmas day, and my world had plummeted. All I did was flounder from one dealership to another. Each time I would excel to being the top man; I would turn around and quit so I could live off my earnings.

Nothing superseded my desire to get high and stay high. Work was just a means to an end. Whatever I could get my hands on, I used to fulfill my need; never once thinking about how all the abuse might be affecting me.

Routinely I'd still visit Kansas City just to check on my father and sisters. My mother's woes were of no concern to me. I figured whatever hell she was suffering she brought on herself and had coming.

Eventually my best friend, Dan Kelly, a fellow salesman would lead me into rehab. Like myself, Dan was a die hard drinker and druggie. We spent our free time mostly frequenting bars and strip joints. It was a plastic world, but we were too mesmerized by the glitz and glitter to recognize it was just an illusion.

Then one night, quite by accident, Dan accidentally threw me through a Plexiglas window at one of the bars. Shards of glass had shredded my leg down to the bone. It took over four hundred stitches to patch me and virtually every doctor who viewed my accident predicted I would be doomed to limping for the rest of my life.

One would think that such an experience would have been enough to turn my life around. Unfortunately it only served to make me more stubborn and reinforce feelings of invincibility.

All the while I'd graduated from snorting coke to injecting it. My future just continued to look dimmer and dimmer. At times I'd even joked with Dan that "this shit is going to kill us."

As lousy as I often felt afterwards, I couldn't seem to stop. The merry-go-round of thrills just kept taking me for a ride.

It wasn't until a three-week period when Dan totally disappeared that I took notice. I truly thought the reason for his absence was because he'd bought the farm. To my surprise he called me one afternoon to reveal he was in rehab. Dan? It didn't seem possible.

He went on and on about how good he felt. Finally he ended with the tired old phrase that if I ever needed help getting clean, he left the invitation open ended. I terminated the call as fast as I could without trying to appear too rude. Rehab was for wimps or losers, not me.

Just because he couldn't handle himself didn't mean I couldn't. Everyone knew pot and coke weren't harmful. After all, they weren't even addictive. I told myself I could walk away any time I wanted.

Along with my errant tirade, I began making little deals with God again. If he'd help me not want drugs and prove his existence, I'd quit. At the time it seemed like a fair trade. But either God was staying quiet or I wasn't listening, because nothing happened.

Life remained in limbo until one morning I awoke to find myself vaguely listening to a Christian television program. At first I wasn't really paying it any mind, but somehow a woman with only one leg got my attention.

She was telling the world how grateful to God she was that she'd only lost a leg instead of her life. The words pierced me. Here was this young, attractive woman saying how lucky she was to only have lost a limb and praising God for it!

It hit me then. I was not the man I wanted to be or needed to be. Instantly I fled to my bathroom. I grabbed my stash of cocaine and flushed it down the toilet. It was a liberating feeling that empowered me to do what I needed to do next. While looking at myself in the mirror, a reflection that was just a ghost of a man, I dialed the number to the same facility where Dan had gone. It was time.

I went in three weeks before my birthday. There was no turning back. Somewhere within the sensible part of my brain I knew if I didn't clean up my act, eventually I would die.

My thoughts flashed back to the present.

"Yes?" I answered, opening my door. Two burly attendants I recognized as Charlie and Danny stood in the hallway. Danny was slightly taller and more fair skinned than his coworker. Both waited for me.

"You're wanted at the office," Danny said.

They weren't hostile but neither one of them was being particularly friendly. Still, as I closed the door, I thought perhaps it had something to do with my birthday. Both guys were so stoic, they would be perfect candidates for pulling off a surprise party.

Being at the center was a turning point. Incredibly the fog I'd been living in had started to lift, so I could see and think clearly. There were many unresolved issues in my life that needed attention. Essentially my teen and adult life had been a numbing experience. Without realizing it, I had been anesthetizing myself. Buffering myself from the world with drugs. But therapy and rehab made me see it was okay to embrace the pain; I would get through it and be stronger for having worked through it.

I knew it was one of the elements missing in my life. Drugs had to stop being my God. I had to regain control over my life. And without the help of others, I'd never be able to do it. So I surrendered myself to the program.

Eventually family week at the center arrived and I was prepared. This time I wanted to see my mother so I'd invited her and the girls for a visit. Finances had precluded me from inviting my dad, but I knew I'd see him later.

My sisters sat with my mother on a multicolored couch in the lounge. I sat in a cushioned hardback next to one end of the couch. The way my sisters and mother were positioned, I was closest to Jodi and farthest from my mother.

The girls both had on jeans and tees. My mother had on her ribbon dress of blue and gold. She wore it often. Apparently it was one of her favorites. I watched her folding and unfolding her hands during our visit. Was she nervous? Fearful?

I knew my mother was ill, but until that afternoon I suppose I had chosen not to see her vulnerabilities and frailties. My counselors were right; in her own way my mother did love me. It helped me to see her in a different light. In order for me to progress, I had to quit holding onto the tentacles of my past that were dragging me down.

Unbeknownst to me, my mother had been at the center the day before. In fact, she'd been discussing me with my counselor. Finally some of the secrets had been revealed. My counselor asked her if there was anything in my past that might account for my drug problems; my mother broke down and confessed the circumstances of my birth. Vital knowledge that had been deliberately kept from me.

Not only because of the promise she'd made to my father and Doctor Thurber, but because she truly believed she was doing the right thing. Now she wasn't so sure.

"So how do you like it here?" Lisa asked. I looked at her. She obviously didn't know what to say either. And what do you say to someone in rehab?

"It's okay, I'm learning a lot," I said honestly. The internal cleansing had been long overdue. But I had to bottom out to appreciate its value.

"Scott, there's something I have to tell you, it's about your father," my mother interrupted the silence. Tears were clouding her face. I was shocked but I thought I knew what she was about to confess.

"I knew it!" I yelled. "I knew it! I was adopted," I began but my mother shook her head.

"No Scott, please listen, it's not that. You're my son, I gave birth to you, that much is true," she affirmed. A wave of resentment blistered my face.

"You had an affair!" I was pointing my finger accusingly. "You!" I sputtered unable to find the words. Suddenly I was standing up scowling at my mother.

"No Scott. Just listen to me for a minute," my mother said, this time raising her voice.

Charles placed a beefy hand on my shoulder. Gently he guided me back to my chair. Slowly my mother told me the whole story between sobs and pauses.

"Your dad and I wanted a baby so bad," she explained. "But we couldn't have one by ourselves. You were conceived through artificial insemination; your real father was a sperm donor. I'm so sorry," she said burying her face in her hands. Jodi leaned in to comfort her. Both my sisters were watching me, waiting.

My mind went blank. Suddenly I felt like I was floating above the lounge, my mother's voice a soft buzz in the distance. All those years trying to find similarities; to understand. It was a piece of the puzzle I never knew existed, never would have calculated. An affair would have been easier to accept. I could feel my heart pounding. With effort, I managed to speak.

"Who is my father?"

My mother shrugged.

"I don't know. It was all done in secrecy. We were never told. We weren't supposed to tell you; we promised," she admitted sadly, and then her eyes met mine. "But when I saw how troubled you were, I knew I had to tell you," she said quietly.

"But why couldn't dad have babies?" I asked, needing to know. My mother got a strange expression on her face between fear and sorrow. Then she blurted out the truth about Beatrice and the price my father had paid for his freedom.

By the time she had finished we were both crying. Suddenly I had a new appreciation for my father. He had raised another man's child. And he had done it with conviction and courage. Not once had he relented or bailed, even when his world had fallen apart. All of that pain he had borne in silence. It humbled me.

"Scott, you have to promise me something," my mother said. Her eyes brimming with new tears, fretting. Her face was puffy, her nose was red. Her face looked wind-burned from crying.

My mother had endured her own hell. It made me realize the terrible pressure she had been under to keep such a secret. At last I understood the force that destroyed our family. I came to my mother. Hesitantly I stopped in front of her. Then I reached out and touched her hair gently.

"What mom? What do you need?" I asked. It was the first time in years that I really wanted to know and listen. She took my hand and squeezed it as she spoke. More tears falling. It hurt to see her body wracked with such a pervasive sadness. In the back of my mind I now understood her bouts with depression.

"Please. You have to promise me that you will never tell your father that you know. He lives for you Scott; it would kill him," she squeaked out starting to blubber again.

"I promise. After all, he is the only father I know," I said.

I couldn't quite bring myself to hug my mother. We had covered a lot of ground, hard ground, but there were old wounds still fresh in my mind. We needed time. My mother seemed to understand. While I hugged Jodi and Lisa she made no effort to embrace me.

Once they left, I went back to my room. I stayed there all day. Never had I wanted a snort or joint so badly. My life had just been turned upside down yet again. When would it get right? In as much as I knew drugs were not an option, I missed the way they helped soothe the intrinsic pain.

It helped me to forgive my mother. Finally I got it; her whole world had been about having a family. But the secret had twisted her too. It wasn't my father's fault that he was an easy mark. That was a bridge my mother would have to cross, and perhaps now she could.

More than anything, I emerged seeing my father as a truly incredible person. On the outside he looked like a simple, illiterate man; but on the inside he was incredibly strong and loyal. And throughout it all, he had refused to cast blame. Instead he had remained a kind and gentle person. I couldn't have had a greater example of fatherhood.

Strangely, the forgiveness I felt for my mother and compassion for my father had induced a new hatred for the government within my being. And strangely, God got credit too.

Upon my release I went straight to the mountains and there amongst the trees and wilderness I cried out to the world: What kind of a God are you? What kind of a God allows the world to be so full of lies and deception? You are not my God!

With that I retreated, thinking I had once and for all washed my hands of religion and God.

16

My Last Visit with Dad

A promise made should be a promise kept, or so I believed. And that was one promise I never broke. Throughout all the tribulations and failures of my life, I had broken so many promises, to loved ones, authorities and most importantly, God. Perhaps in realizing the devastation my family had already endured, the last thing any of them needed was more pain, especially my dad.

Suddenly my visits to Kansas City became paramount. It was clear that time was running out as quickly as sand through an hourglass. My father's mental acuity was fading and his physical health wasn't far behind. In my heart, I knew each day was a gift.

It tugged at my heartstrings with each visit, but I knew if I didn't see him I'd regret it. It was time to start making good on some of the promised changes in my life.

August was hot that year. Kansas City was pretty and vibrant; flowers in bloom and the trees full. I skipped up the steps of the front porch.

It was a relief to be out of the heat, but upon entering Jayne's house there was a smell of incense and kitties that overwhelmed me. If there was anything to be thankful about, it was that at least now my father didn't worry about where his living environment would be. It had been a tough decision letting him go but the right one. Yet I knew I couldn't care for him nor could my sisters.

As much as I didn't want to admit it, it would have been too much for my mother too. She fought with her own demons.

Dad was sitting up on the couch. He smiled as I entered the room. His smile was a good sign. It meant that dad was really there, at least for now.

On his good days, my dad would smile, laugh and joke. He would slap me on the back each time he introduced me to someone I'd already met saying: my boy.

"Hi dad," I leaned over to give him a quick hug. I handed him a small bag. My dad took it, he peered inside, his eyes got big, mischievous, child like.

"Licorice," he said. It was one of the few things my dad really enjoyed. At home he'd rarely splurge to buy it for himself. At least I could do that for him. "Thanks son," he said untwisting the tie.

"How are you doing dad?"

"I'm fine Scott, how's work?"

"I'm doing good. I'm back to selling," I told him, he nodded. Then his eyes seemed to glaze over with a familiar blank look. He was gone again.

Jayne came into the room, she noticed my dad's disposition immediately, she looked at him, compassion showed in her eyes.

"He's been having more episodes," she confided. "He'll be in the middle of something and then," she spread her arms outward. "He's just suddenly gone again," she finished, picking up breakfast dishes from the dining table.

"Thanks for all you do," I said getting up.

"Well, you know I've always liked your dad," she said softly. I gave her a quick hug before I left.

A lot had happened within the last few months. Especially since rehab. It had been the domino I needed to get my life back on track. It seemed so foolish now that it had taken me so long to get help. All the times I had started over. Why was it so hard for me to stay on point?

For all the questions I didn't have answers for, there were some that clearly stayed with me. My life had been aimless and devoid of the spiritual element too long. God had always been there for me, but I had not been there for Him.

Getting to know my mother again was another challenge. But I knew it was a journey I needed to take. Somewhere along the way I had stopped seeing her as my mother and viewed her only as an adversarial force.

Even if the government was screwing the public, my mother wasn't a part of that. The extent of her involvement was her willingness to participate in artificial insemination just so she could produce me. How could I blame her for that?

How I wished she was more knowledgeable about my conception. That whole nebulous world just continued to intrigue and confuse me. It was impossible not to feel resentment towards my genetic father. He was just one more link in the chain of secrecy and lies. He was a mushroom who had done his stealthy deeds in the dark, without a care where his seed had gone. It was all monetary for him.

For all my mother knew, Dr. Thurber could have been just as deceptive. How could she really know that donors were doctors or graduate students? And as she insisted, it would be nearly impossible to trace, shrouded in such secrecy.

Over the next few months I floundered emotionally. Trying to thread together my mismatched world. In the back of my mind I still toyed with the idea of finding my biological father. Primarily to know if there were any health concerns I needed to be aware of.

And yet I knew I was equally a part of the deception I so readily accused everyone else of. Didn't I cheat customers daily? Once I accepted that truth, it became increasingly harder and harder for me to be the selling machine I used to be. I no longer wanted to be the company's top salesman. That translated to me: top swindler.

No, I wanted to be more like the man who had raised me. Materialistically he had a paltry existence, but unlike myself, he had his priorities right, family and God. What did I have to show for my life? I was a recovering addict who had destroyed every relationship I'd ever had.

Yes I had creature comforts. But what comfort were they to my eternal soul? Did they make me a better man? Even a decent man?

Introspection can be a wonderful thing. It helped me wade through the clutter of my world. Immediately at the top of my list was my job. The day I quit, I felt a feeling of euphoria I'd only associated with coke or pot prior to that moment.

Since Thanksgiving was approaching, I decided to invite my father. But when my father begged off, telling me he hadn't been feeling so good. I'd blasted him about being selfish and promptly hung up on him. Immediately shame bit my conscience. With tears falling I called back. This time I ended our conversation with pleasant salutations for the holiday season.

When Thanksgiving arrived, I became even more thankful that I'd called back. I'd just spent the morning cleaning my apartment when Jayne called. I heard her voice on my message machine, quickly I picked up the receiver.

"Hi Jayne," I said cheerfully picking up the phone. "Happy Thanksgiving," I said. "Oh Scott?," she said between sobs. My stomach tightened.

"What's wrong?"

"Scott, your father," I heard her swallow and pause. Fear clenched my being.

"He was standing at the sink peeling potatoes for dinner, he just kept saying a real family Thanksgiving when he suddenly keeled over. I'm so sorry. We called the paramedics but by the time they got here they pronounced him DOA. I'm so sorry," she wailed.

My hand was shaking so much I could hardly hear her. I mumbled "thanks" and set the phone down. Suddenly my world seemed to collapse around me. How could I live without him? He was my mentor, my anchor, my everything. What was I going to do?

That night I cried myself to sleep. Without drugs, without alcohol, I'd slept. Strangely I hadn't even thought about any of it. My thoughts had been consumed only of him.

I was infinitely grateful now that I hadn't told him what I knew. He was my father. He would always be my father.

A blizzard raged across the prairies that Thanksgiving holiday. Snow drifts in excess of twenty feet gave Boulder an eerie surreal look. Like something one would see on a winter scene postcard. Consequently, it took thirty-six hours for me to arrive for the funeral services.

The weather matched my feelings of despair and being alone in an uncaring universe. One by one, family members and friends arrived. Each one was a shuffle of sadness. I watched them proceed to the front of the chapel where my father's open casket was laid.

By the time the reverend called the service to order, there were over one hundred people in attendance. A horrid thought crossed my mind. Would one hundred people come for me?

Seeing so many who had braved the inclement weather was heart-warming to me. I knew with certainty that my father was in heaven. It was the one comforting element about being there.

Pieces of a conversation we'd had months earlier floated through my mind. I could still hear my father's voice telling me he was going to heaven when he died. It had intrigued me, so I asked him how he could be so sure. His face held a countenance of absolute confidence as he smiled and spoke. "Because Jesus died for my sins," he told me. At that moment I didn't feel myself worthy of such compassion.

Hot tears rolled down my face. Jodi noticed and silently asked if I was okay. I nodded. Then I looked at her and Lisa and my mother. All their faces were red and puffy. It humbled me to realize they were sitting beside me. After everything I'd done, all I'd put them through, they were still there.

We would always be family I thought. Harry's spirit would always be near. I closed my eyes; now I could say my goodbye. I said it in a whisper, I'll see you again dad, count on it.

17

Who Am I?

There's an old adage that history repeats itself but for me it not only repeated itself, it would at times be humbling and humiliating. After pledging that my quest to discover my genetic roots was over, I once again found myself embroiled in deep thoughts, just yearning to know. Why couldn't I leave it alone?

Perhaps it was because I needed to know once and for all how much of who I was, how I was, represented a reflection of my gene pool? Were my continuing bouts with depression hereditary also? Were there other medical problems that Doctor Thurber had no knowledge or memory of?

And there were more questions. I heard Doctor Thurber's words tumbling around in my head, my genetic father had donated a lot. Did that mean I had siblings out there? The irony struck me. How much I had always wanted a bigger family. And now it was quite possible I already had one; but if they existed, would I ever know them?

Another Thanksgiving was upon us. As I sat in my mother's house looking out over the billows and drifts of snow and bare trees that encapsulated Kansas City, I felt lonesome. Sunlight made the glare from the snow almost blinding.

I watched my mother, self absorbed in her own little world smoking and drinking her brew. Did my mother's depression stem from the secrecy and her failed marriage? Secrets could be deadly. There was no denying.

She was so detached from the rest of us. Jodi and Lisa were huddled in the kitchen together, obviously sharing confidences. I was happy for them, that they had each other and such a close-knit relationship; but I was also envious. It would have been nice to have had a brother I could have shared my feelings with. I wondered how much it would have changed the course of my life.

"Scott, why are you sitting over there all my yourself?" Lisa teased.

"Who me?" I returned her frivolity.

"Yeah you, come here!" she gestured.

I glanced at our mother. There was a hint of a smile on her face as I joined my sisters. Jodi grabbed my arm once I was within reach and pulled me into their circle.

"How's mom?" she whispered.

"She's okay," I whispered back.

"How long are you going to be in Kansas City?" she asked. In her eyes I saw hope. But I would not be able to oblige. Things were rocky enough for me at work, I needed to get back.

"I'm going back tonight," I told her. Instantaneously both of my sister's glad faces dropped. Obviously it was not what they wanted to hear.

There had been a strange transformation within me since our father's death. In a way, I found myself playing both big brother and a surrogate father to them. Which made leaving more painful.

"What about Christmas?" Jodi asked.

"I might be free," I said being boastfully playful. Lisa poked my side. We all giggled. It felt good to be sharing the holiday with my family without being stoned or drunk. A twinge of sadness ran through me. It would have been nice to have accomplished that feat before my father's death. It would be another question I would someday ask of God, but for now, I would be grateful for my sisters and my mother.

The girls loaded me up with leftovers and goodies to take back with me. But when I left I didn't go to the airport. Instead I spent the night at a motel and in the morning, through the bitter cold found myself parked outside Doctor Thurber's house. The wind chill made it twenty degrees below.

My body hissed at me as I sat in my car parked on the street, new flakes falling. What was I doing? I didn't even know if they were home, nor how I would be received if they observed my car.

They lived in a large two-toned blue and gray ranch-style house on a hill, set back from the main road by a long driveway. A white fence ran around the perimeter of the property. Several horses stood in one pasture area, the trail of their warm breath visible in the bone crunching cold.

Life had been good to Thurber, I thought, surveying his place. Why should it matter now if I asked about my biological father? After all, Harry was gone now. If I could just get a little more information, I told myself.

Lord, if it's your will, please give me what I want, I prayed in my heart. With shaky knees I got out of the car and approached his house. The ice and snow crunched under my step. I clapped my hands together trying to dispel the stark cold.

Taking a deep breath I pushed the doorbell. Mrs. Thurber answered the door almost immediately. She stood in the doorway with her gray hair in contrast to the yellow chiffon dress she had on.

"Hi Mrs. Thurber, I'm Scott Davis. I called awhile back; I've come to see Doctor Thurber," I said. Her eyes narrowed a bit, but none-the-less she moved aside. She lead me to their living room and gestured to a stuffed chair by the piano. Then she left.

The room was expansive, set in dark wood tones. There was a fireplace and on the mantel an arrangement of family pictures. I studied the photographs. Younger versions of the couple and their children. It made my heart ache to know such familial bliss.

Two guns, a shotgun and a rifle were hung next to the chimney wall. And on the two walls that lead into the mouth of the living room, huge paintings. One depicting a bird dog retrieving a duck and the other two of deer in a woodland scenario.

I heard him before I saw him. His appearance startled me. He was gaunt and pale, his blue eyes lacked luster. Breathing was labored and obviously painful. He shuffled in wearing a chestnut colored bathrobe and slippers. Using a hand to balance himself, he slowly eased down on the right side of the mauve couch. He caught the surprised look in my eyes.

"Bone cancer," he supplied the answer to my unspoken question. "I'm dying," he said calmly. Sadness curled around my heart. I felt selfish having come there only for myself. It left me speechless. Doctor Thurber sensed my discomfort and rescued me. "So how do you feel now about the life I gave you?" he asked, a faint spark flecked across his face.

"I'm thankful, grateful. But I still feel like a part of me is missing. Please, I promise to never do anything to compromise you or hurt anyone else but my father, I need to know his name. Please, just for me," I pleaded. "You've just told me that you don't have long to live. But I have possibly another fifty years, and I don't want to spend it without knowing who my genetic father was."

I wondered if I sounded as desperate as I felt. Doctor Thurber was silent for a long time. I listened to the blood coursing nervously through my body, the steady whoosh in my ears. Alas he began to shake his head.

"Scott, I believe you are sincere and wouldn't do me or anyone else any harm on purpose. However, I have to uphold the patient and doctor bond and cannot tell you anything that would breach that confidentiality. It's not my right. I'm sorry Scott, you're just going to have to find your father another way," his words sliced through my hope of finding my biological father.

I nodded. It had been expected, but I had needed to try anyway. I looked at the frail stature of a man that had once been robust. It was enough that I'd even asked.

"I understand, thank you Doctor Thurber. Thank you for seeing me," I said before leaving. Once outside the cold assaulted me, I pulled the tuffs of my coat close around my ears as I quickly walked to my car.

The visit changed me. Over the next few months, whenever I came to Kansas City to see my family, I would also drop by Doctor Thurber's house. Never again did I bring up the subject of my heritage, I only visited.

Then I got the news. After just returning to Colorado from one of my family visits my mother called. Doctor Thurber's battle with bone cancer was over. I became distraught. In the last few months of his life, I'd grown to really care for him. Once again, I returned to Kansas City.

At the funeral procession among a gathering of perhaps several hundred people I made my way to the casket. It was stationed at the back of the church and against the backdrop of organ music cranking out Ave Maria, I said my final goodbyes. As people filed by, I watched them thinking my last opportunity to discover my past was now headed for the grave.

It gave me a weird feeling to be looking at the shell of the man who had been so instrumental in bringing me into the world. A number of emotions gushed out. It made me think how fleeting our existence is on the temporal plane.

Just as I was leaving, a pudgy man with thick glasses and dark hair matted against his head tucked under a brim hat approached me. He had small, beady eyes that blinked nervously.

"Are you Scott Davis?" he asked. I sized him up. Who was this odd looking fellow?

"Yes?" I made it a question.

"I've been asked to give you this," he said handing an envelope to me. I took it, still confused.

"Excuse me, who are you? What is this about?" I asked the stranger already midway to the door.

"Read it, you'll see," he said, then he was gone.

Something told me I should read it alone. It was a single page with only two words typed on it. Simply: Hans Kroenberg. There was nothing else but I knew, I understood. I held in my hand the name of my genetic father.

It was a tremendous feeling of elation. Perhaps as one might feel after pulling off some incredible heist. I'd faced the impossible and won. I repeated the name over and over. Leaning back in my car seat I closed my eyes. For a few moments, pieces of memories fused. Now I had another piece of the puzzle. Another piece of Scott Davis. A tear escaped my eye. Thank you God, I whispered. Finally I was getting it, what it meant to have God in my life. How much better life could be. And I understood, without him, I wouldn't have been able to get through this.

I knew in my heart that the very next time I returned to Kansas City I would be headed straight for the University of Kansas' library. Now that I knew his name, it wouldn't be that hard to track him.

Yet at first the university librarian did have difficulty locating any information. Then she typed in a slightly different variation on the spelling of his name and suddenly it was all there, blinking on the screen in front of us. It felt so good, I was almost afraid to believe it.

She traced him to a small university on the east coast where he was a professor of soil sciences. There were a smattering of alumni news clips about his accomplishments. Apparently he was an internationally recognized scientist.

It struck me, the contrast between us. Hans had been able to stick with everything he did, I had trouble following my pursuits with just about everything. I knew the next step was finding a phone number for him. This time I wasn't getting my hopes up. A lot of years had passed, there was more than a good chance that he might not be there anymore. But I had to try. It was all I had left.

Things turned out better than I expected, he was listed in the little town and now I stood stunned outside a pay phone in downtown Kansas City holding a piece of paper with his home phone number on it. But it was too soon. I folded the piece of paper in half and stuffed it into my pocket. I would need real courage to call.

I allowed myself to share my good fortune with my mother, but no one else. To my surprise, she was both supportive and happy for me. In fact, she even asked me what I intended to do with the information. That was a big question indeed.

My thirtieth birthday was fast approaching and a lot thoughts were running through my mind. What it would mean to me or my life if I did indeed meet him? How I would react if he refused to speak to me? This was, after all, the birthday I had joked about never living to see. That in and of itself made it important, a benchmark in my life.

I no longer had to live dangerously or die young. In fact, I no longer wanted to die. Conversely, I wanted to understand my world and myself better while incorporating God more into my life.

To celebrate my big day, I settled on a rafting trip down the Arkansas River. Because I was making a good living selling cars, I paid for all the accommodations for myself and six friends.

Alas the day arrived and the seven of us stood peering at the turbulent waters that were higher than normal from recent heavy rain. Our guide was a scrawny, wiry fellow with nervous gestures and small, gray eyes. That day he was dressed completely in black, except for the bright orange life vest. He squatted on the bank, sizing up the situation.

My friends and I watched him. Josh and Jason were smoking, casually passing the time. Both of them are big men, you could see it on their faces that they'd already determined that Charlie, our guide, was a wimp.

I inhaled the intoxicating scent of the dense forest woodland and underbrush. It wasn't a particularly warm day, but the view was panoramic, postcard perfect, full of trees and rolling hills divided by a raging river. It was awesome. Being next to so much raw power made me feel like a pioneer.

Finally Charlie stood. He placed a black baseball cap on his head as he rubbed his chin. Then he glanced at me and my party.

"I have to admit, I'm a little nervous about this," he said. "I can't even see the markings I use to guide. Maybe we should go to a quieter stretch," he suggested.

Immediately my pals began to scoff. Not to be outdone, I joined in.

"No," I told him. "I want to go down this part. It's what I paid for and it's what I want," I persisted. Charlie shrugged.

"Well, let's load up then," he instructed us.

Quickly we loaded our packs and a few necessities into the raft. Then I put one foot into the icy water. The shock almost made me rethink my position. It was incredibly cold. I could scarcely feel my toes, it was so sharp. Suddenly my friends looked uneasy.

Realizing they were following my lead I egged them on. One by one they followed suit. Each of them gesticulating at the harsh cold water as they boarded the raft.

No sooner had we departed when the trip immediately turned to chaos. We had barely cleared the first set of rapids when it became evident we were in trouble. The next set of rapids we were approaching was aptly nick named the widow maker. Our guide was sweating and only fear reflected back from my friend's eyes. Fear clenched my gut tightly. If any of them died at the hands of my foolishness, I would never forgive myself.

"The widow maker is coming up," Charlie yelled over the rush of water. "We need to hug the left side," he instructed. "Otherwise we'll run into rocks on the right."

We all nodded, struggling as we dug our paddles into the swirling brown water. But no matter how hard we rowed collectively we couldn't thwart the arm of the river that violently threw us against the canyon wall. The water roared as it crashed over the rocks, the noise deafening.

I could feel my heart in my throat and just before we crashed, I heard the guys separately shouting profanities. Immediately the curve of the rapids flipped the raft. I fought my way to the surface sputtering for air as I noticed my comrades being pulled down the river. But the raft was stuck between the canyon wall and a boulder at the lip of the right side. I clung to the raft. The constant tugging of the river making it harder to maintain.

Farther down the river people waited on the left shore bank where the river opened up and was less turbulent. They were yelling at me to let go. The current was so powerful that it pulled my suit off. The extreme cold combined with the forceful waters was making me feel ill and weak. I couldn't hold on.

Down I went. Deeper and deeper into the dark mouth of the river. It was swallowing me! The harder I fought, the more exhausted I felt. The screaming rapids were hushed by the depth of the murky water. It was as quiet as death.

Fear flooded me as I swallowed a large quantity of water. My God, I thought, my prophecy was coming true, I was not going to live to be thirty after all. It filled me with great sorrow and regret. All the promises I'd made, most of which I'd broken. I had nothing to show for my life, just a screw up and a big, empty void.

Darkness was closing in on me. There was no light at the end of the tunnel as I'd heard of. This must be what it was like for those who never made it to heaven, I surmised. There was no fire and brimstone or eternal torment. Only, cold, stark, black ugly nothingness.

I closed my eyes. My body feeling light. Only the words "forgive me Lord" rotated in my brain as blackness surrounded me.

18

Wrestling with Myself

Before my world swam in darkness, I felt a calm I used to rely on pot to provide. It was as if a giant hand had enveloped my naked body and had gently carried me downstream. I no longer noticed my body being banged against boulders or raked against rocks on the river bottom.

When I came to I was lying on my back, the glare of sunshine in my eyes. My head was pounding along side the pain of my whole body. I felt like one giant bruise. Everything ached. It was an effort just to lift my head.

A cluster of people had gathered around me. Charlie stood beside the paramedics attending me, a guy and a gal. My friends stood huddled behind them, watching.

My only thoughts were one of gratitude. I was so thankful we had all survived. I was alive. Alive! And it was wonderful. In my heart I knew God had heard my cry; he'd had pity on me and spared me.

The female paramedic removed a blood pressure cuff from my arm. She'd been kneeling, checking my vitals. Now she stood and said something to her coworker. They were both tall and blond, but she was nearly a half a foot shorter.

"Welcome back Scott. How are you feeling?" she asked. Even smiling hurt. "Oops, careful," she said dabbing my lower lip with a wipe. I looked at the wipe in her hand, it had fresh blood on it. No wonder it hurt, I thought.

"I'm so sorry guys," I choked. The female paramedic bent over me. Softly she squeezed my shoulder.

"Hey, you're alive. You made it," she said. "Just don't be pulling this again," she teased.

"You can count on it," I told her. And I wasn't just blowing smoke. I had been a drowning man swept up in a torrent of pseudo bravado that could have cost me my life and more importantly, my friend's lives.

Back at home, I knew I needed to start tackling some of my other deceitful practices. Many of which involved work and the art of swindling potential customers into services they did not need or already had. Over the years I'd honed my underhanded practice to near perfection.

Ironically a customer had caught me in the midst of carrying out another sham. I had been trying to get him to purchase an undercoating for three hundred dollars when I knew darned well the car already had one. But unlike most of his peers, the man was shrewd and car savvy. He'd caught the error.

It was a common practice carried out by many fraudulent dealerships. A practice all salesmen were encouraged to push. It was time for me to disassociate myself from such underhanded dealings. I wanted people to trust me, but more than that, I wanted to be deemed a good person.

When I died, I wanted to be remembered kindly as my father had been or even as my biological father, who had at least strived to make the world a better place with his accomplishments. Could I claim that?

But coming forward was risky. I knew it would result in an investigation and most certainly the termination of my lucrative job. It scared me to be without a job and a source of income, but I knew it was the right thing to do. A better man would have done it long ago. It was time to start using some of my faith.

The next day my first stop was the state agency that regulates car dealerships in Colorado. Standing in front of the door I took a breath. Not only would I be exposing my employer, I'd be baring my own soul.

I was met by a portly man who towered over me. He was squished into a pin-striped suit and sat across from me behind his office desk. As I explained the scam he took notes.

When I was finished he pushed away from his desk and gave me his hand.

"You did the right thing Scott. I know it took a lot of courage," he said calmly. I looked into his brown eyes, nearly hidden behind the glasses sloped on his nose.

"I hope you're right," I said more to myself as I left.

Almost immediately an investigation was launched. All the papers headlines read "Local dealerships investigated for fraudulent practices". As expected, many dealerships were fined. As a result, many managers and salesmen also lost their jobs.

It was tough seeing so many of the guys I'd once considered friends suddenly out of work. There was no question in my mind, if they'd known I was the whistle blower, they wouldn't have been too kind to me. By doing it anonymously, they just assumed I'd gotten the ax too. For that I was grateful. I said a prayer to God to help me find a better job and to help my colleagues find their way as well.

For a while, I floundered, trying to discern what the right direction was for me. In the interim I met a woman.

Unlike the ladies who had preceded her, Michelle seemed to genuinely care about me. No matter the skeletons that emerged from my past, she remained undaunted.

In fact, it was actually Michelle who pushed me to continue pursuing my biological origin. Along with other appealing attributes, she was keenly astute. It was easy for her to see I needed answers and closure.

One afternoon while we were casually watching television, Michelle broached the subject.

"Scott, I think you should look for your father, your genetic father," she told me. Her words made me sit up. Hadn't I been thinking those very same thoughts? The piece of paper I'd so carefully tucked in my wallet that contained his number had stayed there for five years. It felt like a talisman. But lately, hope had been replaced by a thorn gouging me to be addressed.

But how? That was the big question. If I just dropped the bomb on him, maybe he'd have a heart attack or hang up on me. Neither option seemed very appealing.

Somehow I needed to convey to him that I didn't want or expect anything except answers and information and maybe to meet him. But that was all. Was it really so much to ask?

Perhaps if he realized I didn't come with a price tag he'd be more receptive. At least I could hope.

"My father will always be Harry just like Jodi and Lisa will always be my sisters, but I would like to meet him, maybe find out if I do have any siblings out there, see what he's like," I stated matter-of-factly. Michelle smiled. Who was I kidding? She saw right through my nonchalant veneer.

Strangely while I was still debating how I might best accomplish my goal, I happened across an article in the local paper about an organization that searched for the birth parents of people who had been adopted.

The organization was headed by Pastor Richard Adkins, an adoptee himself who had successfully traced and subsequently contacted his own birth mother. From there, he had become an intermediary for other souls seeking their biological beginnings.

Such arrangements made it easier for both sides to decide how, and if, to make contact as well as pass along pertinent medical and family history in the event that contact was desired. At least it was a starting point.

Almost immediately I contacted Adkins. After carefully explaining my situation, Adkins agreed to call Kroenberg on my behalf.

A few days later he called me.

"I told him about you and said that he might be your donor father. I told him you want his health history and possibly to meet him, but nothing else. He laughed and said he wanted some time to think about it," Adkins said.

I heard the words some time to think about it playing in my mind. Somehow it still felt like no. Once again I felt defeated and expressed my disappointment, but Adkins wasn't daunted.

"He didn't say no, Scott. That's a good sign, even if it doesn't seem like it to you. You have to understand, most of these men have families. There's a lot to consider. He didn't deny it or hang up, and in my experience, that's usually a good sign," he stated persuasively. His words encouraged me. Perhaps he was right. What did I know about such things? I was a struggling neophyte just trying to keep one foot ahead of the other.

One week later my genetic father did indeed call Adkins, but as luck would have it, the pastor was out. Adkins removed the tape from his answering machine that continued Kroenberg's message and sent it to me.

Ecstatic, I immediately popped it into my own machine and hit the play button. A man's voice with a heavy Dutch accent came on announcing he was professor Kroenberg. Then he stated he and his family had excellent health. So far, so good, I thought. Then the bomb: I would appreciate no further contact. The response I'd dreaded had happened.

Just like that. It was over. All my efforts in vain. How could he be so dismissing? Why didn't he have any curiosity about me. It felt unreal. My heart sank, but I played the message over and over none-the-less. Just because he had no desire to know me, didn't quell my desire to know him.

I had to see Adkins. His office was less than twenty minutes from where I lived, but each mile seemed to take an eternity. I didn't even know what I was hoping to accomplish by seeing him, but still I felt driven.

He patted my shoulder once as I sat on one of the padded chairs designated for visitors. I looked at him.

"I'm sorry Scott. Sometimes that's as far as we get. At least you know there's nothing to worry about medically," he said plainly. I stared up at his caring face. Was that supposed to comfort me? I could feel my head nodding while my body grew tight. Anger was a cobra rearing back its ugly head, preparing to strike. I felt its teeth digging deep into my being.

"What kind of a man is he?" I shouted more to myself than Adkins. The pastor squeezed my shoulder.

"A man of secrets," he said quietly. I just looked at him. Yes, secrets, I thought. And what had secrecy done for my family? The bitterness was overwhelming. I hardly said goodbye before rushing out the door.

It felt like I should have had a marker stamped on my heart, rejected. Then it came to me. Just because he chose not to know me, perhaps I had siblings, they might want to know me. Maybe something good could come out of my efforts after all.

I knew what I had to do. It meant going back to Kansas and prevailing upon the mercy of Mrs. Thurber. There had to be files. I knew it was a desperate act, but I was feeling plenty desperate. No man should be forced to endure such rejection.

Please guide me Lord, I whispered before I climbed into my car. Not even Twenty-four hours later I was pulling up widow Thurber's driveway. As I parked in the carport I hesitated. What right did I have? While I vacillated, I played the tape once more.

"To hell with it, I've come this far," I said aloud.

Mrs. Thurber met me at the door. She was pleasant and affable as she invited me and offered tea. She listened to my request thoughtfully but in the end shook her head.

"I can't Scott,"

"Mrs. Thurber, please," I heard myself begging. "If you were in my shoes, wouldn't you want to know?" I asked setting my cup down. Her eyes held mine. They were tired eyes, eyes that seen a lot in her life time. She set her own cup down. It made her stop and think, then her brows pinched and she began to shake her head once more.

"It's unethical and illegal Scott. I probably would want to do the same thing you're trying to do but I just can't. Those people were assured their privacy. I could get into a lot of trouble by letting you do that. It would ruin my husband's good name, and that wouldn't be right, after all those years of faithful service," she seemed to get reflective, then her eyes met mine. "I'm truly sorry."

I knew I'd been beat and I couldn't even dispute the point. Everything she said was the truth, but it was also true that I deserved to know my heritage, as did all the other thousands of donor children. Why hadn't anyone ever considered our feelings? How such actions impacted our lives?

"I understand," I said deflated, my shoulders sagging with the disappointment. I saw myself out, then sat in my car contemplating. How could I get to those files? There had to be a way.

First on my list was new apparel. I bought myself a dark wool cap, black pants and shirt. Then I dressed in my new attire and when twilight had replaced the clear skies and stars glittered, I walked down the lane that lead to the Thurber home.

The house was dark. My heart pumped with excitement. It was now or never. Quickly I walked around the house to a small door half hidden by mulberry shrubs that entered into the basement. Moonlight draped the snowy yard. I pulled my collar closer. Past visits had made me privy to the contents, all of Doctor Thurber's medical files were stored within.

Suddenly I heard a dog bark. It was just their neighbor's dog, Sadie, but it startled me. For a moment I pressed my hand to my chest trying to quiet my nerves. With two felonies on my record I knew a third would automatically put me into the "three strikes and you're out" category, which guaranteed a minimum of twenty-five years.

Yet I plowed on, determined. I didn't want to lose my freedom; but I had to know.

The door was easy to pry with minimal damage; only a few ravaged strands of wood by the hinge. One might even miss it all together if you weren't looking carefully.

Once inside I flicked on my penlight. It cast a big enough glow to see my way around. There they were; row after row of file cabinets tucked up against the wall.

Suddenly the enormity of my task hit me. There were literally thousands of files including another eighteen thousand that represented all the babies the good doctor had delivered during his forty-four year career.

I lumbered over to the very first cabinet. Slowly I drew the first drawer outward. As I perused the contents of the files I looked for key words, donor, artificial insemination, and especially Kroenberg.

As I thumbed laboriously through each cabinet, I heard Mrs. Thurber getting in and out of bed. She was obviously restless. All at once I heard a crash and the sound of glass breaking. I froze. Had she heard me? Would the next sounds be a phone call to the police?

The sound of my own heartbeat was deafening as it beat at a furious rhythm. Then I heard her shuffling again, apparently making her way to the kitchen, perhaps for another glass.

Just to be sure, I waited another thirty minutes before I resumed my stealthy endeavor. To my delight I found one record that night of a child whose mother had used artificial insemination. The donor had been Kroenberg. She'd had a daughter they named Christy Anderson. I wondered if I would recognize the face that belonged to that name. After all, Kansas City wasn't that big.

The next morning I freely shared the information with my mother. Rather than own up to my deceitful tactics, I told my mother Mrs. Thurber had consented to allow me to look over some of the files.

"Fact is, I have to go back there tonight," I told her. "You wouldn't believe how many files there are. But I do have a little good news," I said. My mother looked up. "I discovered I have a half sister, her name is Christy Anderson," I explained. My mother grew pale.

"Oh my God," she drew her hand to her mouth then whispered as if it were a conspiracy. "Christy was the little girl born a few days after you. She lived next door. I have pictures of you and Christy as babies. They moved away when you were only one," she said her eyes welling up.

I came to her and gave my mother a hug. She clung to me with such frantic desperation; then she looked up.

"There's something else Scott," she hesitated.

"What?"

"Her father was at Beatrice with Harry. He must have been sterilized too!" she gasped, then began to cry. "This is all just too awful!" she sobbed.

For awhile we remained locked in our respective silences, reflective. A whisper of anger began to pester me. Another man sterilized at Beatrice? What the hell was going on? What were they doing over there?

Abruptly my mother bolted to the hall closet where she kept the family photo albums. I watched her flipping through several books until she spied what she had been searching for. She returned with a black and white picture, all of its edges had yellowed with time.

The picture showed two infants placed side by side on a rug. One boy, one girl, they easily could have passed for fraternal twins. Looking at myself and my half sister gave me an eerie feeling. Even though I couldn't explain it, instinctively I knew something weird was going on.

I kept the photo. It was my talisman as I returned to Mrs. Thurber's house that night. It saddened me to know I'd met my sister once but hadn't even known it. How freaky was that?

Eventually I did find my mother's file. From it, I learned that my mother had tried several more times to get pregnant through the same process, but all further attempts had been unsuccessful. Why? If it had worked once, what had prevented it from working again?

The deeper I dug, the more files I produced, until alas I knew I had completed my goal. Kroenberg had produced at least another five children, all girls. Somewhere out there I had five half sisters. It felt odd to realize they would all be women now. All blond, blue-eyed female versions of myself. A chill ran through me.

By the time I reached my car I was breathing hard. I sat in the darkness, allowing my body to acknowledge its fatigue.

I turned on the engine but kept my lights off until I'd made it to the main street. A dim light was being pulled across the dark Kansas sky. The stream of early commuters made me feel lonesome. But then a trickle of hope, somewhere out there was someone to belong to. And I would find every last one of them.

19

My Biological Past

The desire to know where my siblings were got the better of me. My thinking got a little sideways as I began concocting ways to contact them. Nothing else seemed to matter, not nurturing my relationship with Michelle and certainly not work. Ironically I discovered two of my stepsisters had gone to the same high school. I looked them up in the annual.

One of the names took me aback. Not only did I recall this girl, I'd actually been enamored with her. A chilling thought zapped me, where would it have lead if she'd accepted any of my invitations to date her?

Michelle was sitting splay-legged on the recliner half watching television while I poured over the contents of my yearbook. Memories and feelings came out in clusters.

"Oh God, what if we had started dating. What if we'd had sex or even married," I left the thought hanging. She looked at me tenderly.

"But you didn't," she stressed. I looked at her. In her eyes I could see her sincerity, but it frightened me how close we'd come. My stomach felt sick.

Such times made my body ache to be pacified by pot, but I was determined not to give in. In my mind I prayed. Prayed for strength and God's help. After awhile, the craving dissipated.

There was no mistaking the family resemblance. It was scary. I couldn't help contemplating how many other children there might be out there sired by Kroenberg.

There was a much bigger stake to be considered. One that few seemed to appreciate, the consequences of such actions. While I would concede that I believed

Thurber was a good man, a Godly man with honorable intentions, we already know the cliché about good intentions and its consequences!

But it was the repercussions of such actions that concerned me most. The lives that were or will be devastated by such practices. To say nothing of the deceit, lies and secrecy of such procedures. Should anyone have that much power? Presuppose the mind of God? It seemed profoundly arrogant.

Pursuing my birth heritage had a way of making me overly sensitized to every blond-haired, blue-eyed person of approximate age. I couldn't help looking for a familial resemblance.

It even made me question my former love interest, Laurie. Hadn't everyone proclaimed we could have been brother and sister? It disturbed me. How did I know for sure we weren't? Just the thought of it was doing a number on me. How did I truly know she was from Iowa? How did I know Kroenberg's seed just didn't cross state lines?

It made me feel as though I had no control over my life. That I was a puppet in some twisted play, being manipulated at will. The potential terrified me.

There were days I would barely exist in a fog of depression and confusion. It seemed that the harder I sought the truth, the more it seemed to elude me. On those occasions I would pray. I knew it was too big for me to handle by myself. I needed divine intervention.

The torment of indecision ate at me. As much as I wanted to contact my half sisters, I was conflicted. Did I have that right? How would they respond to me? Would they believe me? Were they happy with their lives? And if they were, could I be so selfish as to jeopardize their happiness just to satisfy my introspective quest?

In the end, I chose camouflage. By posing as a member of a high school alumni committee I was able to glean knowledge that one of my sisters lived in New York and another made her home in Michigan. Even when I knew, I still couldn't bring myself to call.

Instead, I decided I pursue Kroenberg. The timing seemed right. Taking courage in hand, I wrote him a letter pleading with him for just a phone call, a letter and if at all possible, a meeting, just one. The minute I finished it I wanted to destroy it. My desperation bothered me. I had always considered myself to be so self-reliant. It made me feel weak, vulnerable, and cautious.

One month later I received a letter from my donor father's attorney. Just looking at the letterhead, the law offices of Jeremy Renfield, made my hope sink. It had to be bad news.

Dear Mr. Davis:

Hans Kroenberg has retained me as counsel and has referred your letter dated the 29th of May to me. I have evaluated the relevant law and relative rights of the parties in this matter. We can appreciate your interest in pursuing this matter, but my client does not share that interest.

We extend to you our very best wishes and hope that having made this contact, you will now be willing to accept and honor my client's request.

Sincerely,

Jeremy Renefield, Attorney At Law

That was it. A thinly veiled threat. I felt anger and sadness moving in like high tide. All my previous assumptions of the professor faded. He wasn't so great. I hadn't been completely unprepared, but the total rejection cut deep. What would be the harm in just meeting him once? Couldn't he understand the importance of such a meeting?

It was as if he were proclaiming to the world that I was a liar, I didn't really exist. What did that make me? A nobody with half a heritage? It outraged me that there was nowhere to turn. I had little or no recourse.

For reasons unbeknownst to me, I was drawn to the library. I became determined to learn more about artificial insemination. Not surprisingly, there wasn't much. But then I found a new book: Lethal Secrets—The Shocking Consequences and Unresolved Problems of Artificial Insemination by Annette Baran and Reuben Pannor.

The more I read, the more I felt at home. This was my life. My world. Somebody was finally addressing my plight. It felt joyously wonderful. But it was one sentence in particular that gave me chills. It was the author's own intention. This is not an indictment of artificial insemination, but an argument for breaking the bonds of silence and anonymity before it tears the family fabric.

I read the words over and over. The words that gave credence to my life, understanding, compassion. They should have been mine. I wanted to make a banner of that declaration, proclaim it everywhere. Somewhere out there, I knew there had to be others who needed the same resolve as myself.

The next few days pasted quickly. My focus was completely within the pages of that book, my story. Within those pages I was learning more and more about my world. I learned that artificial insemination was first practiced on humans in the late 1800's. It seemed impossible visualizing how society was technologically backwards during those days, but doing something so sophisticated.

The practice blossomed until the baby boomer era of the Fifties. By that time, however, over a million babies had been born to fathers whose only contribution to their offspring was in providing sperm.

The facts were mind boggling. Over one million babies! Over one million souls who could commiserate with my plight. Yet, realistically speaking because of the privacy issues, it was unlikely that the majority of my secret brethren even knew the consequences of their beginnings.

I read over another line that seemed to strike me as particularly profound: This practice of intentional deception has placed a strain on the parents. The burden of maintaining such a secret family life has created many dysfunctional families and not infrequently led to divorce.

There it was. Me and my family. We were a part of those statistics. I could feel my throat getting tight. I highlighted the passage and all those I felt most directly addressed my circumstance.

I peered across the room at Michelle, engrossed in some sitcom. Did she have any clue how all of this felt? Affected me? How could she? Would she be able to handle it? Just for a moment, I felt jealous of her family's normalcy.

The deeper I got into the book, the more each chapter seemed tailor made to my family. It delved into the pluses and minuses of artificial insemination and the resulting donor offspring.

On the plus side, legal fathers felt it allowed them to have children. It was also safer and easier than adoption. (I reflected for a moment on my own family's struggles to adopt.) Donors used were usually above average in intelligence. The father's sterility remains private and the child will feel like theirs because they will be sharing in raising it.

But on the flip side, the baby would only have the mother's genes, dealing with the fact that another man's sperm had impregnated their wives, the biological father's IQ could create a chasm between the legal father and donor offspring.

For the women the affects were more subtle, but just as damaging. Many women felt guilty, as if they'd participated in an illicit affair. Many developed an image of the donor father in which their husband's often fell short by comparison.

Further, they proclaimed the relationship often underwent a shift in power where some women grew to feel they didn't need their husbands. It's was viewed as their own achievement.

As a result, the authors concluded, non-genetic fathers might feel less able to parent and set limits, causing the donor offspring to be deprived of full parenting by their legal father, resulting in the donor offspring internalizing the anxiety of his parents and feeling somehow responsible for it and unworthy.

It explained my father's reticence to discipline me. Explained why he'd been so passive, why he'd allowed my mother to become the dominant parent.

It also explained the source of internal anxiety I had battled all my life. Hell, I'm still dealing with it. What a damned mess. A bitterness had been provoked within. I wanted the easy cushion of a joint or a drink. It hurt to be finally realizing why I had felt like a pariah all these years. I wanted to scream. Vent my anger, pain, outrage.

But it was late and Michelle was already asleep in bed. Still, I wanted to get high so badly. I made my way into the kitchen, the thoughts in my head whirling around in a nonsensical fashion.

I opened the refrigerator and spied the beer. Before I could even debate it, I'd guzzled half a bottle. Then, just as abruptly, I drained the remaining contents down the sink and threw the bottle at our garbage container. The bottle smashed against the hard plastic.

Shards of wet glass lay in disarray by the container. Tears fell. I fetched a hand broom and dustpan. As I swept the shiny brown glass onto the mouth of the dustpan I began to weep uncontrollably.

In my mind pieces of the book hissed at me. Pieces about the moral and ethical perspectives. The authors argued that only donors willing to be a part of their donor offspring should be used, and none should be allowed to donate more than three times to prevent unwitting incest and inbreeding. But was anyone listening?

If they could see that donor offspring had a right to access their heritage and meet their genetic fathers, why couldn't Kroenberg? I turned the dustpan upright. I watched the glass drop into the garbage.

Who says you can reject me? Maybe I'll reject you! I threw the dustpan against the wall, my anger driving me. I have a right, I told myself. And I defy you to deny me. Now I could sleep.

20

Learning about Eugenics

It became a fascinating journey to me. Uncovering secrets and covert government and state policies all affecting the lives of countless, faceless lives. Lives the government and society chose to ignore.

At times, it felt as though we were a segregate society unto ourselves. And perhaps we were in some ways; for who could understand the perils and fall out of how it was to be a donor offspring more that we did?

My quest led me to a group called the Authors of Lethal Secrets. The name was appropriate; their very existence was a testament to my story. Through them I learned that the connection between donor insemination and forcible sterilizations imposed by state and governmental regulations was unique to my circumstance. It seemed that they hadn't been aware of the connection before my case. My life circumstances seemed to be opening many doors. It made me feel as though I were a pioneer carving a necessary niche in the world.

Upon their recommendation, I called Candace Turner, a woman who had recently created a support group for donor offspring. It was exactly what I needed, an opportunity to talk to others like myself. Immediately I called her home number in Missouri.

To my delight, Candace was just as excited. The more details I shared about learning the identity of my genetic father, the more enthused Candace became. The group was small, only about a dozen people, and once again I was at the forefront. None of the other members had been as lucky.

"It just about drove me nuts when I found out," she confessed. Her feelings of discouragement were familiar. My mind flashed back to my own plight. Unlike myself, Turner hadn't been privy to the paperwork that had eventually been a turning point for me.

Like myself, Candace was convinced that the secrecy behind her conception had destroyed her parent's marriage. She revealed an upbringing filled with many arguments. The similarities were eerie and haunting.

Hadn't I always believed my screwed up past was a product of all the lies? Now here was my proof. It was too much. I could feel my head spinning. So many thoughts were whirling around in my mind. Pieces of events that seemed significant, explaining another piece of my intrinsic puzzle. In the midst of my introspection, Candace asked a curious question.

"You ever hear the word eugenics? Or know anything about its correlation on our creation?" she asked. My mind went blank. What was eugenics? Why all the mystery? What did that have to do with me?

"What's eugenics?" I finally asked.

What I heard next shocked me. Candace began discussing things like the Nazi's and the Holocaust and population control. If my brain had been fuzzy before, it was on overload now.

The more I listened, the more I began to feel dubious about the sensibility of connecting with her. From her mouth spilled words about Nazi breeding programs, forming a master race and sterilizations of so-called inferior people.

"It was something the Nazis learned from the eugenics movement in the United States," she explained. The United States? All my previous righteous anger with my government suddenly seemed justified. Had a part of me secretly known?

"My dad was sterilized," I confessed feeling shaky. It was all too weird to be true. How could such atrocities have been permitted? Even worse, encouraged? The seed of anger I'd been fighting so valiantly to control suddenly surfaced with a vengeance. An old urge reared its ugly head. God help me, I said over and over silently. I wanted to get high so bad. The truth was too ugly for anyone to accept.

"You see?" Candace spouted triumphantly. But I did not see. I did not want to see. Just the thought of it made me bitter as hell. Unbelievably angry. I could feel the storm brewing, coursing through my blood with each beat of my heart. "And here you are a blond-haired, blue-eyed wunderkind. You and I are products of eugenics. It still exists; don't think it doesn't. Ever wonder why you knew so little? Nobody's supposed to talk about it; not the doctors, not the clinics, nor you and your family. It's all part of the big secret. All hush-hush," she said simply. As if that explained it. But her words outraged me. It was too much to handle. It couldn't be true. It couldn't. For all the negative warts I accredited to my country, never could I have imagines such diabolical roots.

My world was reeling. How could stuff that transpired during World War II be relevant now? This was fodder for B movies or history books, not breathing, living people.

"You're nuts!" I finally shouted, my anger getting the better of me. Suddenly Candace grew silent. Obviously she'd thought I was a kindred spirit, her previous gush of emotion was replaced by a flat statement.

"I'll send you a copy of our newsletter, and if you ever feel like contributing something to it, we'd like that," she said softly. I regretted shouting, but I couldn't bring myself to apologize. The tremendous amount of information was so daunting. I just hung up.

I didn't know what to think. Clearly Candace was a true believer, but it all seemed so distorted to me. A giant conspiracy? It made me feel paranoid just considering it. And yet within myself, I knew it had a ring of truth. What would be her motivation for lying? For proliferating such propaganda? Hadn't their explanations been right on target?

Maybe if my own parents had been able to talk to someone, or if it hadn't been so clandestine, perhaps some of the pain could have been avoided. The more I thought about what had happened to my father and the subsequent way my birth's conception was handled, the more Candace made sense.

One morning while I poured myself a cup of coffee, Michelle approached me. She was very good for me in that way. She encouraged me to release internal demons, express my feelings, things I tried to run from. In as much as it hurt, it also helped.

"Well," I told her. "They're not going to be able to keep their dirty little secret anymore. Not if I can help it," I said defiantly.

She wrapped her arms around me. As we shared the coffee a plan began to materialize. I knew what I had to do. What I wanted to do. But first, I needed to apologize to Candace.

Turner was wonderfully understanding. It was no surprise; she knew the feelings of shock and anger well. When I hung up I felt infused.

Next step: the media. Denver has two large dailies. I called the Rocky Mountain News. My call was passed to a bored and tired sounding reporter. I told him just enough to peak his interest.

We agreed to meet the next day at a local restaurant. Over coffee I told the reporter, a Mr. Vance with a southern accent and a white, neatly trimmed goatee a watered down version of my story. I figured that was potent enough. Even though he had a tape recorder going, Vance still took notes. I watched him write.

He was definitely from the old school and used to taking notes. During my story telling, I omitted most of my drug and relationship woes and intentionally negated revealing the details to my father's sterilization. Nor did I provide any relevant facts on how I managed to obtain the information on my genetic father.

It was my opinion that the reporter already had plenty to go on. The next question would be to learn how well he managed to convey the facts.

When the story was released I felt like a celebrity and a rebel. That somehow I had struck a blow for my father. Although it felt good to be getting some of the ghosts out in the open, my genetic father's rejection continued to be a blight on my world. I just couldn't leave it alone.

Through Candace, I began meeting other donor offspring. Each time their stories seemed to mimic my own; broken homes, dysfunctional families, tormented lives filled with drugs and an unyielding relentless search for meaning.

I felt compelled to write Candace a letter. It would be my contribution to the newsletter, or as much as I was capable of at that time in my life.

Dear Candace:

I'm sorry this letter will be reaching you so late. It seems that I either don't think about it at all, of being a donor offspring, or I'm obsessed with it. I wish I could find a happy medium.

I think presenting this problem to the world is right in time with other hot issues like abortion, surrogate parenting, embryos, and all that other high-tech stuff, just to name a few.

I also think that DI's should either be regulated in an honest and open way, or it should be abolished. As for myself, I feel luckier than most and do not see my story as tragic, but rather a very sad commentary of our times. I was fortunate enough to come to a family that really loved me.

I'm not angry anymore. Just sad that so many thousands of DI's are out there and unaware of what is truly going on. It is terribly unfair. And people need to hear this. I am so grateful that my mother was honest with me, even if it did take her 28 years to do so.

As much as I'm able, I and going to stir the kettle. I'll write more as I feel like I have something to say. Thanks for letting me share.

Sincerely,

Scott

I kept my word. I called everyone I could think of trying to generate some interest. Slowly it began to unfold.

Then one sweltering afternoon in August while I sat in my apartment with sunlight peeking under the closed shades and listening to the steady whirl of the AC, I received an important call. It was from a man proclaiming himself to be the producer for the Joan Rivers talk show. Apparently someone had sent the station clips from the Rocky Mountain News.

"We want you to come to New York and do a segment with Joan," he continued. In my mind's eye I could see River's making me out to be a buffoon. I scowled.

"I don't want to come out there just so she can turn my life into some kind of joke," I told him.

"No, no," he assured. "This is more of a variety show. We're going to do some of everything. But we're treating this as a serious subject," he continued. "We're taping this on September 8th. Can you make it?"

In spite of the qualms still rumbling around in my head, I knew I had to do it. When would I ever get another chance for national exposure? It was just too great of an opportunity to pass up.

"Sure," I heard myself say.

One week later I was sitting on a crowded Alaska Airlines flight. Nervousness churned in my stomach. I contemplated what I should and shouldn't say. I wasn't prepared to out my genetic father or expose my father's sterilization, but there were plenty of other issues I could address.

Suddenly the plane started shaking as it ran into turbulence. Almost immediately the warning light to fasten seat belts began to flash. I watched people all around me grip their seats and exchange worried whispers. I held my breath and said a silent prayer: God, I know you didn't bring me this far just to have my life stop now. I have a story to tell first.

Miraculously a few minutes later the plane stopped shaking. The turbulence had passed. I wanted to share my faith to the world. I knew God had intervened.

The celebrity-like service was heady. The producer had arranged to have a limousine waiting for me at the airport. A small, mid-eastern descent guy held a sign with my name on it next to the glass double doors. When I acknowledged the sign, he whisked me away to a plush hotel across from Central Park.

Inside the expansive suite was a full bar, a panoramic view of the park and a decor done in medieval trappings. It was easy to feel complacent as I lounged, lazily soaking in the view and sipping on a gimlet.

At first glance of the bar, I told myself I would treat myself to one drink only. After all, I couldn't lose my focus of why I'd come. But I told myself one drink was fair.

The next morning the same driver escorted me to the studio. To my surprise, Rivers was poised, professional and articulate. She asked serious, intelligent questions. And by focusing on her, I was able to block out the fact that the show was being viewed by millions.

As a bonus, I remained their guest for another night before returning to Denver. I knew I was pampering myself a bit, but it was a feeling that I hadn't experienced before and my heart had a need to soak up more of my new ambiance.

I raised my glass in a toast. "Here's to you dad, I hope you saw me on television," I said aloud. Then it struck me; I wasn't sure which father I was talking to. A pang of sadness jabbed me. Would I always be so conflicted?

21

Kindred Spirits

If there was anything propelling me during those dark days of soul searching it was probably the fact that at least I made good on my promise to stir the kettle. Throughout 1990 I took it on as my personal cause to campaign against the secrecy behind donor insemination. Following my appearance on the Joan Rivers show, I appeared on Geraldo and appeared in numerous newspaper features.

True to my nature, I found myself clipping and filing each and every item in notebooks where I had placed the details of my previous search for my father and sisters. Consequently, my personal scrapbook was growing right along with my trek for truth and justice. What started as a stark, nearly barren notebook was now a plumb book full of details, nostalgia and clippings. Chronically all the benchmarks of my quest.

Before long, I had been elected president of the Donor Offspring group. My involvement continued to grow as my notoriety soared. But with my new proclaimed successes, came an increasing amount of pressure to be completely forthright. I had carefully dodged or omitted details about my father's past and I certainly hadn't been honest about how I'd acquired the information on my biological father. I felt tremendously torn.

My car salesmanship was replaced by a new business selling coupon books and recycling services. I had a full sales crew and made my living by reaping a percentage of what they made. In as much as I had made up my mind to abolish my previous deceitful behavior, I still wrangled with my own egotism from time to time. It didn't help knowing I could sell anyone anything. At times it was a huge struggle to allow my good guy side to prevail; knowing it would be so easy to increase profits ten fold by utilizing just a few of the old tricks. During such moments of weakness I would find myself calling upon God for inner strength. It was getting easier to talk to him. My faith might have been a bit wobbly yet, but not my voice; that was resonant and clear.

But as time wore on my head focused. I found myself thinking more and more about the half-sisters I had not contacted. I liked to daydream about meeting them, that somehow we'd be like one big, happy family. Blood thicker than water and all that. I just hoped they would share my enthusiasm. With that thought in mind, I decided it was time to reach out to them.

Whatever I expected or hoped would be, I was bitterly disappointed. I met with skepticism, disbelief and detachment. When some opened up, they revealed similar backgrounds of dysfunctional families, divorce and troubled lives. More pain.

After the brief initial interest or correspondence or telephone conversations, the enthusiasm seemed to evaporate. They were not brother and sisters in any true meaning of the words. There was no connection beyond genetics. I would not have my ideal family. I would have no family at all, but for my adopted sisters and depressed mother.

Disappointed, at last I came to the first name I had discovered in Mrs. Thurber's basement, Christy. She was the little girl who had lived next door when we were both infants. Born a week apart, I hoped that we might find something in common, some trait that might bring us together.

It was actually my mother who got her telephone number. As it turned out, my mother had her own interest in locating her former neighbors and finally succeeded in January 1991. What she told me though was anything but encouraging. Christy's mom was not well, she had spent time in a psychiatric hospital with severe depression; her father had died at a young age, after the two had divorced.

Christy had been raised by her grandparents, and then tragically had subsequently been sexually molested by an uncle. As a means of coping, her own youth had been ruled by drugs, depression, and disastrous relationships. The striking similarities hit me. Beyond association, without a doubt we were brother and sister. Her life was mine and visa versa. It hurt me and gave me a brain hurt to realize how many others out there were going through the very same things. When would the lies stop? Who would be there to help them?

Mom told me this while we shared coffee in her tiny kitchen. Of course she was smoking. Her ashtray was loaded with butts of all the dead soldiers she'd already had. The table, like everything else in her house, was littered with used coffee cups. It reminded me once again that my mother was battling her own demons, spending most of her days sitting, smoking and drinking coffee, lost in depression.

"If I had just been a better wife," she said breaking into tears. "More understanding. Your father didn't deserve to be treated the way I treated him. It wasn't his fault. But we couldn't talk about any of it, it was supposed to be a big secret and we didn't dare bring it up, even between ourselves.

Maybe if we had just told the truth when you were old enough, we could have faced it together. But Scott, I was so scared. I'm just so sorry."

Mom sobbed, holding her face in her hands. I put my arm around her shaking shoulders. A deep understanding coursed through me. My mother was as much a victim as I had been.

Just then the cuckoo clock chimed. I watched the wooden bird rotate on its perch three times then disappear behind its tiny door.

"It's not your fault, Mom," I said softly. "This was done to us. All this secrecy, all the lies and deception, you and dad both did your best by us kids. We love you and that's what matters."

"Do you Scott?" she asked. The words took me by surprise. For the first time in a long time I really saw the age and wear on my mother. Her tired, bloodshot eyes held my gaze. How could she think I didn't love her?

A wisp of guilt flowed over me. Why wouldn't she? My mind flashed to tidbits of ugly shouting matches we'd had. How many times had I told her it was all her fault?

"Of course I do Mom. I'm so sorry you ever had to doubt that," I squeezed her shoulders.

"I'm sorry I wasn't the mother you wanted or needed," she added before more tears began to spill.

"Please stop," I stroked her gray hair. It was coarse and thick. She buried her face in my shoulder. I held my mother, wondering why it had been so difficult to do such a benign act for so long, but also knowing. We had both conquered many demons within our mother and son relationship. I could feel myself starting to choke. The need to leave was becoming overwhelming.

I would need time to absorb our new-kindled relationship. Not knowing exactly what that even meant, or what it would mean in the future. But knowing we had gone as far as we could for now. Perhaps sensing my reticence or dealing with her own reservations, my mother moved back. She extracted a handkerchief from the pocket of her sweater and dabbed her eyes, then she blew her nose.

"Thank you son," she said softly. "Let me get you Christy's number," she said. I watched her padding down the hallway in her slippers. The same old ratty blue and white terry cloth slippers I remembered as a child. They had to be threadbare by now. A prickling sensation of sadness shot through me. Why hadn't I ever replaced them? Why hadn't I ever noticed before? She emerged with a piece of paper.

I left with Christy's telephone number and address in hand, but still unsure of what to do. This would be the last chance for establishing some sort of relationship with my genetic family. But did I have that right?

Christy lived in Kansas City. The first thing would be deciding whether to drive by her home, hoping to catch a glimpse of her or just call. Covert actions won out. I pulled onto her street nervously and looked for house numbers until I found the right one.

Children were playing in the front yard. No doubt her children, which would make them my blood nephews and nieces. A weird feeling filled me. To be so close to relatives without having the luxury of just saying hello stung me, but it was too risky. I'd have to temper my enthusiasm.

I decided to be prudent and park the car about a block away. Getting out, I surveyed the neighborhood as I walked up the sidewalk and past the children who looked at me with curiosity. The family resemblance was remarkable.

"Hi," her little blond boy said.

"Why, hello" I replied as I reached the front door to knock.

A man answered. It wasn't what I'd expected. Encountering a husband hadn't been a part of the plan, how could I explain what I was after? It was easier to lie, so I did.

"Hi," I said. "I'm looking for Tony Smith."

"There's no Tony Smith who lives here," the man answered politely. He was tall, dark featured and stocky but friendly enough.

"Oh, I'm sorry," I replied trying to sound sheepish. "This was the address I was given. Sorry to trouble you."

"No trouble. I hope you find who you're looking for," he said before ushering the children inside. I hurried down the sidewalk, stealing one more look at my half-sister's children.

I told myself I needed to leave it at that, but the knowledge I now had about my extended family made me bolder. Two days later I called the telephone number, but to my disappointment I only got their answering machine. Instinctively I left a brief message saying only that their families had once lived next to each other and would she please call.

That evening, Christy indeed called.

"Hello?" she said tentatively. "This is Christy."

"Oh my God," I said hearing the excitement in my voice. "I can't believe I'm talking to you," I gushed.

"Why?" Christy sounded apprehensive. "What's going on?"

I took a deep breath. Then hesitantly, while saying a silent prayer, I began. Now was the moment of truth. "I have reason to believe that you're my sister," I said softly, hearing my heartbeat raging in my chest as I waited.

Silence. Had I scared her away? Oh God, please no! Not after all this time, all I've been through. I found myself begging God to rescue me, have mercy.

I was terrified she would hang up, hurriedly I told her my story. When alas I had finished there was more silence. What must she be thinking? That I was a quack, a fake? Finally she spoke.

"I don't know what to believe," she confessed honestly. "I was once told that I was adopted. But an uncle hinted that my mother had an affair and I was the child of her lover." Suddenly Christy grew angry.

"Why are you calling me?" she demanded. Her words were bitter, accusing. Not unlike how I envisioned I would respond to such news. "Why are you doing this? I spent years in and out of a psychiatric hospital trying to deal with my childhood. Now, I finally have a family, a wonderful family with a great man I love very much. I don't need you to tell me this. I don't believe you!"

Her anger stunned me. In as much as I'd had high hopes, I understood. Something intangible existed between us I knew. Whether we ever saw each other face-to-face again, it would always exist. It was our pedigree. The old cliché haunting us, that blood is thicker. Now what have I done? It was easy to blame myself. And I did, fearing my contact might send her back into therapy.

"It's okay, Christy," I said. "I won't bother you anymore. I just think it's important to know where we came from, that it's important to know the truth. I understand where you're coming from. But if, someday, you ever want to find out for yourself if I was telling the truth, call Mrs. Thurber and ask for you mother's records."

With that, I gave Christy my Denver number and hung up. Well, that's it, I thought, I'll never hear from her again. This was all a mistake.

Tears appeared out of nowhere. I let myself feel the emotions. The sadness, the disappointment, the void. Why God? I needed to understand.

It was only one week later, while I was lounging in my Denver apartment, that the telephone rang.

"It's Christy," said the voice being recorded. I picked up the receiver.

"Hello?"

"What you said, it's true isn't it?" she asked. Her voice was shaky, uncertain.

"Yes," I answered.

We talked that night for several hours. I was stunned to learn that she'd already heard the truth from her mother with whom she'd had no contact since early childhood. More broken lives, I thought.

"She's a sick woman. She mentioned artificial insemination, but I didn't want to hear it," she admitted.

"That's understandable. I didn't want to believe it at first either," I owned up to my own struggles.

The complex's night yard lights kicked on, giving the grounds a weird yellow glow. It made me realize how long we'd been talking. It was wonderful to be talking, sharing with her. To belong.

We hung up with the promise to talk again soon, perhaps even meet. I set the receiver down, feeling better than at any time since my quest began. We really seemed to connect, even if the memories shared dredged up old wounds that were hard to deal with. There was solace in knowing I wasn't dealing with them alone anymore.

"Maybe there really is something to genetic connection," I told Michelle just as she walked in the door, home from work. She gave me a quick kiss before wandering off to the kitchen. I knew that look, she was famished. The light from the open refrigerator door framed her inquisitive face. She grabbed a yogurt and fetched a spoon from the drawer.

"How do you mean?" she asked settling next to me. She scooped out a spoon.

I paraphrased my earlier conversation with Christy.

"I feel something different."

"What?" she asked putting a spoonful in her mouth. She sucked on the spoon, contemplating.

"I'm not sure I can explain it," I professed. "At home, peace?" I threw the words out. We exchanged looks. I saw in her eyes a deep understanding. She got it.

A month later, I heard from Christy again. She was flying from California back to Kansas and had a stopover at Denver. Casually she'd asked, did I want to meet."

"God yes!" I exclaimed. I arrived at the airport an hour early. Watching the sea of people arriving and departing reminded me momentarily of standing in the airport with my mother while waiting to claim Lisa. I wondered if I'd recognize her, if she'd recognize me.

Just then she was there. Her blue eyes staring at mine. We both smiled. I gave her a big hug. It felt as if I'd never been separated from her. We went to the coffee shop on the corner.

Once again the words just flowed. This time Christy wanted to dwell more on the future—hopes for her kids and her husband and how she seemed to finally be putting her life together. We parted that afternoon as friends.

But as time passed, Christy's husband began to question whether contact with me was a good thing. He questioned her. Who was this Scott fellow? Why was he uncovering all these things from her past that she'd hoped to put behind her? According to him, it was better if certain things remained buried, meaning me and our connection. His arrogance made me incensed. How could he possibly understand our struggle? What we'd already gone through. What could any typical person understand coming from a traditional family? Bitterness and resentment burned within my being.

Eventually Christy told me the words I dreaded, and I was devastated. How could I let go now? Now that I had a genetic family? Had so valiantly fought the odds to find? Before I could answer Christy's letter came.

Dear Scott:

To be perfectly honest, I have strong mixed emotions and thoughts concerning how you found me and the possibility of having a half-brother.

If we do share the same father, in reality we are strangers and do not share the brother/sister relationship any normal family would or for that matter what I share with my sister. Regardless of what information you may have, we can never nor should you expect, these developments to lead to any type of true brother/sister relationship.

I grew up and was raised always knowing the people raising me were not my true parents. I was told my parents were not responsible enough to take care of my sister and I. I went through a period of searching and trying to discover my roots, so to speak, a few years after I graduated from high school.

After finding my mother and learning from her that it was possible I was an off-spring of artificial insemination, I dropped the matter and resolved to myself that the past is the past. I turned my attention to the present, letting the future bring whatever. It was after putting it behind me, that I met and married my husband. We have built the kind of life I had always dreamed of. A nice little house, three beautiful children and the warmest relationship anyone could have with their in-laws.

I can appreciate what you have gone through and what you had to do to come to terms with it, but I feel my privacy has been invaded. I am not prepared to adopt a new brother. I thank you for filling in the gaps of how it is I possibly came about.

I'm most grateful that the person you claim is our genetic father is of a sound medical background and has no major medical history problems. This has always been my main concern with not knowing my own medical history, especially for my children. Aside from this, I do not feel there is anything further I wish to know about my past and I would appreciate it if you would not continue pursuing this further as far as I am concerned.

I wish you the very best life has to offer.

Christy.

I could hardly read the last line because of the tears. It couldn't have hurt more if she'd shot me. It was as if someone was closing the book on my life. There would not be a large family with a shred of historic past. No blood nieces. No blood nephews. No sister. Nothing. I was a pariah, ostracized again.

All I'd managed to do was frighten her off because of my damned obsession. That closing line had sounded an awful lot like the closing line from Kroenberg's lawyer. So final.

Months passed slowly. Then one rainy night as I listened to the steady drumming against the apartment roof, I started missing my family, feeling that hole in my heart. It compelled me to call Christy. I wanted to apologize and promise her that the matter was closed, but much to my chagrin I discovered she and her family had moved, leaving no forwarding address.

For the rest of the evening I neatly filed away the notes I'd made from my conversations with her along with those of my other half-sisters. I had been abandoned again.

22

Abandoned Again

After Christy's letter, I could feel myself withdrawing. It was a fight not to become more and more distant with Michelle. Each day I feared digression and the toll it was taking on my hard-earned progress.

For all of that, I was functioning as if my body had a control for autopilot, as though someone or something else was controlling my body and speech, while in my heart I curled away from the feelings of abandonment. Work wise I was covered, I had my sales spiel down pat and could say it in my sleep. For once I was thankful for my arrogance, that I had trained others to be equally competitive which allowed me to make a lot of money off their commissions. A nice car. A nice apartment. Cushions to assuage my wounded heart.

Work became my new narcotic. Often I stayed up nights until three a.m. working on new sales schemes, existing on four hours of sleep. As long as I kept working, I wouldn't have to face just how miserable I felt.

Whenever thoughts of my genetic father and sisters arose, I would bitterly push them down along with my feelings, telling myself I didn't need that family crap anyway. It's nothing but fights and heartache.

The temptation to push Michelle away and revert to using, was magnanimous. Each day brought me to my knees. I pleaded with God over and over for strength, courage and conviction. But I could feel my world crumbling, and it terrified me to realize that all I'd fought for could be shattered so quickly, as if nothing had ever changed.

Anger brought me back to the library. It was time to do more research. Redirect my rage, put it to work helping me. Candace had planted a seed, a seed called eugenics. At the time it seemed too far-fetched, but now I wasn't sure. I needed to know for my own sense of well being how much was truth and how much was exaggerated or false.

Casually I opened the dictionary. There it was, Eugenics: the movement devoted to improving the human species through the control of hereditary factors in mating.

Immediately I reacted, slamming the dictionary shut. So what? The word existed. That didn't mean Candace was telling the truth about all that other stuff, like the Nazis and sterilization programs. It was preposterous! I stormed out of the library with a nagging feeling. If I was so sure she was wrong, why was I so afraid to look? Why was I so afraid to face it? What could be so cryptic?

Not knowing only fueled the anger inside me. Anger I often vented on Michelle by saying mean, hurtful things deliberately designed to make her cry. The intrinsic war raging within was making my daily life a burden to endure. I knew my thinking was out of sorts, but I couldn't seem to calm the raging seas within my soul.

Then one Sunday morning, quite by happenstance while idly reading the classified section for property sales, an ad caught my attention. I had no idea why. I mean, it wasn't as if I were really considered buying any. But that ad stayed me. It was for mountain property near the high-plains town of Fairplay.

Affordable, it read. "Two bedrooms, 40 acres, well, septic, $26,000," and best of all "owner will carry."

Instinctively I called. Within an hour I found myself driving to the mountains. It was owned by an older couple in their sixties, the Kellies. They met me in Fairplay to lead me to the land.

"It's our mountain getaway," Mrs. Kelly confided. "It was God's gift to us, but my husband's having a harder time these days with the altitude and all."

They were a wonderful couple. Both were gray and fragile, and yet they each maintained an internal sparkle. They possessed a peace with themselves. It made me a tad bit envious. Their relationship was a model of marriage. They'd been together for nearly fifty years. And here I was, some bum that couldn't make it past a few.

Soon I saw why they spoke of the land with such love. It was forty acres of high-plains prairie nestled up against the mountains. Every direction provided a beautiful view; grasslands, forest, mountains. Hawks soared above the rippling grass and birds sang in the sagebrush. It was majestic.

It turned out that Mr. Kelly was a preacher. Whenever they were staying at the property, he gave guest sermons at the little church in Fairplay.

"I feel closer to God here than anywhere," he told me as we drove up to the house. Was this why I'd been drawn to that ad? Was God talking to me? Taking charge of my shambled life? I prayed it was true.

Easily I could visualize myself putting up fence, chopping wood, or enjoying a cold beer on the front porch. There was such a peacefulness there. I fancied myself sitting on that porch reading the Bible as white, pillowy, clouds drifted across the blue expanse. Where had that thought come from? Then, I knew it was my mother's words ringing through me, it was my chance to get closer to God, a chance to put my life in order and diffuse the anger inside.

"I want it." I said without even seeing the interior of the house.

For the next few weeks, I went up every Sunday to hear Mr. Kelly preach in Fairplay followed by trips to look over the property. By April we'd closed the deal. Unlike so many things I'd done throughout my life, buying the land felt right.

The house was simple, devoid of electricity and running water. Its only heat source was a well-preserved cast iron wood stove. Furnishings were as modest as the amenities; a bed and couch. But that first day of ownership, as I sat on the porch and watched deer browse near a stand of Aspen trees, I felt it again; this was God's country and probably as close to heaven as I'd ever get. The thought of Harry came to mind. If there was a heaven, I had no doubt his sweet soul would be found there. Thinking of him resurfaced old pain. I missed him.

In the weeks ahead I discovered it was possible to run most of my business from the property. I spent nearly all of my time at the property. I found the trips to Denver, which were only ninety miles, cumbersome now. It felt strange. I had been accustomed to traveling a lot; now all I wanted was the rustic hearth. Michelle made an effort to engage me, but her visits were merely me going through the motions of a relationship. I waited for my time alone.

As I chopped wood for the stove and cleaned up the property, I began to notice my muscles were growing harder, my resolve stronger. There was an added bonus of living at nearly 10,000 feet in altitude: it made it nearly impossible to smoke pot. God was keeping me on the straight and narrow. Even my mind began to clear. Amazingly enough, I found I enjoyed the sensation of going for weeks without so much as a beer. Clean living appealed to me more than I had ever imagined.

Summer passed quickly and soon the nights began to grow colder. Mornings I could see my breath well after sunup. Evening frost kept the ground hard and brittle all day. Each step I took my feet would crunch under me. Soon I realized I would have to spend more time in Denver whether I wanted to or not.

I was aware that winter in the high country was bound to make my property inaccessible some of the time; and living without electricity or running water was too difficult to endure for very long. Sensing it might be some time before I could return, I decided to do something to acknowledge the peace and personal growth I'd achieved living there.

When I'd initially moved to the property, my collection of pornography had accompanied me. Not just the magazines and videos, but also the photographs of former girlfriends I had persuaded to pose provocatively in the nude.

On a September night with the air crisp and cold as crystal, I carried it all outside to a bonfire. Millions of stars twinkled overhead in the clear night sky. For a lingering moment I looked at the pile of photographs and films.

"You are not part of my life anymore," I said aloud. Then one by one I fed them to the fire. Sparks rose, flickering like tiny red stars until they blinked and went out.

Finally, it was all gone, and with it an intrinsic burden lifted. Still, I did not leave but stood watching the pulsating embers of fire glowing red, then orange, before turning black. When alas I returned to the house, I looked at the bare shelves where my magazine and film collections once stood. I took my bible, carefully I placed it facing outward. Now I could sleep.

23

Stark Facts

In 1993, I started looking for another project. Once again I was feeling restless and needed my work to be a reflection of my evolution. I settled for offering environmental services. It seemed like a good fit for how I was feeling at that time in my life. Thus I went into business with a guy by the name of Clint Hanson. Hanson was an easy-going, wiry little guy with midnight, curly hair. Dark-rimmed glasses hid most of his inquisitive brown eyes. To look at him, he seemed to be of some Asian descent.

Our business was mostly comprised of collecting aluminum cans and glass. We talked about honesty and integrity being integral for customers and each other. Almost as an afterthought, I mentioned my love for reading the Bible and my goal to live as a Christian. Surprisingly I felt at ease explaining to Clint why it was so important to me to be an active Christian, rather than just providing lip service.

"I'm a born-again Christian myself." Clint confessed after I'd revealed my philosophy. "Why don't we pray together and get this thing off to a good start. Those words made me feel closer to him than I'd felt to most of the friends I'd had as a youth.

Unlike them, Clint was not interested in what I could provide for him, the next score, the next party, the next lover. He cared about God, our world, life and me. A huge contrast to what I'd grown accustomed to. The change was refreshing.

Immediately I liked the idea. I'd been talking a lot more to God, becoming more and more convinced that I would be forgiven for my past. John 3:16 in particular comforted me. The passage came to mind, For God so loved the world that He gave His only begotten son, that whosoever believes in Him, should not perish but having everlasting life. It was perfect.

Fall came to the high country in the form of a pleasant Indian summer that year. The forest trees were ablaze with fire engine reds, pear yellows and russet browns intertwined with the deep, lush green of dense lumbering pine trees. Alas, I felt like my life was coming together.

Good things were definitely happening. My new business showed promise. I was reading God's word more and more and applying it to my daily life. Only on rare occasion did I take any pills anymore, even though there was nothing in the Bible prohibiting it. Still, I only allowed myself to have something when I felt like I really needed it. There was nothing recreational about it.

Being amongst the expansive mountains and thin air, I could feel my anger dissipating like a summer rainstorm. But at the same time, it was replaced by questions. Why? I spoke to the night stars: would a loving God have allowed what happened to my father?

He was, in my estimation, a good and decent man if ever there was one. How could this country, a country Harry Davis loved so profoundly, have allowed such things as sterilization programs?

Finally one evening as I admired the sunset beyond the mountains in a glorious display of reds, pinks and oranges blending, I recalled a conversation with Candace Turner and my brief encounter with the world of eugenics at the library. Back then I'd been too disturbed, frightened and weary to look any further. Now I needed to know the truth.

Now I knew it couldn't be avoided any longer. Already ten years had passed since that fateful day when I'd learned the truth about Harry, and four years since contact with my genetic father had been brushed.

There were still times when I found myself suddenly wondering about Kroenberg. What did he look like? What had he done with his life? Where had he and his people come from? Sometimes I even permitted myself to fantasize Kroenberg had miraculously relented and asked to meet me.

It wouldn't be too much, just to pass on information, acknowledge that I was a part of his heritage. Such thoughts would often end with me getting into a huff that Kroenberg would die before the fantasy could come true. At such times, it was hard not to sink into that murky world of depression. Sometimes deliberately

I'd hurt myself by believing a hundred years could pass and such a thing would not happen.

I just couldn't understand all the secrecy. What was everyone afraid of?? Then it came to me, that curious little word. Eugenics.

Almost as though some invisible forced was propelling me, I found myself entering the doors of the Denver Public Library. This time I was looking for more than a dictionary definition; I wanted everything I could find on the subject.

The first book I happened upon was already thirty years old. The Human Heredity Handbook by Amram Scheinfeld published in 1956. It reflected the disfavor into which eugenics had fallen following the demise of the Nazi terror in Europe.

The more I read, the more I became astounded. Candace had been right, there was a connection. Then he came across a section on the use of sterilization in population control. There it was.

If someone had slapped me, it couldn't have hurt more. I stared down at the words describing my life, my world. It was incredible.

"This is the most extreme method of birth control," Scheinfeld had written. "Such operations are legally authorized in twenty seven American states and in some European countries, mainly Scandinavian, in cases of individuals who are mentally defective or insane and are likely to produce mentally defective offspring.

"Sterilizations also are authorized in a number of other cases involving serious hereditary defects and in some states, chiefly California and Indiana, for habitual criminals, habitual sexual offenders and degenerates. (The latter sterilizations are chiefly for social reasons, since there is no proof that such persons are products of defective heredity)."

Scheinfeld noted that from 1907, when the first American sterilization law went into effect in Indiana, until January 1955, some 57,218 legal eugenic sterilizations were performed in the United States. "Of these, about half were for mental deficiency, 44 percent for insanity and the rest for other cases."

I gasped; 57,000 sterilizations up to 1955! How many more had there been since? The term "mental deficiency" stayed with me. That was the scarlet letter used to dismiss my father's rights, despite the fact that he clearly wasn't retarded, something Beatrice hadn't even bothered to explore. Their only concern was maintaining some misguided notion of a perfect society.

Just revisiting the facts in my mind made my face blister with outrage all over again. What gave them the right to play God?

Time and again I returned to the library, looking for new material. Eventually I found the book The Surgical Solution, by Philip R. Reilly, an attorney and physician-geneticist.

Reilly wrote that the practice of involuntary sterilizations ground to a halt in the 1960's. Still, it had gone on long after the "science" of eugenics had been discredited by Hitler's excesses. But it had flourished in the period between the world wars.

"A small number of eugenicists capitalized effectively on the national concern over the dramatic postwar influx of immigrants from Southern and Eastern Europe and growing uneasiness about the northern migration of American blacks. The resurgence of sterilization programs was closely tied to the popular demand to limit immigration. It is no accident that a second wave of state sterilization laws, targeted at a different threat to "race," were enacted at the same time."

It was during this time, Reilly noted, that Adolph Hitler was writing Mein Kampf in a German prison and was quite taken with eugenics, which were mostly espoused by American and British proponents. I found the timing curious. Each paragraph was more grotesque than the proceeding. It appalled me to consider Hitler had contrived some of his worst atrocities from ideas spawned in America.

Old suspicions of my country and government came charging back. No wonder I'd been a rebel. It made my goals and feelings seem noble now.

I pressed on, reading more of the material that turned my stomach. "To prevent defective persons from reproducing equally defective offspring, is an act dictated by the clearest light of reason," Hitler had written. "It's carrying out is the most humane act of mankind. It would prevent the unmerited suffering of millions of persons and, above all would, in the end, result in a steady increase in human welfare."

I snorted. It was incredulous to me that society had ever bought into such propaganda. Since when had Hitler been worried about the suffering of millions and or increase in human welfare? Everyone knew where Hitler's compassion had led. But what shocked me more was that Hitler had only taken American ideas one step farther.

Even U.S. Supreme Court Justice Oliver Wendell Holmes, a supposed champion of the little guy, wrote in a 1927 upholding Virginia's involuntary sterilization law: "It is better for all the world if, instead of waiting to execute degenerate offspring for crime or to let them starve for their imbecility, society can prevent those who are manifestly unfit from continuing their kind."

"Yeah, like my father," I muttered under my breath. "But you were wrong, he was a great man!" I said aloud. It was puzzling to me how people could believe such garbage, despite the fact that scientific research showed that sterilization had little affect on the rates of mental retardation, crime, poverty or any of the other traits eugenicists hoped to stamp out. But was anyone listening?

Reilly pointed out that various organizations such as the American Eugenics Society and the Human Betterment Foundation, which had appeared to champion the cause of sterilization and eugenics. Battle lines were drawn between those who argued for more money to help the disadvantaged and disabled to those who protested, claiming such money would be better utilized by spending it on the gifted.

It seems eugenics was so popular in the years between the world wars that country fairs, particularly in the Midwest, held the so-called "fitter family" and "better baby" contests where judges conferred over human pedigrees to determine the most eugenically positive families. Just like the best cattle, chickens and pigs, the winners were awarded blue ribbons.

The statistics made me bitter. Contemptuously I wish the founders could have been forced into participating in human breeding barns. It would serve them right, I thought. I forced myself to read on.

In the years shortly before World War II, the eugenicist movement split into two branches: those who advocated "negative" eugenics involving sterilizations and abortions for the poor; and those who, more conscious of public relations perhaps, advocated "positive" eugenics. These people believed in such things as programs to convince minorities and so-tagged defective segments of society to stop having babies through birth control and abortion, while contrarily encouraging educated whites to have more children and educating them on the need for popular mate selection.

Hitler's excesses had made the movement change its rhetoric. No longer could they talk about creating a superior race of humans without conjuring images of Dachau and gas chambers. But the post-war influx of immigrants and the increasing immigration of blacks to northern cities made many whites susceptible to the more positive aspects.

Reilly concluded that despite setbacks, the concept of eugenics, in particular sterilization programs, remained "surprisingly strong" into the modern era. He offered, as proof, legislation to force welfare mothers to accept sterilization in exchange for food stamps and efforts to sterilize prison inmates in exchange for reduced sentences. What a humane society indeed!

As I read the words my thoughts became a blur. It felt like something I should have been reading from a science fiction novel. Old anger returned. Even pills didn't help. Who were these people, these eugenicists?

Had the United States gone crazy? Had states like Kansas been secretly pursuing eugenics policies when they sterilized my father in exchange for his freedom? It all made sense.

After all, weren't sperm donors selected for their superior genes, the children of doctors, intellectuals, college professors? Hadn't I come out blond and blue-eyed, the perfect prototype for what Hitler had envisioned? It made me feel as if I were part of the plot. Suddenly I felt dirty, as if an indelible blueprint had been stamped on my soul. It was scary to realize I was an indirect product of that distorted world.

I reacted by trying to get the word out. Instinctively I began calling radio shows whenever there were discussions even remotely connected to eugenics. Debates about abortion; about a prisoner sterilization bill in the Colorado legislature; about Planned Parenthood, they were all fair game.

In my research, I had discovered a small book titled, Margaret Sanger: Father of Modern Society by Elasah Drogin. The book described Sanger's life as a political activist, first as a champion of the poor but later then later flip-flopping to describe the poor and uneducated as "human weeds."

In 1942, stung by her earlier association with German eugenicists, Sanger changed the name of her organizations which advocated sterilization programs, abortion, and birth control for the poor from the American Birth Control League and Human Betterment Foundation to Planned Parenthood International.

How appropriate, I thought. The Planned Parenthood of the Rockies agency just a few blocks from my Denver apartment was the offspring of the eugenicist movement. No wonder Planned Parenthood put its clinics offering abortion and birth control in poor, minority neighborhoods. Politicians claimed it was for better access for people without transportation; but suddenly all I could see was how the agency was still championing the ideals of Hitler and Sanger more than fifty years after the Holocaust.

Payment for our arrogance, I told myself. Thought you could play God, didn't you? I heard myself mutter.

All at once it came to me. My role, my purpose, the reason for all my tribulations. I was to be the messenger. And I knew exactly what I was going to say.

24

The Promise Keepers

The more time passed, the more I became convinced that the eugenics movement permeated modern society. Artificial insemination. Eutelegenesis, the supposedly benign effort to increase the intelligence of the species through calculated gene selection. Abortion for the asking. Surrogate parenting. As far as I was concerned, it was another part of a huge conspiracy. It was a subtle and sometimes not so subtle form of manipulation.

Some kinds of people are better than others just because of the luck of their birth? Who had decided that? Maybe the same group that had decided that my father, because he wasn't a genius, or rich, or well-educated, shouldn't have children.

If my voice was one in the wilderness before, I was on a crusade now. I decided it was imperative that any chance I got to tell my story and about my discovery I should just go for it. Reporters and television producers were eager to meet with me, whenever they called I always began with the same question. "Ever hear of eugenics?" Of course very few had, to which I was only too happy to enlighten them.

Eventually my research led me back to Kansas City. During one of my visits I returned to the public library. I studied the history of the Beatrice state home where my father had been sterilized.

Beatrice seemed disconcerted about openly and unabashedly heralding their sterilization program of the Fifties. In fact, it was easy to find old clips about the Human Betterment League of Kansas welcoming Dr. Clarence Gamble. It was horrific to read how the founder of baby products giant Proctor and Gamble had been a chief pioneer in the human genetics field. There was Gamble, praising Kansas' efforts regarding the inmates of its institutions like Beatrice, where more than 753 people had been sterilized between 1918 and 1965 before the sterilization program was abolished. I wondered if there were others that hadn't been recorded. How could I really ever know?

Proctor and Gamble? Oh my God; it sent my thoughts reeling. What other diabolical horrors lie behind door number two? I knew that every few years the company had to deal with recycled rumors that its famous "man in the moon" logo was associated with devil worship, but this was a much greater evil and it was real. Yet at the time, no one seemed to care, as if it had all been forgotten. Well, I didn't want them to forget. The public had a right to know what grotesque practices had gone on unmonitored and unchallenged. And worse, what the impact of such nightmarish deeds had on its hapless victims.

Pensively I visited the institution. It was like stepping into a Vincent Price stage. Most of the buildings had an eerie and gothic feel to them. All they could tell me (or would, I wasn't sure which) was the year my father had been discharged.

Casually I wandered about the campus, studying the old brick buildings. Some looked like pretty homes, nearly normal, but it was the ones that smacked too much of a prison, complete with bars across the windows, that got me. History had it that the institution had shrunk dramatically over the years. Its citizens no longer were required to work the fields or dairy herds.

Its inhabitants seemed to be comprised only of the mentally retarded and mentally ill who were most disadvantaged and didn't fit into the modern concept of community-based programs. Watching shuffling lines of the severely retarded ambling between buildings equated my thoughts to prison once again. Just as easily, I could see a row of inmates on a chain gang.

It was with some relief I recognized that the institution had become a champion of the rights of its inmates. While it didn't erase the anger for their past record, especially what they'd done to my dad and my family, it did help. Maybe, alas, somebody in charge had finally understood how inhumane their former practices had been. After all, weren't we all God's creatures?

My ongoing crusade landed me on radio and television shows such as Geraldo, Hardcopy, NOW and NBC News. My efforts as a spokesman were duly recognized by my colleagues of Donor Offspring, who opted to elect me president year after year.

One morning, I was sitting at the table drinking a cup of coffee when a headline caught my attention. I dropped my cup.

"Oh my God," I cried so loudly that Michelle rushed from the next room to see what had happened. She peered at me with a worried look. I stood frozen in the middle of my dining room glued to an article I found incredulous. The premise of the story revealed how the U.S. government had conducted experiments on the mentally ill in the Fifties, like exposing them to radiation. It was the stuff of bad science fiction books, only this was real. Tears filled my eyes. It was totally unbelievable. As if all my worst fears about the government had suddenly been proven to be true. How did they get away with such atrocities?

Completely outraged I immediately wrote to Beatrice demanding to know if my father had been a part of some experiment sanctioned by the government. Could that be why my father was so deathly afraid of people in uniforms and clinic coats? And why he refused to even go to a dentist? It certainly would make sense.

Further investigation threatened to destroy the peace of mind I had found in the mountains. Everywhere I looked, the world seemed to be full of lies and deception. No wonder kids no longer seemed to have any morals, I thought. Looking at what they had for role models explained volumes.

Politicians who lied. Couples who cheated on each other. Rap musicians glorifying violence, rape and hatred. An entertainment industry that saturated in vice and guns. It was hard not to feel self-righteous.

The only question left was why weren't more people making the same connections I had? How could they be so blind? Of course, I reminded myself, I was coming at this from a personal viewpoint, about as close as a guinea pig to the scientist.

It disturbed me immeasurably that some of the people I talked to even argued that maybe eugenics wasn't all bad! Maybe criminals shouldn't have children. Maybe welfare mothers should be held accountable for their little mistakes. The fact that we needed social change was a given, but endorsing eugenics? Could they be serious? It would be like voluntarily choosing Hitler for leadership.

But it doesn't stop there, I'd argue. Before presenting Hitler and what he'd done with it. For that matter, what it had done in my own case. I had felt the effects but, not knowing what caused it, turned to drugs. It had inhibited my ability to trust people, especially those who loved me. Starting with my genetic father's rejection. Onto my "Dad" Harry, and my complete inability to connect with him. Even my mother had been unable to fully love a man who couldn't give her children through the act of love. It was obvious she harbored anxiety about the reality of her situation, but my dad had just been another victim. Beyond being sympathetic, what could he do?

I was becoming obsessed. Most days it was all I could do to keep the business running, while I actively rallied against the government. Feeling the need to withdraw, I retreated to my mountain home frantically hoping to find God again in the breeze and the sunsets. But anger blocked me by encompassing me like a shell. Little did I know that I soon would be distracted from such thoughts.

One afternoon, I drove down from the mountains to my business partner's office. Increasingly my partner had been slow getting the commission checks out to me. I needed the money to make mortgage payments on the mountain home and cover payroll checks I'd already issued to my sales crew so I couldn't afford to wait on him.

I'd had it in mind just to drop in to pick up my check. Actually I was in a bit of a hurry because I wanted to go with a friend to a new Christian program for men. It was called Promise Keepers, an organization formed by the University of Colorado's football coach Bill McCartney.

I was more than aware that anger was destroying me. Besides, I liked the sound of Promise Keepers' stated purpose of Christian men taking responsibility for their actions. Responsibility to live God's word as an example to other men.

But when I walked into my partner's office and asked for my check, Clint just shrugged. "I don't have it," he said.

"What do you mean you don't have it?" I barked back feeling panic beginning to rise in my throat. "I have to have the money. I already wrote checks to pay my guys."

"That's your problem," Clint said.

For a moment I just stood dumbfounded. This was the same guy who only a few months before had gotten down on his knees to pray for our new partnership. A "born-again" Christian. Now he sat there with a half-smirk on his face. He's scammed me.

It was too much. I felt tears of anger coming to my eyes and didn't want to give Clint the satisfaction. Instead I swallowed hard and jerked Clint to his feet by his lapels. That got his attention. Suddenly he wasn't smiling. Instead genuine fear shone in his eyes.

"You son-of-a-bitch! I need that money! Where is it? What have you done with it?" I growled at him caught between urges to strangle or throttle him.

"I spent it. The commissions have been down and I just spent it," he squealed. For a moment I remained. My face pressed against his. I could smell his fear. The adrenaline and rage were scaring what piece of my rational mind I had left. It would be so easy to really hurt him. Suddenly I pushed him away, throwing him hard against his swivel chair. Just from the force he nearly fell off the chair. Then I ran out.

In the car, my hands shook as I popped a couple of pills. I couldn't deal with Clint, not then. I knew if I faced him again, more than likely there would be trouble. I sped off to pick up a friend to drive to Boulder's Promise Keepers meeting in the university football stadium. I desperately needed that meeting now. I needed something to make sense out of the confusion in my world.

The gray skies didn't help my mood as I drove. I'll probably lose the ranch and get sued by my crew, I thought. Fear embraced me. All those checks were going to bounce. All those men with families that were counting on that paycheck and all Clint could do was arrogantly smirk? It was incomprehensible to me. How could he be so myopic? So cold?

By the time I reached Tyler's house I wasn't sure I felt like going. After all, I'd just been screwed by a supposed Christian. The last thing I wanted was to hear a few thousand brag about being responsible men of faith. But Tyler didn't have a car and I knew if I didn't go he couldn't. So I went with the thought that at least I would keep my promise. Just because Clint was a backstabbing s.o.b., didn't excuse me.

Together we barreled up the interstate between Denver and Boulder. Dodging between cars as if they were standing still, I drove like a man possessed.

In route it began to rain. Suddenly lightning flashed. Thunder boomed. The weather seemed to be trying to match my mood. I yelled and cursed other drivers, flipping off anyone who got in my way, oblivious to Tyler's presence beside me.

"Hey, Scott, cool off, it'll be okay," I heard the terror in his voice. He had a Promise Keepers tape and put it into my car stereo hoping the message of God's love would calm the situation. Instead, I reacted by ripping the tape from the deck.

"Lies! Lies! Lies! Just shut the fuck up," I spat. "Sit there and let me work this out."

Tyler fell silent. I continued my wild trek toward Boulder. I truly felt possessed, as if all the demons I used to imagine sitting on the doorstep of my mind had found a way in. Lies. Deceit. They were all there, along with the eugenicists and my business partner.

Miraculously we reached Boulder safely only to find that there were no parking spaces within a twelve-block radius around the stadium. Promise Keepers officials had said they expected 50,000 men to attend. It was hard to believe.

I drove around in the pouring rain cursing. Nothing was going right.

"I'm not going," I told Tyler. "I'll let you out near the stadium, if you can find a ride back to Denver." Tyler got out quickly, thankful to be alive.

"Hey, Scott," he said kindly, "I can always go to tomorrow's. If it's not right for you today, let's just go back," he offered. His thoughtfulness moved me. I knew I'd just been an ass. I'd endangered both our lives because I was angry.

The CU stadium loomed ahead. I nodded. Then suddenly, a block away from the main entrance, there was a parking spot. Other cars drove right by it. Somehow the other drivers hadn't seen it.

Skillfully I maneuvered my car into the spot. It was such a relief for something to go my way after such a poor start. I took it as a sign for an impending change. Maybe it was meant to be, that I was supposed to go to Promise Keepers, after all. I gave myself a moment as I rested my head on the steering wheel, gathering my thoughts. Tyler reached over to pat my shoulder. "It really is going to be all right," he said.

I raised my head. Something was different, and I knew what it was. The rain had stopped. All around him, on the sidewalks, striding down the street, in groups or pairs or walking by themselves were men headed for the stadium.

Slowly we got out of the car. Steam was rising from the streets as the sun broke through the clouds. Everything seemed so fresh and new; the colors brighter, the air cleansed, a rebirth.

I took a deep breath and exhaled slowly, letting the stress evaporate with the rain. "Let's go in," I said. Tyler sensed the difference, he smiled and nodded.

Inside the stadium, I saw only men. Someone was already at the podium leading a prayer. As the evening wore on, there were more speakers all saying the same thing. They talked about family values and living a life according to Christian virtues. No more talking about it, they said, the world needed them to just do it. No more excuses.

For the first time I really looked around. Everywhere guys were crying, or hugging, or on their knees praying. Hesitantly at first, I began praying, asking to find peace. Soon I was overcome by the sound of 50,000 men singing Amazing Grace. As the words and voices resounded around me I could feel myself being humbled. God had brought me here to heal me.

Amazing Grace, how sweet the sound, that saved a wretch like me. I once was lost but now I'm found, was blind but now I see.

Before I realized it, I was singing too and felt that at last I was finally able to see. The next day, I returned to the stadium to relive the emotion. It was a hot day; temperatures on the field reached into the 90s.

Call it the heat. Call it delirium. But in the midst of praying, I heard a voice. It wasn't like a voice in the wilderness. It came from within, or maybe it was just my heart, but the voice spoke directly to me.

"Don't worry about who your earthly father is," the voice said. "I'm your father. You haven't always noticed, but I've always been with you and will be with you forever.

"Just follow me. Have faith in me. Give your anxieties and your fears to me." In that moment, I willingly surrendered to God. Never again would I ask God for things in exchange for promises. From henceforth I would be a promise keeper. And like a mountain climber finally taking off his heavy pack, it felt as though some great weight had been lifted from my shoulders.

That evening, I returned to my modest Denver apartment. Michelle was out and I was grateful. How could I explain what was happening. I was afraid she wouldn't understand.

I had decided that it was time to truly give myself to God. It seemed like I'd tried just about everything else, but none of it worked. Not the pills. Not the pot. Not my crusading on behalf of my father.

I went to the bathroom and opened the medicine cabinet. There stood row after row of pill bottles in colors from blue to pink. There was something for every occasion. Happy pills, calming pills, sleeping pills, and more pills to keep me awake.

Carefully I gathered all the bottles and emptied them into the toilet bowl. For a moment I stood there looking at the rainbow collection that had governed the ups and downs of my life for so many years. Then with all the flourish of a burial at sea, one by one, I poured the contents of each bottle into the toilet and flushed. My grand finale.

I watched them being swished away, knowing there would be fallout. I had been warned by more than one physician that if I ever stopped taking the pills, I should do so over the course of several weeks, weaning myself gradually.

It struck me suddenly that I'd been addicted to the pills for more than half my life. There was no more time to waste.

True to form, the withdrawals proved to be pure agony both physically and psychologically. If I wasn't puking, I had cramps from the harsh diarrhea. As if that wasn't enough, I experienced anxiety attacks. My throat would tighten and I'd wind up fighting to breath. My whole body ached as though I was caught in the throes of a three-week flu. My stomach twisted like a wet towel. Making matters worse, my skin crawled. Invisible minuscule lizards plagued me beneath the surface of my skin, trying to wiggle free.

In the worst moments, I turned to the Bible, hoping beyond hope for a calm amongst the raging seas of my being; but in response sweat dripped from my brows onto the pages.

"And God so loved the world..." I desperately whispered. My brain screaming in torment, it compelled me to scream aloud. "...that He gave His only begotten son..."

I begged God to ease the pain. "...that whosoever believed in him..." I begged for the suffering to end. "...should not perish..." Ever so slowly the torment subsided I gave a heart felt thanks. "...but have everlasting life."

It took nearly a week, but finally it was over. For the first time in what seemed like forever, I could see clearly. I had to leave Denver. The air was dirty, the streets haunted by drive-by shootings and drug dealers. I told myself I needed a place to recover and rediscover my relationship with God. Denver held too many bad associations, too many temptations. There were too many demons on my doorstep at the foot of the Rocky Mountains.

I put the mountain property up for sale. It was an easy sale. The very first guy who saw it fell in love and bought it. It was good to see the same feeling in another man's eyes that I'd felt. Still, it was hard. The land had represented the first real steps I'd taken toward salvation. It was there that I'd destroyed the pornography in a ceremonial fire. It was there I'd felt the real presence of God and heard a voice urging for change, before it was too late.

But now it was time to move on. Other changes needed to be made. Sadly, I knew one of those changes was with Michelle. I found myself watching her sleep at night. I knew without a doubt that I loved her. She knew me better than almost anyone, except perhaps my mother. It was indisputable she had been there through the frustrations, the highs and lows of finding out who my genetic father was, and throughout my many ill-fated attempts to find my sisters. But she was uncomfortable with Christianity. She thrived on the lifestyle of the city and smoked pot like a chimney. I smoked too, but only regular cigarettes now.

Now that it was clear in my mind that I needed to leave, I needed to decide where and when. I thought of going home to Kansas. The timing seemed right. I knew my mother was feeling poorly. Her years of chain smoking had finally caught up to her and she was battling emphysema, fighting for every breath. She needed me.

Yes, I would go home; come full circle. Like a snake shedding its skin against rocks and branches, I would rub up against my past, face my fears, my many mistakes and emerge a new man. But first I would start by finishing what I had started with my first contact with old Dr. Thurber. I needed to find my biological father.

25

Meeting Kroenberg

Driving has a way of being a formidable opponent, especially when you are tired and have been driving steady for over twenty hours. After awhile, all roads and scenery seem to blur in distinction. By the time I pulled off the interstate and into the small, east coast town I was exhausted. I'd driven half way across the country by myself, not knowing what I would find or do when alas I arrived. Except, at the very least, to have the opportunity to walk the same sidewalks, stroll the same college campus, breath the same air as Hans Kroenberg, my genetic father. Sometimes it baffled me that I was so obsessed. Why did it have to be so important to me?

Michelle had urged me to go. She knew that I would never be whole unless I went. But I knew she knew by sending me, there would probably no longer be a place for her in my life. My healthy side cried that my unhealthy side couldn't let go, and as a result, was costing me another relationship. But the problems were incontrovertible; we were going in opposite directions.

Stars filled the sky by the time I arrived. Darkness wrapped around me as I pulled into the motel parking lot with the red neon sign flashing vacancy. How lucky was that, getting a room at the only motel in town?

The place looked like a sketch of the 1950s, down to the free post cards at the front desk showing the motel with vintage cars parked out front. Had Kroenberg ever stayed at the motel? Perhaps when he first arrived in town with his wife. I decided it was likely, maybe even in that very room. It served a purpose if only to amuse me.

Whatever I wound up doing, I decided it would not involve Professor Kroenberg. The man had made it plenty clear that he didn't want to meet his "son." It still troubled me, but I had no right forcing myself upon him. That night it was impossible for me too sleep. I was living off adrenaline.

First thing the next morning I went to the university library where Kroenberg had worked as a professor until retiring a few years earlier. At first I found very little. A tiny photograph in the files of the professors in my father's department. Their faces were so small they were hardly distinguishable from one another.

I felt disappointment creeping inside me. Would this lead to another dead end? But then unexpectedly the librarian emerged with a thick file. She had a spinster-ish look about her, mousy brown hair wrapped tightly in a bun on top of her head. She offered the folder to me with a broad, infectious smile.

The file was full of news clips and articles detailing his many accomplishments. Obviously the man had led a rich and full life. Apparently, my biological father had not just been some drab soil scientist, lecturing his days away in classrooms. He was internationally renowned. An expert in his field who other countries had begged to visit to assist them in setting up agricultural and soil conservation programs. Among his accomplishments he'd been a civic and university leader, chosen as teacher of the year by his students and as man of the year by his colleagues. I was impressed.

Adding to his esteem, he was also known for founding the largest tax-exempt retirement community in the East, which was now his home. I found it all very interesting and a little disheartening. Where were all my accomplishments? What did I have to show for my life?

Buried under articles and clippings, I found a photograph. It startled me to see how much I resembled my genetic father. Slowly, one by one, I made copies of everything, telling the librarian I was a former student of Kroenberg writing a paper about the man. That seemed to please her. Apparently Kroenberg had been well liked by just about everyone. She was obviously was among his admirers.

With my own plump file in hand, I finally left the library, prepared to go back to Colorado. But first I had a need to explore the streets of the town. I went into a corner bar and pretended that my father had also sat on the same stool and enjoyed a cold beer. I wondered how people would react if I told them I was Hans Kroenberg's long lost son. The thought made me smile.

A football game was going on the television screen. Did my father enjoy the game? Maybe even keep up with my favorite team, the Kansas Cornhuskers? Would I ever know?

As I again poured over the clippings, I felt a distant flush of pride. That was my genetic father's accomplishments. Suddenly I felt overcome with a familial urge. I wanted to shout: that's my Dad. It angered me that I couldn't.

Within a few minutes I was quietly nursing a beer. Once my brain caught up to my senses I quickly discarded it. On a whim, I'd trotted to the corner store and purchased a six pack. Those days are behind me, I reassured myself with shaky hands. Not sure if my body believed it, but none-the-less I put the rest of the beer in the room refrigerator.

For a while I stretched on the bed watching the neon sign blinking red shadows across my window. I tried to convince myself that my cup was finally full. But the more I said it, the more it rang empty.

Hans Kroenberg had not been the father I'd known. He was just a production mill for sperm who could care less about what one spermatozoa among millions had become, or the troubles I had gone through as a result of his actions that had brought me here; the drugs, the heartache, the anger.

All of a sudden my pride was washed away. Strangely, I felt like a thief. Hadn't I crept into town, taken all I could without asking the owners? And wasn't I preparing to sneak back out? The feelings hung around me all night and carried over into the next morning, even as I packed and drove out of the motel parking lot. But by then, resentment had replaced anger and guilt.

The irony of my situation struck me, my biological father had spent the entirety of his whole life giving to others, other countries, other students, his community. Yet, he wouldn't give me the time of day.

"Quitter!" I yelled, chastising myself inside my car and slammed my hands against the wheel. "You came this far and now you're going to quit before finishing the job?" For a while I played alternating parts of woe is me and devil's advocate.

Kroenberg didn't want a relationship. Well, that was okay, I didn't want one either. Nor do I want to debate the morality of what he's done. But by God, I am not going to slink out of town, as if I had never existed in the first place. I deserve more than that.

Immediately I started searching all the hotel, store and business lots for a pay phone. On the corner of a Dunkin Donut shop I spotted one. I extracted his telephone number kept safely in my wallet all those years and dialed.

Then I held my breath as I watched a couple driving past in a 57 Ford pulling a horse trailer. Nervously I swallowed.

"Hello?" a thick, Dutch, male voice answered.

"Uh, hello, Dr. Kroenberg, this is Scott Davis."

Nothing but silence followed. I began to fret that this was a mistake. I continued. "I was in town and wanted to stop by and say hi."

To my surprise Kroenberg said okay, but my elation dissipated almost as quickly as it as surfaced. He probably thinks I'm one of the thousands of college students who took his classes. Undoubtedly, former students probably stopped by and said hello all the time. I conceded he hadn't made the connection with my name on the telephone to the disturbing letter I'd sent years ago informing him who I was.

Finding the retirement community was a cinch. The grounds were beautiful, peaceful, speckled with Aspen trees surrounded by immaculately kept lawns. There were wide streets and comfortable but modest homes. Care had been taken to keep the place pristine. One thing I noticed almost immediately, it was devoid of children.

Finally I pulled up to address I'd anxiously scribbled down. For all of his accomplishments, Kroenberg lived in one of the more modest homes at the end of a long sidewalk. A 15-year-old car stood in the driveway. Cheap too, I thought wryly.

I got out and walked to the front door. I rang the bell surveying his neighbor's homes while I waited. A stout blond woman answered the door. She looked at me suspiciously. Just for a moment I wondered if perhaps she had remembered my name. She must be his wife, I surmised.

"I called just a minute ago," I stammered. "I just wanted to stop and say hi to Dr. Kroenberg." Then I stopped talking, not sure what else to say.

The woman curtly turned, and in an accent as heavy as her husband's called out, "Hans, you have company." She left me awkwardly waiting on the porch.

Shuffling proceeded the figure that appeared on the other side of the screen door. The old man opened the screen. Before I could stop myself I gasped. I might well have been looking at myself in another thirty years.

Kroenberg was wearing little half-glasses for reading and now tilted his head forward to look at me. There was a slight frown on his lips, but his blue eyes seemed kind.

"Yes? Can I help you?"

"Hi. I'm Scott Davis."

An uncomfortable silence ensued. Fear gripped me again, it had been a mistake.

"Scott Davis" Kroenberg repeated, furrowing his brow. "Where do I know you from?"

My mind raced. I could feel myself wanting to choke, bolt. And yet, here I was, three feet away from the Holy Grail of my existence, the key to my past and maybe my future, but I couldn't think of anything to say. Words failed me during my most critical need.

"Kansas City, Kansas," I finally blurted offering my hand. For a moment Kroenberg stood suspended. What would I do if he didn't take it? Just as I was starting to feel foolish, he did take my hand and held it firmly but there was a quizzical look on his face. He was obviously trying to determine what child of an old friend from Kansas this might be, but was getting nowhere.

God, help get me through this, I pleaded. Then I gathered my courage and locked eye contact with him and said, "Do you remember, Dr. Thurber?"

Suddenly, Kroenberg's eyes grew wide. His hand went limp. He started to say something but nothing escaped his lips.

His reticence suddenly made me confident. "I just wanted to thank you for the gift of life. I don't want any money. I don't expect any relationship. And I won't bother you again."

"I just needed to meet you," I said earnestly. Kroenberg's face was solemn, but he said nothing.

With that, I shook his hand once more and let it drop. Then I turned around, squared my shoulders and marched confidently back down the sidewalk without looking back.

26

Discovering Peace in Weston

I drove away and headed west a happy man. I had accomplished the impossible. How many donor offspring could claim as much? That they'd met their genetic father? Signs for Kentucky, Indiana and Iowa zipped by like mile markers instead of states. I was floating on my own intrinsic cloud. Every mile that passed beneath the wheels seemed to strip another layer of my past from my soul. By the time I reached the familiar rolling hills of eastern Kansas, I felt reborn.

It was glorious to be leaving behind the ghost that had haunted me since my twenty-eighth birthday. Now, ten years later, I was more convinced that ever that society needed to examine the ramifications of eugenics. But I no longer felt that I needed to bear that cross alone.

In fact, since joining Promise Keepers, I no longer felt that I had to bear anything alone. God was my constant companion now. The voice that had called out to me at Promise Keepers remained like an eternal flame. I remembered the voice, the message: Have faith. Give me your fears, your anxieties. Faith in a God that forgave the sins of my wayward past and loved the promise of my future had been tantamount toward restoring my personal faith in humanity.

Shortly after my return to Colorado, the state legislature soundly defeated a bill to offer prison inmates freedom in exchange for sterilization. It was a very personal victory; one I had lobbied for before embarking on my quest to find my father. Old fears were disproved; the public had not voted in favor of old fears held about crime and violence. But in the end, the legislators recognized the bill for what it was. Eugenics, even if they had never heard the word before.

There was so much more to do. Not a day went by that there wasn't some headline in the newspaper or some television expose that struck a nerve. Each reference felt like a personal affront to me. There it was in bold face type staring at me defiantly:

In Virginia, infertility doctor Cecil B. Jacobson admitted to fathering as many as 75 children while telling patients he was using an anonymous sperm donor program.

In Texas, a legislator asked his constituency whether they favored sterilization for women on welfare. They voted yes by a 3-2 margin.

In Los Angeles, a white woman sued the largest sperm bank in America for mixing up the sperm of her late husband ten years earlier with that of a man of a different race whose child she bore. While another woman battled with her dead lover's family over the right to use his frozen sperm.

In Maryland, legislation was introduced to make welfare payments to women with two or more illegitimate children contingent upon the mother's sterilization. It failed by a thin margin.

In California, at the University of California-Berkeley, home of the most prestigious fertility clinic in the world, embryos were stolen and given to other couples without their knowledge. Some were sold for genetic research and many remained unaccounted for, the scandal covered up.

Baby-making was big business, it seemed. An estimated 170,000 to 175,000 donor inseminations were occurring annually, resulting in an estimated 15,000 to 20,000 donor births. Most of these donor offspring, however, would never be told their true heritage. It disturbed me greatly that they could suffer my plight all over again.

With little or no regulation of the industry, it was a mad dog left to gluttony and greed. Each new tidbit left another scar on my soul. Suddenly I understood my role: I was born to champion the cause, whether that meant lobbying Congress, or speaking out wherever I could find an audience, I was the messenger and my efforts against eugenics were my message.

I knew I couldn't necessarily stop people, but perhaps I could get them to at least listen. And if they listened, together there wasn't anything we couldn't do. My mind flashed to the old cliché: Each journey of a thousand miles begins with the first step. This was my first step.

However, I knew I would first have to leave Colorado. It was time to stop toying with the idea and just do it. Colorado represented my past, but Kansas was my future. As much as I loved the mountains, it was time to go home. I was also yearning for someone to share the new Scott Davis with. Someone who shared my rekindled faith in God, someone to have children with.

When I mentioned moving back to Kansas to Michelle, she balked. She loved Colorado and the city. The illicit hub of its nightlife was her lifeline. I couldn't fault her for being caught up in the illusion. Thank God I'd finally emerged victorious from that dazzling mirage.

I hardly ever had a joint of marijuana with her. More and more I saw it for what it was, a crutch I'd soon leave behind. Unfortunately my progression was her undoing. Because I had given up drugs, we had less and less in common. We were drifting apart.

Peace and quiet was primary to me now. I needed a place where I could openly meditate on living a Christian life. A place from which I could rally forth on my crusade to warn the world about eugenics; demand that society regulate the baby industry, and return to recuperate.

Suddenly, I was overcome with a need for haste. Knowing my mother's health was declining fast, I gravitated in her direction. According to her doctors, cigarettes had robbed her of ninety-five percent of her lung capacity. Just thinking about it disheartened me. I could hear death creeping in little by little each time I called. Her ragged speech, labored breathing. Time was running out. I needed to see her.

Whenever I thought about how the government and tobacco industry conspired to cover-up the devastating affects of cigarette smoking, it unleashed that old demon, anger, to return. But I was determined to keep going towards the light. I could mourn for my mother, I could be there with her as she rejoined God, but I couldn't let her situation be my undoing.

I received about $20,000 for the mountain property. During the next few months I found myself driving back and forth to Kansas to look in on my mother and hunt for some property where I could settle down.

I knew I didn't want to reside in Kansas City. While it was still small compared to Denver, it embodied too many city qualities for the life I wanted (and needed) to live now. Maybe I could find something in one of the many farming communities that surrounded Kansas City.

It happened that while visiting my mother one Sunday and randomly perusing the newspaper, I noticed an advertisement for a house out in Weston, Kansas. The name caught my attention because of pleasant memories cruising the rolling hills of that little farm country on my motorcycle as a youth. The asking price was $19,000, which was right in my price range so I decided to see the property.

Most towns in Kansas sport water towers and church steeples that emerge from the trees atop the highest hill. Weston was no different.

Immediately I was enchanted with the tiny streets, just wide enough for cars to pass. On the corner of Main Street stood an old opera house and the town's only bar. A tiny post office building that looked slightly larger than a child's playhouse was the only place one could get mail. There was no home delivery.

The day I chose to investigate, it was hot and humid. It made my adventure a sticky and uncomfortable one. Yet viewing every yard with a little garden and a stand of corn helped to improve my disposition.

I rolled down my window to inhale the heavy, dense air with the fragrance of ripening ears. Families gathered at the tiny town park where children chased each other and the adults lingered around talking. They looked up, watching the new car driving through their town, but instead of the suspicious looks like I expected, they waved at me as if we were old friends. Their gesture of friendliness sold me.

I could live in a place like this, I said aloud as I smiled and waved back. By the time I arrived at my destination the realtor was waiting outside. Instantly I was disappointed. Instead of one of the quaint farmhouses that made up most of the town's homes, it was a squat, ugly box. That wouldn't do.

The realtor was an elderly lady who easily could have passed for my mother's sister. Immediately thoughts of my mother washed over me. I tried to focus, feeling sadness permeating me.

"It just doesn't feel right," I told her.

"I understand," she said squeezing my hand. It was refreshing to see how genuinely nice she was; unlike the trademark hustle I'd become desensitized to from my car sales days.

"Thanks," I said quietly as I watched her leave.

Before leaving I decided to take a little detour to a road below what had apparently been the old high school, but was now boarded up and empty. Not enough kids, I thought sadly.

Then it occurred to me that most of the town's businesses were boarded up, the grocery store, auto repair shop, the feed store. Like many farm communities, the town was slowly dying. It brought my mother back to mind.

Near the end of the road, I came to a tiny old house. From the outset I knew it once had been a beautiful wood bungalow with a nice front porch. But it had been allowed to fall into disrepair and its beauty was like a wilted rose.

A Harley Davidson motorcycle was parked on the lawn. Trash and pieces of automobiles lay strewn about. Bits of aggressive bushes grew through the front porch making it appear even more unruly. Even the gutters were rusting and the whole building was in dire need of a coat of paint twenty years ago. Along with the chaos, was a beat up For Sale sign mostly hidden by the tangle of weeds and shrubs.

Something prompted me to stop the car and write down the telephone number on the sign. Once I got back home I called the realtor. I didn't need to ask why it hadn't sold; that was only too obvious, but I was curious about the asking price.

"Oh, that place," the realtor said. He hesitated. Was that a good sign or a bad one? "Well, it needs a lot of work, but the owners are only asking $13,950," he said plainly. It was below the market value but I didn't question it, given what I'd seen earlier.

Instinctively I made arrangements with the realtor for the next day. When we arrived, the current occupant was there. A big, burly man in biker garb. He reminded me of Bear, the man who had introduced me to marijuana more than twenty years earlier. It seemed strange to realize twenty years had escaped me so quickly.

Remembering Bear gave way to a host of mixed feelings, most of them negative. That had been a woeful time in my life. It hurt to remember. My biggest regret amongst it was in succumbing to his invitation. I contemplated the enormity of it. How pot had cleared the path for harder drugs. It was not a time I looked back on with any fondness.

The man invited us in and then left. There were oily motorcycle parts here and there about the small living room. Grease and dirt was on everything. A bottle of Jack Daniels whiskey lay on its side on the tattered carpet and drug paraphernalia lay on kitchen table. A eerie sense of deja vu came over me.

But yet, I could see possibilities. And I loved the town and the way people nodded or waved when I visited. I want it, I thought, but to the realtor I heard myself say, "It's not worth $13,000."

The realtor agreed. That started a series of haggling between myself and the owners. Eventually they agreed to $7,250. We sealed it with a handshake. Weston was that kind of place.

27

Leaving Colorado

The plan was for Michelle to join me in Weston the following March. At least that's what we told ourselves. But as that fateful day in October approached, I knew in my heart it wasn't going to happen. An emptiness settled into my soul. A man alone, abandoned, lost again. I knew it was old thinking, but I couldn't help it.

I still loved her, that much was true. But it was the sort of bond that two old friends shared. We rarely made love anymore. Even the friendship, which had been the strongest part of our relationship, had become strained.

It was as though we had taken two different branches of the same river, and we could only see each other from a distance. Me on one metaphorical stump waving, and her on another. The tragedy was that we could still see each other, but we would never be meeting again. The current direction our lives were headed just kept sweeping us farther apart.

Colorado would be referred to in the past tense now. It was time to leave. I should have left long ago and not just because my mother needed me. It was the next logical step in my personal journey.

I needed to break clean. Cocaine had been a ghost since that fateful conversation with my mother and the revelation of my past. The pornography had been stripped away, thank God, destroyed in a shower of sparks high in the mountains. My personal sacrifice.

The Promise Keepers had given me the courage to flush pills down the toilet and the faith not to replace them. But meeting my father had let loose another dam that held anger.

One by one, I had been exorcising the demons that had gathered at my doorstep. Drugs. Sex. Lies. Deception. Anger. It had been a gradual process of one step forward and two back. Whenever I heard other Christians claim to have been "Born Again," as if their transformation had been instantaneous, it made me laugh. Somebody wasn't being honest. Either they never had that far to go in the first place, or they were kidding themselves. The road to forgiveness and redemption was traveled one slow step at a time, and more often than not there were setbacks, or as I deemed them, potholes in life's highway.

Even now the old demons lingered near, waiting for a moment of weakness to get a foot in the door. There was still marijuana to contend with; these days I wasn't using as much, but occasionally I still depended on it for that moment of calm.

I knew I was far enough along to realize the calm of marijuana was actually just another illusion. It didn't make problems disappear. It only disguised them in a haze of sweet-smelling smoke so I wouldn't have to deal with them. The problems were always there, waiting for me once the drug wore off.

Ironically it was the morning of October 18, my mother's birthday, when I realized the road I was to travel wouldn't include Michelle. She enjoyed pot and cigarettes way too much to give them up. And she'd grown increasingly uncomfortable with my spiritual quest.

I would be driving five hundred miles to Weston. But it was so much more than that. In time I knew she would make her own way when she was ready. And wishing she was ready to join me now wouldn't make it so.

So that morning I stepped out of our apartment for the last time. My stomach grew tight. I wanted to yell: Michelle come with me, don't you realize what you're doing? What you're doing to yourself? But I knew it would have been in vain. How much would I have listened before I was ready? How many years had it taken me to get to this point?

I looked around at the graffiti-covered walls and empty liquor bottles in the alley. Dirty brown air hung over the city, barely allowing slivers of sunshine through. I kicked bottles out of my way. My ears were bombarded with the shrill sound of sirens and car horns, people yelling and cursing. How had I lived like that? Some things I definitely wouldn't miss.

Slowly I climbed into the U-Haul truck. It contained all of my worldly posses-sions, my stereo, computers, photo albums and perhaps a dozen notebooks con-taining research on eugenics.

Behind the truck I would be towing my car. The cats, King and Bubby were in their pet carrier on the front seat, strangely quiet. Unusual for the vocal felines, as if they too realized the seriousness of the moment. And maybe they did.

One last look. Michelle was standing on the balcony, she looked down at me. That was the defining moment I truly knew it was over. My heart wanted to leave my chest and fly to her. I knew we'd both hurt for a while, it was inevitable. But how do you tell someone you've outgrown them? She would always be a friend. But I would go on.

With tears flowing freely I waved. I left with the image of her staring longingly down at my reflection in the rearview mirror. I would carry that image with me forever. For a while I was nearly blinded by my tears.

Michelle had offered to let me take our marijuana stash. But I declined, instead rolling three small joints. I smoked one heading out of the city for Interstate 80 that would take me most of the way through Colorado and Kansas.

Please God, I heard myself praying. Part of the sadness I knew was the same old fear of being alone. Michelle might not have been the woman I was seeking, but she represented security and probably understood me better than anyone in the world except perhaps my mother. Immediately I wanted to turn back. What had happened to all my strength, faith? Suddenly I became so overcome with emotion that I pulled off to the shoulder. While cars whizzed by I just let myself feel the feelings, weeping pitifully.

Bubby and King began to meow. Could they sense my pain? Feel it? I opened the door of their carrier and pulled them out one by one. King began to climb me but Bubby let me hold him. I clung to him as he purred. Then I put him back in the carrier and retrieved King curled on the floorboard.

"Thanks you guys," I said putting the truck in gear.

I could always ask her to join me. But as I drove across the high, golden plains of eastern Colorado, heading toward an unknown future, the tears over Michelle began to dry. A new fear emerged. I didn't know anyone in Kansas anymore. Most of my friends were married, out of touch, dead, in jail, or had moved away.

It occurred to me I owned a home in a town where I knew no one. Everyone seemed friendly enough, but would I feel that way after I lived there full time? And how would I ever meet a woman to spend my life with? A Christian woman? Never again would I live with a woman unless I was married; I wanted to know a potential mate before sex got in the way. But how would I find her living in po' dunk Weston?

It was scary and unnerving. Suddenly I realized I had smoked my second joint as the big truck bounced and lumbered east. The cats meowed softly. I turned my eyes to the great blue expanse of sky. Clouds cut into the paintbrush crimson horizon and floated like icebergs across heaven's sea.

"I know I've mad a lot of promises, Lord, and broken a lot of promises," I said above the roar of the highway. "But I made a promise to turn from my old ways. I need you to help me keep that promise now; and to place my trust in you, because I can't trust myself. Please help me. I am a small man, nothing without you. And I'm afraid, afraid of what is happening to me," I pleaded softly.

As I prayed, sadness and fear seemed elevate my heart as though they'd escaped into the clouds. Before I realized, I was smoking my last joint as I crossed the Colorado, Kansas border. I held my breath through closed eyes, savoring that one last puff, then slowly let the smoke escape. I inhaled deeply. Already the air felt different, wetter, fresher. The afternoon sun seemed to be massaging my road-weary muscles.

I accelerated towards my destiny. A sea of emotions washed over me. Good and evil colliding. It would have been profoundly arrogant to assume I was out of the woods. I might have left Michelle and Colorado behind, but all those ugly demons were still inside me, needing to be purged. And yet, strangely, I felt as though I'd closed the last chapter of a book. A story of a broken man filled with lost opportunities and broken promises. But there was still a chance for a happy ending. The marijuana wore off with each click of the odometer, I felt a growing sense of worry. Could I really do this? Why was this time so much harder? I began to question myself.

The interstate veered off into a two-lane highway that took me toward Weston. The sun was a yellow mushroom with crimson trim sinking lower in the sky. On either side of the road were lush green fields of beans and corn stretched as far as one could see across land that rolled away like gentle ocean swells.

Air was heavy and thick with moisture. A sense of growing things filled my nostrils. I passed abandoned farmhouses and wondered what dreams those pioneers must have had. They must have had fears about the future too, but held on to call forth God's bounty from one of the most fertile places in the world.

The U-Haul truck rolled past the New Holland dealership with its rows of combines and tractors. As I left central Kansas for the eastern part, the land began to change, the swells became more pitched. Cottonwoods and elm grew along sluggish creeks. Small towns could be captured in the distance by their water towers and church steeples.

I could feel myself growing more excited. No matter what it took, I would make a life out here where it could be so simple; simple was good. I'd find peace from the demons that plagued me. At least that was my prayer. It meant no more drugs, including pot. No more living in sin with women, any woman. And most of all, I'd care for my mother like I had tried to care for my father, my real father. But this time I would be successful. Not only with my family, but my friends and in faith as well.

Ten miles from Weston, the land pitched and rose like stormy seas. There were more trees, more wild vegetation across the flats and unplowed land. Giant irrigators seemed to crawl across the farms like enormous insects.

When I'd left Colorado I'd meant to make it to Kansas City to visit my mother. It was her birthday after all. She was only 65 years old and dying. But fatigue made me go to Weston.

As I was entering, I came over a rise, and there, to the right, I saw the silver water tower and church steeple of Weston, population six hundred and sixty-eight. I looked in the rearview mirror. The sun was slowly setting as the skies had burst into a painter palette of orange and red, bathing the tired little town in a surreal light.

I passed over railroad tracks that seemed to cross every Kansas town ever built. I continued past the tiny post office, the old opera house and the town park.

People in the town's park stopped swinging their children long enough to see the U-Haul truck. Others leaned forward on swings or front porches. They waved at me as if I were an old friend. It gave me a sense of belonging, community, acceptance. Finally.

"We're home," I shouted to the cats my faithful companions, who meowed anxious for release. The sun was becoming a haze in the far West, back in Colorado.

"Thank you God for bringing me home. Please make this work," I prayed aloud. The weight of my journey suddenly seemed to catch up to me. I was so tired that for the night I unrolled a sleeping bag on my living room floor and called it good.

28

Stumbling to Stay Straight

I awoke shaking. Apparently one sleeping bag wasn't sufficient to keep myself warm in Weston at night in late October. On top of that, a less than wonderful stench permeated my senses. I knew that smell. Where were King and Bubby?

Wriggling free it was hunt and seek time. Naturally Bubby and King were nowhere to be found. It never ceases to amaze me how pets know when their owners are pissed at them.

It didn't take me long to find their handy work. It reminded me of the need to get the utilities turned on and get to a phone. It was my plan that while the utility companies were busy getting me connected to the community, I would visit my mother.

I left town that morning feeling Weston was everything I'd hoped it would be. Quiet. Peaceful. Friendly. It felt as though I'd taken a step back in time. Life here was suspended in the good old days, time stood still. It was the sort of place where folks were surprised at an inquiry if they locked their cars, even at night. It was wonderful to witness such trust and abandon.

Lisa and Jodi were at the hospital when I arrived. Both of them ushered me outside mom's room in the ICU. By their expression and hasty actions, I knew the prognosis wasn't good.

"Scott," Jodi hugged me. Lisa stood back, solemnly watching. "Where have you been?" she asked with tearful eyes.

"I only got in last night," I explained.

Jodi joined Lisa; they took a seat in a row of padded chairs that ran the length of Mom's room outside the waiting area. Lisa cleared her throat.

"Mom had a bad night Scott, they resuscitated her twice. We tried calling you but Michelle said you'd already gone," she said quietly blinking at me. A sea of emotion was burying me. In as much as I tried to tell myself I couldn't have changed anything, a wash of guilt enveloped me. I was failing my mother just like I'd failed my father. Why hadn't I left sooner? Hadn't I known that things were over between Michelle and I long ago?

I'd been so self absorbed in the wonderment of Weston that I hadn't thought of much else. It was so foreign to me to be living in a place where one walked to the post office just to get their mail. Then to be greeted by an abundance of smiles, polite salutations like hello, or how are you, by all in one's path and meant sincerely.

"What did Doctor Thatcher say?" I asked Lisa, the more composed of the two. Jodi remained in a heap trying not to cry while tears continued to fall. A tremendous sense of big brother clicked and overtook me. I wanted to protect them.

"Maybe a few weeks," she said soberly. I took a deep breath.

"We're going to get through this, okay? I promise," I told them. Immediately we were locked in a unit hug. Then one by one, we filed into mom's room.

Her color was ashen. The look of death. Monitors blinked and beeped, indicative of her status. I sat on the edge of her bed and took mom's right hand. Her heart monitor immediately beeped. She knew I was there. I forced back the tears.

"I'm here Mom," I said softly. From the corner of my eye I could see Lisa comforting Jodi, both of them were sobbing softly. "Lisa says you had a scare last night. I'm really sorry I didn't get here sooner, but I'm here now, okay?" I looked at the monitor expecting a response. Instead her fingers close around my hand. She'd heard me.

Trying to be strong for them was singularly the hardest moment I'd ever faced. It took more fortitude than being in jail or being rebuffed by my genetic father. They were my true family, and they were counting on me.

"Do you need anything Mom? Can I get you anything? Do anything for you?" her hand went limp as the monitor screeched to life. My heart did a flip. Fear was suffocating me. I didn't want her to die. I needed her to live. She was slipping away.

Jodi and Lisa flanked me, collectively we watched her intently.

"Should I get the doctor?" Lisa asked.

"Yeah," I told her.

As Lisa vanished among the milieu of hospital staff Jodi sat opposite of me and took Mother's left hand.

Doctor Thatcher was a fossil of a man. He came in carrying my mother's chart. He seemed to be checking something before he set it on end of her bed and began reading her equipment. After he'd satisfied a curiosity he had, he turned to us.

"Doctor Thatcher, how is she?" Jodi asked. His tired, elderly eyes looked at her.

"Well, she'd fading Jodi. But we expected this," he said simply.

"Can't you do anything?" Lisa asked.

"Like what? She has end stage carcinoma in her lungs compounded by pulmonary edema and stage three emphysema. All we can do is make her as comfortable as possible," he admitted.

"But she sounds like she's drowning," Jodi whimpered, referring to the steady gurgle heard along with the beeping and humming of medical equipment.

"She is," he confessed very stoic. Then Doctor Thatcher grabbed my mom's chart as if to leave.

"But?" Jodi gasped?

"We could suction her lungs again but they'll just keep filling up. At some point you have to decide what is more humane. It's very painful for her," he explained.

"But doesn't the fluid hasten her death?" she countered. For a moment he was silent. We all knew the answer before he said it.

"Yes. If you want her lungs to be suctioned I'll give the order," he said waiting on Jodi.

"Yes," she said. Just then Mom squeezed my hand. I looked at her, her eyes were closed but a single tear rolled out.

"No, she doesn't want it," I said.

Jodi shot me a look like I'd just ordered Mom's execution. Maybe I had.

"Scott!" Lisa and Jodi chimed.

"She squeezed my hand," I explained. Simultaneously their eyes flickered from her to me then at Doctor Thatcher.

"I want her to breathe!" Jodi said defensively.

"She doesn't want it Jodi," I looked at Lisa for help but it was clear from the look on her face that she wanted no part of it. Thatcher stood patiently observing our trio debate. In my heart I knew mom had spoken to me as best as she could. Maybe I hadn't been the model son, but this was my chance to honor her final request.

"Jodi, it's Mom's wishes, we need to respect that," I stated firmly.

"No, you just want her to die," she insisted. The words stung. I knew it was fear and grief talking, clouding her thinking, yet it still hurt. How could she think that? I was beginning to feel miffed that Lisa was remaining neutral.

When it became obvious we were not reaching a happy medium, Doctor Thatcher finally intervened.

"It looks like you need some time to decide. I'll check back later," he said. Then he squeezed my shoulder and left. I looked at my mother, I knew she'd given me a sign but Jodi was not able to accept it. My mind was spinning, what to do? How could I honor my mother's request but stave off a bigger fight with Jodi?

"Would you talk to her?" I looked at Lisa. She looked at both of us. By the look on her face she didn't want to get in the middle. But by being a family member she was in the middle.

"Jodi?," she said softly. "I think Scott's right, it would be prolonging mom's agony," she touched her sister's arm. But Jodi withdrew.

"No!" she yelled before abruptly leaving. Lisa's eyes held her own resignation on the matter.

"Thanks," I said. She nodded.

"She's going to think it's us against her now," she said with a wry grin. Sadly I knew she was right, but I was equally confident Jodi would get over it once she regained her reasoning powers and realized keeping our mother alive was not in the best interest of mom. It was that intangible need for offspring to stay connected to their parental source. I couldn't fault her for feeling such devotion, but it was weighing on me. Each minute I remained, watching mom's respirator pumping oxygen into her lungs, IVs dripping nourishment into her weary body, it continued to drain me.

"Lisa, I've got to go home," I told her. She cocked her head, looking at me squarely. Her eyes telegraphed worry. She was probably afraid I would revert back to old behavior. She was reading me right. I wanted nothing more than to get high, but she didn't need to know that. "I left this morning with instructions for the utilities to be hooked up, but I think I better at least check in, in case they need me for anything," I explained. It was partly true.

Even before I exited through the big glass doors of the hospital, I knew I was running for the devil. The impulse was so huge that no amount of logic could rescue me.

Stepping out into the chilly air I paused. My only thoughts were concentrated on how I would score.

29

The Ad

For a while I drifted. Instinctually steering the car towards familiar taverns and bars I used to frequent. Finally, in a heated rush, I hurried inside one I'd often gone to for quick connections.

Immediately I ordered a beer, but before I could take even a swallow I began to notice faces from those former days. Drunks and druggies, numb and oblivious to the world. It hit me. Nothing had changed. They were still living the same day they'd lived starting nearly twenty years ago.

How had I lived like that? Why had I lived like that? It humbled me to realize the abyss I had emerged from. There was no doubt in my mind, I was one of the elite lucky ones.

Suddenly one face stood out amongst the crowd. It was Bear, my old partner in crime. An eerie sense of deja vu enveloped me. From the sloppy way he was handling himself at the pool table, I could tell he was both wasted and drunk.

An overwhelming urge hit me. I wanted to thrash him for introducing me to a world that had lead me into that murky underworld for so long. Yet I was equally filled with sadness. Another soul who would never know their potential.

At that moment he looked right at me, but there was no connection. His eyes were glassy and bloodshot. He was looking at me as if I weren't there. And perhaps I wasn't to him. Had I been like that? Briefly I wondered, thankful I wasn't there now.

Their eyes were lifeless pools drained of all meaning and substance. Men falling all over themselves, half had peed themselves, totally unaware of their wet pants, they contented themselves groping anybody that would allow it. The women were so lost they were indifferent to strange men pawing them. Watching their pathetic existence made me want to vomit. That had been me, my world.

I ran a finger over the lip of my beer, dew ran like a pearl down the side. It would be so easy. And a part of me wanted it so bad. But in my being, I knew, something inside me had turned a corner. I didn't need to get drunk to anesthetize myself from the world. I wanted to be a part of the world. I knew I had a contribution to make and I was determined to do it. I would be my father's son, not Bear's protégé.

"Hey buddy, we don't need chair warmers," the bartender reprimanded. His remark snapped my attention back to the present. I gazed at him; he was glowering at my full bottle.

"No, I don't suppose," I said getting up. I slapped several dollars on the counter and left.

Immediately the cold air affronted me. But it was a refreshing blast. It helped me to keep my focus. I walked quickly across the lot towards my car. Two couples were laughing, swaying, heading for the entrance.

I wanted to tell them to turn around, that they'd lose their frivolity if they went inside, but I didn't. How much would I have listened? I climbed inside my car. I could go home now.

There was a lot to think about. My mother being tantamount. Tomorrow I would talk to my sisters, straighten out misunderstandings between us. But for tonight I would go home and refocus. I hadn't come all this way just to digress.

I slept good that night, awaking refreshed and ready to tackle the world. It was blissful having heat again and lights. Simple things one takes for granted. Only the phone wasn't on. It would be a few more days. I scratched King's head affectionately then showered and shaved.

For the time being, I'd work on fixing up my home. Clearing the brush. Fixing loose and broken boards. Scrubbing. Painting. This place was a carpenter's goldmine; there was a wealth of work that needed to be done. I began by taking out the old cabinets and replacing them with new oak ones that reflected my tastes. Next I'd install new carpeting. I still had money from the sale of my house and marketing business. It wasn't much, but it would tide me over. Living in Weston didn't require a lot, thank God. Besides, there wasn't a doubt in my mind that I could get a job as a dishwasher someplace if I had to. Whatever it takes, I told myself as I sat on the front porch.

Thus became my routine: renovating and visiting. Then home to relax. But evenings were my high life, just soaking in the painted sunsets and good clean air. And the hushed drum of locusts in the fields clashing with laughter of children carefree playing hide-and-seek or kick-the-can in the neighborhood. There was a peacefulness here that Colorado lacked.

One particularly beautiful evening I decided to go for a walk. As I strolled past the simple houses and undeveloped neighborhoods without thinking, I headed to the baseball field.

Standing on the clay colored dirt, the same feeling flowed over me as I'd felt the first time I laid eyes on it. It smacked of a scene from the movie Field of Dreams. The baseball field was neatly mowed, its base paths carefully raked dirt but it was the outfield surrounded by fields of corn that really got me. A sense of surrealism pervaded.

An old timer sat on the bleachers facing the field as I approached.

"Did you know that Bob Cerv used to play here?" he asked. He faced me shielding his eyes from the sun. "You're maybe a might young to remember Cerv. But he played for the New York Yankees, with Mantle and Maris back in '61 when they won the series. He got his start right here." He told me, his eyes glistening. He turned to the field as if he could still see them. So many boys dream of being in the big leagues, and one who had finally made it.

Watching him reminisce, I wondered if that had been his dream once.

Like many farm communities, Weston was just holding on. The small farmer that had been primary to the backbone of this community had been bought out by farming corporations or bigger neighbors. Businesses had struggled, as the townspeople often headed to bigger towns where there were better selections and lower prices. Consequently it left fewer families. Kids left for college as soon as possible, or anywhere else to get out. If they returned at all, it was only for the holidays, depriving Weston of potential growth.

But recently a trend was emerging, changing the status quo. Like myself, quite a few of my neighbors worked in Lincoln but lived in Weston.

The old man spoke again.

"There's been a lot of baseballs knocked into that corn over the years. Sometimes I can't find em' again until after the harvest, if at all," he chuckled.

I nodded following the old timer's gaze. There was a sense of hearth here. Alas, I'd found the town of my dreams. I could see myself growing old in Weston.

"I'll bet. Good night," I said nodding politely. Since it was early yet, I decided to wander up to the water tower and watch nightfall descend on the town.

Lightning bugs twinkled in the twilight as I neared the cemetery. Occasionally I paused to read the tombstones of pioneers who had established the town more than a hundred years earlier. Are you up there with my father? I looked at the great expanse of the night skies. Maybe even watching me? I tried to imagine what would happen when my body lay in the ground and I came to the gates of Heaven.

"And why should I let you into my kingdom, Scott?" God would ask.

"I know I failed often to live by your word," I would say. "But I know I can go in because you sent your son to die for me with the promise of forgiveness," I would reply, unafraid. Forgiveness. If any word stood out in importance in my life that was it.

And lucky. Lucky to be alive. Lucky to have had a family who loved me. Forgave me. Lucky to have found faith before it was too late. The only thing missing was someone to share it with.

For all of its attributes, Weston is not a place to meet single women. For a while at Christmas I reunited with Belinda, my high school sweetheart who had stayed in contact with mom through the years. She came to visit mom one day without knowing I was there.

Life hadn't been kind. She'd married twice and endured as many divorces. She was now a single parent raising three children. She was still beautiful, reminiscent of the girl who had captured my heart in high school. We started to date, trying to pretend we could pick up where we had left off. But it was an illusion. We had gone down separate roads and there was no turning back. Friendship was ours, but that special spark was gone, leaving me feeling alone and unlovable once again.

In as much as I was disappointed, I was also relieved. My heart knew I needed to start with a clean slate when I met the woman of my dreams. On a whim I decided to try the personal advertisements in the Lincoln newspaper. I didn't hold out much faith in it working; after all I'd been there before with the Denver personals.

Before I could talk myself out of it, I went to the local newspaper's classified office and got a form. I stared at the blank page. Nothing was happening, what should I say? What would make my ad stand out? Catch the eye of the woman I sought? The woman I wanted would be hard to find, one in a billion, it gave me an idea.

Then I picked up the pen and wrote. It began, "One in a billion?"

30

Meeting Joan

Before I knew it, a year had passed. Mom was still holding on and I was still single and lonesome. Just for something to do, I found myself wandering around a video store in Columbus, Kansas. I'd pick up a movie, peruse the contents then put it back on the rack and picked up another.

While the personal ad had been amazingly successful in terms of volume, eighty-seven women had called, hoping to meet that "one in a billion" man. Most of them were nice enough, but lacked that special something. It surprised and saddened me to see how many were single mothers alone willing to settle for security. Dreams had been abandoned long ago. I wondered if love really even factored into it.

But none of them were for me. Some voiced open descent on Christianity. And if I were to be honest, I was equally repelled by their lack of faith. I didn't consider myself an evangelist, but the right girl had to be able to share my faith.

Whenever I got downtrodden, my mother tried to cheer me up.

"You'll find someone to love, Scott. Just take your time and keep your eyes and your mind open," she told me while looking at me tenderly. I'd missed a visit the week before and was now trying to catch up, thankful mother was still here for me to spend time with.

"I hope you're right," I told her adjusting the pillow behind her head. Mom was just an ashen shadow now. My sisters and I knew each day was a gift. But the day would come soon when my mom would be reunited with dad.

"I am," she said before sputtering. Mom had "fits" now, as we referred to them. They were bouts of choking and coughing that were coming more frequently daily. Each episode tugged at my heart. Seeing my mother so frail was difficult.

I snatched a couple of tissues from the box on her utility tray and gave them to her. Through tired and tearful eyes, mom breathed thank you. I could feel the emotion building. It was taking everything within me not to cry.

We were closer now than at any point since childhood. Spending time with her had allowed me to realize her life had been a hard one too. On one hand, she had never lost her faith in God, but she had struggled with her own demons: depression, cigarettes and caffeine. After divorcing Harry, she had never gone out with another man, never went looking for something better. At one point she'd even confided she'd never stopped loving dad. Hearing the words changed me. There had been times when I was sure she hated him and me.

It took me years to realize that the same forces of secrecy and deception tearing at me had created as much havoc on the foundation of their union. They'd never really had a chance; they were victims too.

Mom told me often how she looked forward to seeing him again someday in heaven, sooner than later, she feared, because emphysema was robbing her of her very breath. Those damn cigarettes, I thought.

She'd quit them several years ago, but the damage was done. The once beautiful and robust woman had been reduced to an eighty-five-pound skeleton. At times it was hard to recognize "mom" within the shell that existed.

Mom had no reticence in discussing her demise. We often talked of death; she knew she didn't have long. But her faith was strong and unwavering. There was no fear or sadness in her eyes as she spoke of seeing Harry again. If anything, it seemed to console her. I commended her strength. Would I have such conviction when it was my time?

"He'll be standing there with that silly grin," she said confidently. "And I'll walk up and say, "Harry, I love you. I always did, and I'm so sorry," she said softly, lost in her own world. My mother had her own regrets. How she'd treated dad, myself and to a lesser degree, my sisters. It was the same forgiveness, I had searched for, something lost that now was found, just like the song Amazing Grace.

But unlike myself, she'd never lost her faith. And now it was that faith predicated on the promise of forgiveness that was carrying her.

I knew it pleased her to see my new relationship with God. The change was nothing short of remarkable. Being caring and thoughtful, I had blossomed into the baby boy my mother would always see in me. It moved her that I called daily and visited almost as often.

Now, she prayed she'd live long enough to see her boy happy. She wanted to see me settle down with the right woman who would love and support me. Maybe there'd even be enough time to see grandchildren. She had always loved babies. She boasted I would be a good father; I prayed she was right.

As caller eighty-seven came and went, my heart sunk. I prayed it wouldn't be much longer. "I'll call a hundred before I give up," I said silently. "Then a hundred more. Lord, I'll wait as long as I have to, but please, let it happen."

As time went by, the weather had once again shifted. Snow and ice were on the horizon under gray clouds. Each day I forced myself to continue the charade that I believed it would happen. But I couldn't lie to God, he knew I had pretty much given up.

Two weeks later a friend from my high school days asked if I'd be interested in meeting a young woman he knew. I shrugged, why not? It couldn't be any worse, I thought, so I gave her a call. But she was out of town. Another disappointment.

It would be a couple of weeks before we could hook up in January. Starting 1995 auspiciously. Even then, it had not gone smoothly. In the interim we talked on the phone. We were learning about each other from snippets of conversation. Both of us feeling that it probably wouldn't go anywhere. We were from different worlds.

Still we made plans to meet in Columbus, some ninety miles north of Kansas City, at a video store the woman said she managed. My mystery date's name was Joan.

Driving through a snowstorm, I arrived early. If possible, I wanted to check her out. It wasn't that I was so enamored of physical beauty, but I felt I could tell a lot about her as a person if I was able to watch her unobserved. So I played detective fiddling with movies I had no interest in until I gathered up enough courage to ask an employee if Joan had arrived. The employee pointed to a tall, blond woman.

It definitely wasn't love at first sight for either of us. The past year had been diffi-cult for Joan. Her boyfriend of nearly a decade had proved himself unfaithful again and again. Then her sister, to whom she was very close, had been diagnosed with breast cancer and Joan had spent the end of 1994 at her side as she under-went chemotherapy. The emotional anguish and effort it took to run the half-dozen stores she actually owned, not just managed, had taken its toll.

She's a beautiful woman, I thought when I saw her; leggy, with a great figure, and pretty blue eyes. But her countenance lacked luster, leaving her looking tired and lonely. In truth, she had given up on finding a man who would be faithful; a Christian man she could count on. She had only agreed to the blind date because her friend had spoken so highly of me.

Her friend told her about my unsuccessful bouts with the personal columns and had even gone so far as to show her my ad. In spite of misgivings about looking for love among the personal section, there was something about my ad that struck her. "One in a billion?" it started. She read over it several times.

She was equally skeptical about my phone message. Yeah right, she'd said aloud after listening to it. She'd even scoffed thinking: Don't they all think they're something special?

But it was that intangible something that haunted her. What if I was that one man who could make her happy? She would reveal to me later that it was as if she was watching a stranger, as she picked up the telephone to call back.

Since moving to Weston the year before and giving up marijuana, I had con-verted to healthy living. And probably like most new converts, I was guilty of being overly zealous. After all, I was feeling good physically and wanted someone who also took seriously keeping the soul's temple in good shape.

"So what do you look like?" I heard myself ask during one of our conversations. Immediately I blushed, thinking I'd just put my foot in my mouth. It didn't come out as I'd meant it. Afraid she might think I was just another jerk looking for sex and not anything deeper than physical appearance, I quickly tried to change the subject by suggesting we meet. Reluctantly she agreed.

I hung up feeling elated. I'd just pulled a rabbit out of the hat. Now I needed to make that rabbit materialize.

A few days later at the store, I seriously entertained thoughts of slipping away. I was riddled with insecurities. Could I really do this? But then she smiled at one of the customers, a soft, warm smile that permeated the store. Immediately I felt encouraged and decided it was time to introduce myself.

Two months later, on Valentine's Day, I surprised us both by proposing. This time it felt right, as though we had known each other all our lives and had just been waiting for the right moment to connect. I told her right away that it was important to me to have a Christian marriage according to the tenants of Promise Keepers. My suggestion was right on target since she wanted a Christian man who lived his life according to the Bible. Unlike Michelle and my other less than compatible partners, Joan and I truly seemed to be seeking the same goal. Just knowing that she shared my virtues meant more to me than I could express.

We went down the list: someone Christian, faithful and wanting babies. She did, though at 38 years old she worried that her biological clock was fast running out of time.

With most women, I delayed telling my life story. With Joan I dropped the bomb after the second date. If she was going to think I was crazy and dismiss me as others had, I figured I wanted to know sooner than later before my emotions would be involved.

But Joan had a personality to match her looks; a strong woman who'd fought and scraped to create a successful business, she was intensely compassionate. Something inside told me she could be trusted with my deep secrets. She found it fascinating.

Joan also met my mother and to my astonishment, they hit it off like sisters. Watching her laugh with mom convinced me she was the woman I would spend the rest of my life with. Someone to love and be loved by.

Throughout the courtship we abstained from sex. It was difficult at times. The more convinced we became that we were in love, the more we ached to give each other that ultimate gift. And yet we were equally convinced that if we could sustain the relationship without the narcotic effect of physical love, we could build something that would last forever.

In truth, Joan's family and friends had reservations about the suddenness of the engagement. The video stores had made Joan financially secure. How could she be so sure that I wasn't just some gold-digger?

Right away I made it known that I was not interested in her money. I even compromised on one of the most important aspects in my life just to make the relationship work. While it had been my hope to share my Weston home with her, I was aware her business life was important, and she enjoyed the attributes of cities. Maybe by being with her I could learn to appreciate elements of city life I had grown to disdain.

So I sold my little place in Weston and a little piece of my heart to be with her. I would never again let anything get in the way of making a commitment, especially with a woman who shared my family values. God had given me another chance. I was going to be worthy of that gift.

We decided to switch roles. Figuring if I stayed home I could take care of the house and, hopefully, the children while working on my campaign to lobby Congress for more regulation of the baby business and subsequently to warn the public about eugenics. It was an important campaign, the public needed to know.

Joan agreed. Whatever anyone else might think, we were in love. Six weeks after we met, just like my own parents, we were married in the church by the same minister, no longer young, who had rescued me some twenty years earlier from prison. Complete with my mother, beaming and crying in her wheelchair, acting as our witness.

Our coupling got its first test right away. Just as we were set to leave on our honeymoon, unexpectantly my mom suffered a stroke. Reinforcing my belief that Joan was the right lady for me, it was she who insisted mom live with us while she healed. And it was Joan who pushed me aside to take her on shopping trips or to the beauty parlor, knowing how much those trips meant to my mom. It humbled me. She treated mom better than I had for so many years. It made me feel blessed.

Finally it was time for mom to return home, she'd hid her disappointment until I prepared to leave. She knew as newlyweds we needed some time alone, still it had been one of the most precious times of her life. As I bent to kiss her goodbye, she suddenly held me fiercely against her.

"Scott," she cried, "I wouldn't have made it without you."

"Mom," I said as tears began to fall, "if you hadn't wanted a baby so bad, I couldn't be here for you."

Life was incredible. Joan seemed more loving everyday. In turn I found myself so eager to please, so eager to understand. I wanted to fulfill her every need, be the sensitive man she'd never had.

In the mornings we would get up and start the day, side-by-side saying our prayers like children. We thanked God for many things, but most of all each other. Each sunny day the sunshine seemed a little brighter, warmer, just for us. Even mundane things were less tedious because we shared them.

Joan adored the way I cut out photographs of infants and toddlers from magazines and pasted them around the house, on the bathroom mirror, on the side of the refrigerator. She never knew where the next one would turn up. That was why after six months of trying, it was such a disappointment when we hadn't managed to conceive.

It led to outside help. With much reservation, we wound up at The Swedish Medical Center for Reproductive Medicine in Denver.

The center was like a thousand doctor's offices. People sat perusing magazines in the waiting area while a receptionist took vital information behind a credenza.

"Mr. Davis?"

I looked up at the nurse in a purple smock. Nice color, I thought, better than the old green and blue I was accustomed to. Cheerier. Which seemed appropriate considering this was the place where infertile couples came to realize their dream of having children through the miracle of science.

The middle-aged nurse escorted me to a room and then left. There were Playboy magazines and the little cup she'd left me with. The irony hit me, after everything I'd been through, everything I believed, here we were in a baby-making clinic.

Picturing my wife's face brought a pang of fear. What if I never see her again? What if something goes wrong? I'd be alone again.

Joan willingly prepared to undergo an operation just to have our baby. It felt like deja-vu. My mother, willing to have some stranger's semen planted in her so that she and Harry could have a baby. I could appreciate her need so much more now. Understand the struggle.

I kept reminding myself however, there was a difference. This child would know its father. I was determined it would not suffer as I had. There would be no secrecy. No lies. And these were my genes being fused with Joan's genes, the doctor was just helping a little. Science didn't have to be bad; it could work miracles, God's miracles. It just needed to remember where to draw the line on the ethics end.

It took me no time at all to do what was necessary. I left the cup along with my hope for the future. Then the same nurse returned me to the waiting room.

Time seemed interminably slow. It was impossible not to worry. What if something had gone wrong in the operating room? I'd never forgive myself if something happened to Joan just because I wanted children.

Then I heard it, like a whisper in my brain. She wanted children too, a voice reminded me. I looked around. There was no one, only strangers patiently waiting their turn. The voice sounded like my mother's. Before I could give it anymore thought, Dr. William Schoolcraft, a young, boyish-looking medical director, walked in.

"Joan came through with flying colors," he said immediately answering the question I hadn't verbalized. "And, while there are no guarantees, the two of you are perfect candidates for this procedure.

Suddenly, my heart was soaring. Cocaine had never felt this good. I ran to the recovery room. Joan sat propped up, she smiled weakly. We both started to cry.

31

Barbara Goes Home

In the early morning hours of September 17, 1995, Joan Davis was jolted out of her sleep by a scream. She had never heard a sound so full of anguish and heartbreak. She knew instantly that it meant someone had died. Dawn was barely breaking, but it would be a grim day.

Joan hadn't heard the telephone, perhaps because I'd managed to catch it on the second ring. It was my sister Lisa, calling from Kansas City. "Mom's heart stopped," she sobbed. For a moment I couldn't breathe. All the air had been sucked out of me.

It wasn't as if mom's death had been unexpected. We'd been watching week by week as her health steadily declined. She had spent her very last summer in a Kansas City nursing home. Reality hit me. How terribly sad it all was.

Originally in August, we still garnered hope as she haplessly tried to return to her house but it was impossible. Her severe emphysema had robbed her mobility. Just a year earlier she had been reduced to only twenty feet without requiring rest to catch what little breath she had left, then it dwindled to ten feet and eventually barely five.

The nursing home became a necessity. Mom couldn't even fetch the pills she desperately needed to breathe better. At least at the facility someone would always be around if she needed help. It had hurt me to see her struggling so futilely to hold on to her sanity while engulfed in so much despair.

The home's ambiance was a reverberation of women's shrieks, the groans of patients suffering, and confused Alzheimer's patients muttering as they wandered along. Making its inhabitants acutely aware of demise and death.

To pass the time, and perhaps try to make sense of the twists and turns of her life, my mother had started writing her biography. It brought her joy to recall falling in love with the shy, young man who had courted her at the drugstore lunch counter so long ago. And tears as she remembered their tragic ending. All the same she kept any sorrow she felt contained. Throughout her final days she remained cheerful and happy to see Joan (who she insisted call her Mom) and I. Confident she would be going on to a far better place.

Only a week ago, it appeared she was doing better. Leading to something of a family reunion, my sisters and their spouses had all come to Kansas City for the week. We went out to dinner every night, watched videos, and talked about old times, making future plans.

Everyone was excited about the prospect of Joan and I having a baby. A date had been set for Spring 1996 to attempt the embryo implant. Mom, of course, had been the most excited. She hoped the child would be a tow-headed little boy, just like his father.

So, though it was expected, when the moment death came it was still a shock to the family. Joan found me in the kitchen, howling like a wolf who had lost its clan, inconsolable. She just held me and let me cry. She understood my need to release the pain.

The day of the funeral, it was cold, overcast and dark; a precursor of the winter to come on the plains. It depressed me further as I approached the open coffin where my mother lay in state. She looked beautiful; like the young woman from our family photographs I'd been pouring over since her death, now tucked safely away in boxes. I couldn't stand to see photos of her smiling face anymore.

And yet she reflected such peace now; no longer racked by coughing fits, nor gasping for each breath. A life senselessly stolen by cigarettes.

For a moment I could feel that wellspring of old anger trying to bubble up. The tobacco industry was nothing but a pack of liars and murderers. It incensed me, they'd not only kept her broke but killed her as well. But something inside stopped me, helped me catch myself. I knew mom wouldn't want me using her death to resurrect old demons. She believed in getting on with life, in making babies, and in love. She wouldn't want me to be consumed by something that could no longer be helped.

Thus I turned to go back to my seat but quickly whirled again to kiss mother's forehead.

"Goodbye Mom," I cried softly, "Thanks for giving me my life. I will love you, always," I whispered as a tear cascaded down my cheek.

By the time we'd ventured out to the graveside I began to feel a little better. She was being laid to rest next to my father. There had been a time when I would have been so sure it wouldn't happen, back in the bitter days of the divorce. But Barbara had insisted that she be placed next to the only man she had ever loved, their bodies together, as their souls would be in heaven.

Nearly a hundred people attended the funeral, many from her church. Barbara had been known for her gentle ways and willingness to help anyone in need. Now they came to pay their respects. I opened text for the service that would be performed. It was a poem that read:

"Death is nothing at all, I have only slipped away into the next room."

"Whatever we were to each other, that we are still. Call me by my familiar name, speak to me in the easy way which you always used. Laugh as we always laughed together. Play, smile, think of me, pray for me. Let my name be the household word that it always was."

"Let it be spoken without effort. Life means all that it ever meant. It is the same as it ever was; there is absolutely unbroken continuity. Why should I be out of your mind because I am out of your sight? I am but waiting for you, for an interval, somewhere very near just around the corner."

"All is well. Nothing is past; nothing is lost. One brief moment and all will be as it was before, only better, infinitely happier and forever."

I liked that, the words flowed over me, warmed me like fine Brandy. Someday it would be my duty to tell my own children about my parents and their devout love for their kids. I'd speak her name with love and when the pain was not so fresh, laugh at the old memories. Mom would never be far from thought.

But right now it was hard. I was more than grateful that Joan was by my side, holding my hand while the minister delivered a sermon about Jesus preparing a home for Barbara Davis. That was my wish.

"Preparing a house to be a home was something that Barbara knew all about. Home, family, children these were the joys of her life."

"Scott, Lisa and Jodi, it is a tribute to your Mom that you rise up and call her blessed. And you were blessed to have a mother like Barbara; a woman who put a family together in perhaps an unconventional way." he continued.

Over the hum of conversation I nodded, remembering how she complained the saying was wrong. It wasn't that blood was thicker than water when it came to families; but love was thicker than blood. "Love is what makes a family," the minister continued.

I thought about the family Joan and I hoped for. We would try the embryo transplant once, if it was God's will we'd have a child. Otherwise, we'd already sent for the paperwork from the Holt Adoption Agency, the same agency that had arranged for the adoption of my sisters, Jodi and Lisa. It wouldn't matter; love was what made a family.

"Barbara wanted to go home. We celebrate Barbara going home," the minister said. "Peacefully, she died in her sleep and awoke in God's kingdom. For her, the promise has been fulfilled and she is truly home," he concluded.

Home. I closed my eyes thinking of it. Memories of mother looking out her picture window waiting for glimpses of me or my sisters coming to visit flashed in my mind. She was always quick to welcome us home. It made me realize how lucky we'd had been. How many families could claim that?

Too many families torn apart by the vagaries of life never get the chance to reconcile. There had been a time when I believed I hated her; so unaware of the forces that had driven her then. But the truth had set us free, allowed us to love again. And I was thankful.

Suddenly the service was over. I looked up into the bleak gray sky, but now it didn't seem quite so depressing. Instead I imagined Barbara and Harry holding hands, looking down on us with smiles on their faces, joy in their hearts. Harry would be pointing me out to the other angels, "That's my boy," and Barbara would be laughing.

I wiped the last tears from my cheeks. As I noticed how warm Joan's hand was in mine. "Come on, honey," she said. "Let's go home."

32

My New Life

I stepped out into the bright winter sunlight. As I shielded my eyes from the glare of the freshly fallen snow I stood, reflecting over my life. Kansas City had become a mural of white, spread out across a huge canvass. It was beautiful, but not without a bite.

My life had gone full circle. There had been so many changes, both disturbing and life altering. But through it all, I had survived. I was alive.

There were elements to my life that would never be repeated and things I had learned that I didn't need to have my nose pushed in them any longer to understand the message. It amazed me to be standing, in tact, daunted by my son's diagnosis but not broken.

In days gone by, such news would have unraveled me to the place of ruin. At least I could be proud of that much, knowing I had truly grown. But I knew in my heart as I looked over the great expanse of white and started walking, beginning my morning workout, I had not accomplished this alone, I owed everything in my life to God.

Without his constant presence, I never would have championed the tribulations nor conquered my vices. More than likely, I would have become another statistic. I would have died young, miserable and in silence.

I had much to be thankful for, including the sense to forgive my mother, which in turn, opened my heart. I couldn't imagine now how empty and void my life would have been if I hadn't. I was one of the lucky. I had lived to tell my story, to continue on, to carry my heritage along.

Knowing there would always be battles to overcome, but feeling confident now that I could tackle them. It felt strange at times to realize the same man who used to run away from problems no longer ran, but rather embraced them.

Perhaps the shift in focus accounted for some of the change. Realizing that not everything was about me. Realizing how much Preston needed me, needed us. And he would need us badly if he was going to have any semblance of hope for a normal life.

So many things had been revealed to Joan and I by happenstance. Our journey of discovering buried truths about seemingly innocent inoculations carried out daily on the unsuspecting masses was just the tip of the iceberg. We truly believe had Preston not been vaccinated at such an early age, he would not have developed the crippling autism and health problems that ensued after his shots.

No one knew and there would be no one to help while we dealt with his tiny body night after night, week after week, wracked in pain, writhing in agony from horrible stomach cramps to diarrhea to vomiting.

At times we were both spent just trying to help him hold on, not sure if the tiny thread sustaining him would be enough, or if he would soon be joining my mom and dad. Without a doubt, they were some of the hardest days I've ever endured. And what hurt me more was the knowledge that he didn't have to be subjected to it. He shouldn't have been subjected to it. Simple knowledge could have prevented him from being another medical statistic. When would they learn? Where will it stop?

With myself, my close calls had been my choosing, but what choices did a six month old baby have? And how much more helpless.

It would be so easy to be bitter. So easy to justify the righteous anger. But it wouldn't change our circumstances. Preston would still be autistic and I would still be a donor offspring. Only prayer and faith can carry me.

Now here I was reflecting over the defining moments in my life. Noticing the stark differences in my son several years later. Seeing him struggling to articulate the simplest of words, while other toddlers were free spirited children expressing themselves so easily. It hurt.

But the man inside could face the hurt. It is never easy seeing your precious child wrangling to perform such little tasks or master words, but I know he will. He will conquer his demons as I have, because he's my son. And I will be here to help him, as my father tried to help me, would have helped me, if I'd let him.

Joan has become his lifeline of knowledge, learning everything she can about autism. About the connection between vaccinations and children developing autism as a result of taking shots.

We are sure that had we not embarked on that process of giving him shots, Preston would have continued to progress as any child his age. But once the shots were administered, his world became a bubble we had to learn to permeate piece by piece.

Joan had to teach our pediatrician and doctors. We have been met by every form of cynicism possible, but still continue to prevail. Knowing that just as it is my job to be a messenger, it is hers also to illuminate the medical profession about this evil and sometimes deadly tradition that snatches the very life from so many innocent children.

I finished my workout and returned home. Joan and the kids were in the living room. Ashley was playfully pulling on Preston while Joan just looked on. Immediately I laughed. This was my life now.

"Hi guys!" I said. Both kids looked up. Instantly Ashley was in my arms followed closely by Preston. There had been a time when Preston wouldn't hug me, now he welcomed my affection. He'd come so far.

Already I could see improvement with him, but it had taken hours and hours of steady work. Work to improve his speech, motor skills, and health. Being a parent had turned my life upside down and inside out. And yet there was nothing I would change. I loved them all dearly. He was worth the extra effort, they all were.

I know in my heart some chapters in my life are ending, but others are just beginning and I will be there for each and every one.

33

Epilogue: The Obituary

Two years later....

I always believed that someday I would have another chance to build the bridge between my father and myself that I'd always wanted. I always believed that we could have a real and father/son relationship. Even if this relationship would last just for one single day. Even if it had come down to an hour or so in a coffee shop.

You see, after a lifetime of imagining and trying to guess the truth with only scattered clues to work with, I knew that if I could find the truth in his words then I could spend the rest of my life using that truth to build a foundation in my life. I blamed myself for that failure without ever understanding why. Now that I had begun and now that I'd actually gotten somewhere—I found him. I believed that more things, better things, were to come. I had beaten the odds more than once and refused to give up. I had been told by countless people to give up and I never did. Anyone who has ever known what they want more than anything else in the whole world knows what I mean when I say that come what may, that fire in your heart never dies and there is no water in this world that can extinguish it. To give up is not only unthinkable, it is impossible. It would be like trying to be a different person than the one you are. And perhaps to a certain extent I became blinded by this belief, this fire in my heart. This fire was love and love never gives up. Love always believes, love gives you the power to build bridges, even if the chasm is so wide and deep that you can't even see the other side. This is why after all my research, all of my discovery, the twists and turns it had taken and the repeated shock of truth played out over the whole course of my life, that seven simple words from in an e-mail from my younger sister on the eve of my birthday, exactly twenty-one years later to the day of my mothers revelation, would bring and end to my journey:

"Did you know that Hans Kroonberg died?"

I felt my heart shatter into thousands of microscopic pieces. I tried to hold myself upright but fell to my knees. I tried to catch my breath, but instead from inside me came an animal sound which I could not stop. It got louder and louder until I was wailing like a wolf. It tore the air around me with sounds that have no name.

There are no words to describe my grief. I had lost my natural father, and for a moment again lost the fire in my heart, the drive that always kept me going, the hope that had sustained my life, if ever so meagerly, and it was never coming back.

I again had failed the test. Like the fool I have so often been, I allowed my fear of rejection take me past the door of opportunity. I didn't try hard enough. I wasn't good enough. I blew it. No second chance. The verdict was read. Guilty…

All of the horrors of my past came swelling up again. The hollow depression, the anger, the confusion. I could barely control the surging emotions and desires, the desire to just sit down and smoke a joint. Do a line. Drink some booze. Numb myself to the pain of the universe. But I knew that this was no longer me, and within moments those demons left.

How would I now obtain what other people, normal people, call closure? I imagined his family gathered in Georgia, grieving, consoling each other, remembering him proudly and laying him to rest in the bosom of a community grateful for his service as a citizen.

My family. My father. Part of me was reaching out from my world he never wanted to know. Me. The arms in my heart were stretching, trying to get all the way across the country to Georgia, to the only people in the universe who could feel his loss in a way that approached the way I felt.

I wanted to reach across to my people and say I am one of you, and I need you too. I need you now just like I always needed him. The chasm was still there. I had failed to build the bridge and it remained.

I went searching on-line for his obituary. Within moments I found it.

OBITUARY—KROENBERG, DR. HANS

KROENBERG, Dr. HANS.: Dr. Hans Kroenberg was born in Rotterdam, The Netherlands in 1922. During the Nazi occupation of the Netherlands in World War II, he served with the Dutch Resistance and had a number of life threatening encounters with the Nazi occupying forces. Upon the liberation of Europe by Allied Forces, Dr. Kroenberg established what was to become a life-long personal goal—to repay the American people and armed forces for helping Europe regain its freedom. In 1948, Dr. Kroenberg and his wife, Margaret, immigrated to the United States as a first step toward achieving his goal. He entered Cornell University on a Presidential scholarship and received a B.S. Degree in Agronomy in 1951. He received a Ph.D. from the University of Kansas in 1956. He went on to become a Professor Emeritus of Soils at Georgia Tech where he was involved in research and teaching from 1956 to 1987. Dr. Kroenberg taught over 6000 students during his 31 year career at Georgia Tech.

At Georgia Tech, Dr. Kroenberg was an early proponent of the study and protection of the natural environment. He led the way to the establishment of an environmental minor, a departmental name change from Agronomy to the Department of Crops, Soil and Environmental Science, and an explosion in enrollment in these programs.

He also served as the founding President of the Faculty Senate whose goal is the enhancement of the role of the faculty in university governance. He was elected as a national councilman of the American Association of University Professors and was often called upon to solve conflicts in the university community. However it was not his distinguished academic career that Dr. Kroenberg viewed as his greatest achievement during his life. It was the founding and development of the Warm Hearts Retirement Community in Atlanta, Georgia. From 1974 until his death, Dr. Kroenberg dedicated himself to the establishment and growth of this non-profit community for the elderly. It was a realization of his goal to make a meaningful contribution to American society in gratitude for America's sacrifices in liberating Europe during World War II. Today, the community is home to some 500 elderly residents of all economic strata. Warm Hearts provides a range of living environments including independent living, assisted living, intensive nursing care and Alzheimer's care.

The community sits on 200 acres of rolling wooded hills near the Georgia Tech campus. Dr. Kroenberg conceived of the community, raised funds to acquire the land and chaired the Board of Directors of Warm Hearts for 30 years. He never accepted any compensation for his work on behalf of Warm Hearts and contributed generously to the community from his own personal retirement savings.

Dr. Kroenberg received numerous awards during his career including the Georgia Tech Award for Teaching Excellence, the Distinguished Citizen of Atlanta Award by the Greater Chamber of Commerce of Atlanta, the Citizen Recognition Award from the Rotary Club of Atlanta, and the Hank Johnson Award for Leadership.

Dr. Kroenberg is survived by his wife, Margaret Kroenberg; his daughter, Roeli Kroenerg; his son-in-law, Scott Fullton, and granddaughter, Alison Fuller.

A memorial service for Dr. Kroenberg will be held at the Atlanta Central Presbyterian Church in Atlanta, Georgia at 2 p.m. Saturday, January 24, 2004. The family will receive friends at 3:30 p.m. Saturday following the service in the Karr Activity Center at Warm Hearts. Those wishing to make memorials are encouraged to make a donation to the Warm Hearts War Memorial Fund, c/o Warm Hearts Village, 2607 Warm Hearts Drive, Atlanta, Georgia 24060.

Arrangements by McCray Funeral Home Atlanta.

Copyright (c) 2004 The Atlanta Times
Record Number: 0401240001

And again came the tears and the sounds that I cannot describe. This man was my father. He was my blood, my being. I am a little piece of this. This is me. In one long paragraph I'd received more information, than I'd uncovered in all of my years of searching. Over the last twenty years all I'd been able to do is uncover tidbits, factoids that didn't allow me to see much more than accomplishments, and now an anonymous newspaper reporter managed to tell me who he was. Finally there was something I could grab onto and fix in my mind, a person to put behind the face that I'd seen, startled, all those years ago.

In some way I can't describe, the big question mark in my life resolved to an understanding of a person. A warm and caring human being. Even if many questions would remain, my doubt was in some way changed, informed by an idea of a man. Instead of "who?" my question, without my really being aware of it, shifted to "how?" How can I form more of a mental picture that will allow me to resolve this and let me move on with life? How can I build the bridge in my own heart?

Now as I looked across the chasm that had defined my life I had a new perspective. My natural father was gone forever and with him went many opportunities, but I saw him in myself the way most people see themselves in their children. In a way, now that I looked across the chasm, I saw myself looking back at me. And as I stood in front of his headstone on a brisk Georgia morning some days later, I took comfort in knowing that my father had given me the greatest gift a man could ever give his son. The gift of life. Ultimately his gift to me may have been detached. It did, in fact, lack almost every aspect of human relationship, but the essential gift of genetics. It made me his son and it makes him my father and nothing in this world has the power to change or alter that.

In the months to come I would begin to understand for the first time that my father wasn't an uncaring brute, nor was he an irresponsible philanderer, a power-mad bureaucrat or the incarnation of demonic forces in our society. None of these scenarios fit the picture generated by his obituary. I evolved the picture of a man who donated his sperm almost fifty years ago to help a childless couple conceive just like he'd done so many things to help other people in his life. The man wasn't a monster, he was a scientist and he believed that his techniques could help produce a healthier world and happier people. The gift he sought to impart to my family he gave anonymously and attached no strings.

The more I had found out about him, the more I found about myself. A great chasm that had always existed in my heart was being closed up, filled in with firm ground. I was able to focus and see things around me in a way that finally made sense.

I thank God today for allowing me to find the tidbits, the puzzle pieces, that eventually emerged as a whole picture and I thank him for igniting the fire that kept me going for so many years in my heart. I thank my mother's husband, my childhood father for his unselfish love. And I'm thankful, finally to the man who's genetic information I contain.

Even though it took a lifetime to find out what that information was…

Bibliography

The Nazi Connection: Eugenics, American Racism, and German National Socialism
by Stefan Kuhl. Oxford Press ©2002

Preaching Eugenics: Religious Leaders and the American Eugenics Movement
by Christine Rosen ©2004

The Surgical Solution: A History of Involuntary Sterilization in the United States
by Philip R. Reilly, University Press ©1991

Margaret Sanger: Father of Modern Society
by Elasah Drogin ©1979

War Against the Week: Eugenics and America's Campaign to Create a Master Race
by Edwin Black, ©2003

IBM and the Holocaust: The Strategic Alliance between Nazi Germany and America's Most Powerful Corporation
by Edwin Black ©2001.

Henry Ford and the Jews: The Mass Production of Hate
by Neil Baldwin ©2002

About the Author

Scott first approached me about assisting him with his book about three years ago. Once I read about his life, I was hooked. It became apparent to me that the information contained within and his triumphant story but turbulent journey needed to be shared.

From the author of the Sci-fi thriller, *The Model Male* and *Voices From The White Noise.*

Marsh continues to write and create in Battle Ground, WA.

0-595-32000-7